Modeling and Analysis of
CONVENTIONAL DEFENSE IN EUROPE
Assessment of Improvement Options

Library of Congress Cataloging in Publication Data

German Strategy Forum Workshop on Long-Term Development of NATO's Forward Defense (1984: Bad Godesberg, Bonn, Germany)
 Modeling and analysis of conventional defense in Europe.

"Proceedings of the German Strategy Forum (DSF) Workshop on Long-Term Development of NATO's Forward Defense, held December 2-4, 1984, in Bonn/Bad Godesberg, Federal Republic of Germany"–CIP t.p. verso.
 Includes bibliographies and index.
 1. Europe–Defenses–Congresses. I. Huber, Reiner K. II. Title.
UA646.G47 1984   355'.03304   85-23233
ISBN 0-306-42227-1

Proceedings of a German Strategy Forum (DSF) Workshop on Long-Term
Development of NATO's Forward Defense, held December 2-4, 1984,
in Bonn/Bad Godesberg, Federal Republic of Germany

© 1986 Plenum Press, New York
A Division of Plenum Publishing Corporation
233 Spring Street, New York, N.Y. 10013

All rights reserved

No part of this book may be reproduced, stored in a retrieval system, or transmitted in any form or by any means, electronic, mechanical, photocopying, microfilming, recording, or otherwise, without written permission from the Publisher

Printed in the United States of America

Modeling and Analysis of CONVENTIONAL DEFENSE IN EUROPE

Assessment of Improvement Options

Edited by
Reiner K. Huber
Federal Armed Forces University, Munich
Neubiberg, Federal Republic of Germany

PLENUM PRESS • NEW YORK AND LONDON

PREFACE

This book presents a collection of contributions to a workshop on "*Long-term Development of NATO's Conventional Forward Defense*" to which the GERMAN STRATEGY FORUM (DSF*)) had invited some 50 systems analysts and defense experts of the United States, the United Kingdom, the Federal Republic of Germany and the SHAPE Technical Centre. Held in Bonn from 2 to 4 December 1984, this workshop was to provide a forum for the discussion, at a non-political expert level and in the light of available analysis results, of proposals for the improvement of NATO's conventional defense capabilities. In addition, it aimed at arriving at some recommendations as to which of these proposals deserve to be studied further and what methodological deficiencies must be alleviated and information gaps closed for an adequate assessment.

The idea to organize this workshop has been discussed ever since 1980 with several defense systems analysts in the US and the UK who shared the opinion that, with a view to the immense global build-up of the Soviet threat on one hand and the stringency of defense resources in most NATO countries on the other, there is no reason that could permit us to dismiss any proposal promising improvement without careful study. Rather, ways and means must be found to discuss and assess, free from interference and in an environment that does not imply any political weight, innovative ideas that frequently tend to get dismissed by the national defense organizations primarily with a view to presumed adverse political implications within the alliance. However, it is quite possible that some of these proposals exhibit positive aspects which outweigh such implications. But we will never know unless there is a chance to study and compare them to the existing concepts, preferably by means of quantitative analysis.

---

*) Founded in February 1983, the DSF (DEUTSCHES STRATEGIE-FORUM) is a private nonprofit society devoted to the promotion of scientific analysis and interdisciplinary debate in the field of security policy in order to provide for a better understanding of the principles and world-wide inter-relationships of the security policy of the Federal Republic of Germany and to contribute toward the evolution of a comprehensive overall strategy. Its chairman is Ambassador (ret.) Dr. Rolf Friedmann Pauls.

Thus, this editor is deeply indebted to the GERMAN STRATEGY FORUM and its chairman, Ambassador (ret.) Dr. Rolf F. Pauls, for agreeing to sponsor this workshop under its charter. Special thanks are extended to the excecutive chairman of the DSF, Lt.Gen.(ret.) Lothar Domröse and to Maj.Gen.(ret.) Alexander Frevert-Niedermein for assuming responsibility for all organizational arrangements and to the DSF-staff, in particular Mrs. Herta Kaufmann and Captain (ret.) Alfred Lindner, for a perfect effort in the administration of the workshop.

Last but not least, I have to thank the authors, session chairmen, assessment group members and panelists for their contributions to the workshop and the preparation of these proceedings. And I must not forget my secretary, Mrs. Carin Flitsch-Streibl, for her diligent work in preparing the manuscript. Also, I am indebted to Plenum Publishing Corporation for the patience and helpfulness throughout the production of this book.

Reiner K. Huber

Neubiberg, April 1985

CONTENTS

Rationale and Structure of the Workshop on 'Long-
term Development of NATO's Conventional Forward
Defense' 1
    Reiner K. Huber

Part I

BASIC PREMISES FOR THE EVALUATION

The Nuclear Relationship: Conventional Defense and
Nuclear Posture in the Strategy of Deterrence 5
    K.-Peter Stratmann

Criteria for the Evaluation of Conventional Forces
and Quantification 15
    John W. Gibson

Part II

CONCEPTUAL APPROACHES TO THE ASSESSMENT OF ALTERNATIVES

Game-structured Analysis as a Framework for Defense
Planning 25
    Paul K. Davis

Assessing Alternative Strategic Concepts 55
    John Elliott

System Dynamics as a Conceptual Framework for Long-
term Defence Planning Initiatives 59
    Richard G. Coyle and Rex Goad

Part III

ANALYSIS OF IMPROVEMENT PROPOSALS

Analyzing Alternative Concepts for the Defense of NATO 83
    Milton G. Weiner

On Reactive Defense Options - A Comparative Systems Analysis of Alternatives for the Initial Defense against the First Strategic Echelon of the Warsaw Pact in Central Europe 97
    Hans W. Hofmann, Reiner K. Huber, and Karl Steiger

Some Long-term Trends in Force Structuring 141
    Walter Schmitz, Otto Reidelhuber, and Klaus Niemeyer

Part IV

ASSESSMENT GROUP SUMMARIES

Military Rational and Operational Robustness: The Impact of Emerging Technology and Experimental Tactics on the Future of Infantry 167
    Phillip A. Karber

Politico-Military Assessment 193
    John Despres

Technology Implications 197
    Vincent P. Roske Jr.

Economic Implications, Cost and Manpower 201
    Michael G. Sovereign

Assessment Methodology and Modelling 205
    Robert Farrell

Workshop Participants 208

Index 211

RATIONALE AND STRUCTURE OF THE WORKSHOP ON 'LONG-TERM DEVELOPMENT OF
NATO'S CONVENTIONAL FORWARD DEFENSE'

        Reiner K. Huber

        Institut für Angewandte Systemforschung
        un Operations Research Fachbereich Informatik
        Universität der Bundeswehr München
        D-8014 Neubiberg, Federal Republic of Germany

For various reasons, NATO's conventional weakness is increasingly becoming a cause of deep concern to most Western defense analysts. Some argue that, due to the lack of operational reserves, the Western Alliance would be confronted with the nuclear decision too early to lend sufficient credibility to strategic nuclear deterrence. Others claim that American strategic deterrence has indeed become ineffective for the Western Alliance ever since the United States have lost their nuclear monopoly. An extreme view suggests that the employment of American 'tactical nuclear weapons' (TNW) in the defense of Europe should not be acceptable to the United States unless she makes it absolutely clear to the Soviet Union that under no circumstances will her strategic forces be used in a military conflict in Europe. Thus, unless the conventional imbalance is significantly reduced, nuclear war confined to Europe will become an ever more likely possibility.

There is many a proposal to remedy this situation. They encompass the entire spectrum from postulating a completely new strategy for NATO to a more reinforcement of all or some of the force elements within the existing strategic framework of 'Flexible Response'. Be it as it may, except for some unilateralistic disarmament approaches favoured primarily by various 'peace-movements', most of these proposals have three things in common:

(1)   They aim at reducing the conventional imbalance (without necessarily agreeing on what a conventional balance implies);

(2)   Rather than by structured quantitative analyses, their claims are usually supported by qualitative arguments based on expert judgment, at best, or on unsubstantiated beliefs, at worst. Also, in most instances the arguments focus on purely military effectiveness criteria, often on a tactical level, disregarding the implications with respect to their (political, economic, and demographic) feasibility, robustness to varying environmental conditions (such as threat and budgetary restrictions), crisis stability and crisis management, arms control and others;

(3) Insofar as they require more or less major changes in force structure, operational concepts, and strategy, they tend to be dismissed by the national defense administrations in most NATO countries on the (political) grounds of possibly adverse consequences with regard to alliance cohesion. Hereby, it is often forgotten that, rather than presenting designs for near-term improvements, most proposals must be viewed in a long-term context describing potential objectives for the *evolution* of NATO's conventional forces.

While it cannot be denied that there is some validity to certain counter-arguments, at least in a near-term context, several of the proposals may exhibit features that by far outweigh such implications in the long-term. In addition, focussing on near-term improvements without proper regard to long-term objectives may jeopardize the attainment of attractive long-term options. Also, with a view to the rather immense global build-up of the Soviet threat on one hand and the everlasting stringency of defense resources on the other, there is no conceivable reason that would permit not to discuss and evaluate, preferably in quantitative terms, any promising proposals. In order to allow for a maximum exploitation of innovative ideas, such evaluations need to be done in an environment that does not imply any political weight and is free from interference.

For these reasons, the German Strategy Forum invited some 50 systems analysts and defense experts from the United Kingdom, the United States, the Federal Republic of Germany, and the SHAPE Technical Centre to discuss the framework and conditions for the long-term development of conventional defense in Central Europe; to review available analyses on various proposals that have been made for the improvement of NATO's conventional posture; to identify methodological deficiencies to be alleviated and information gaps to be closed for an adequate assessment; to arrive at some recommendations as to which proposals or elements thereof should be studied further and how the requisite efforts might be implemented and coordinated.

In four parts, this book presents the contributions to and the results of this effort which was organized in form of an expert workshop under the chairmanship of this author.

Part I contains those papers addressing basic premises for the evolution of conventional defense. Part II discusses three conceptual approaches for the assessment of force improvements and innovative concepts. Part III presents three papers discussing the methodologies and results of operational analyses on a series of improvement proposals the assessment of which is then summarized in Part IV.

In part I, *Dr. K. Peter Stratmann* of the Foundation for Science and Politics in Ebenhausen, FRG, analyses the interrelationship between conventional defense and selective nuclear employment options in maintaining a credible deterrence. He concludes that the discussion of conventional improvement options must explicitly consider these synergisms lest deterrence should become jeopardized. *John Gibson* of the SHAPE Technical Centre addresses the issues involved in the assessment of the conventional balance between NATO and the Warsaw Pact such as perceptions of the opponent's strategic military threat and their translation into operational concepts; multiple objectives due to linkages with the TNF posture; criteria related to conventional defense and deterrence; long-term constraints and uncertainty.

Part II starts with *Dr. Paul K. Davis* of the Rand Corporation in Santa Monica, Calif., USA, who points out the necessity to base NATO's defense planning on a diversity of alternative scenarios and assumptions about the nature of modern war and on concepts akin to global military-political war gaming. To this end, new analysis approaches and techniques are required.

One such technique is presently being developed in Rand's Strategy Assessment Center which *John Elliott* of the US Army staff's Long-Range Plans Division considers as a potential candidate methodology to support the "Army Strategy Processing Model" (ASPM). In his paper, Elliott discusses the so-called "Colloquium on Alternative Strategic Concepts" which is to provide a forum for the discussion of innovative strategy proposals respectively operational concepts, subsequently to be tested through the ASPM. Finally, *Dr. Richard G. Coyle* and *Rex Goad* of the SHAPE Technical Centre use the example of a hypothetical military conflict in NATO's northern region in order to illustrate the Systems Dynamics technique for the qualitative and quantitative description of the complex interrelationships of strategies and issues such as mobilization, readiness, reinforcement, follow-on force attack, air defense, infrastructure, logistics, command and control, and crisis management.

The improvement proposals and alternative defense concepts discussed in the three papers of part III may be grouped into one of three principal categories:

(1) Improvement of the traditional force structures through a modernization of equipment including the requisite adaption of operational concepts;

(2) Reinforcement of traditional force structures through the introduction of new structural elements;

(3) Introduction of entirely new defense structures and operational concepts.

All three of the concepts analysed by *Dr. Milton G. Weiner* of the Rand Corporation fall within the last category, while those evaluated by *Profs. H.W. Hofmann* and *R.K. Huber* and *Captain K. Steiger* of the German Armed Forces University Munich and *Dr. O. Reidelhuber, W. Schmitz* and *K. Niemeyer* of the Industrieanlagen-Betriebsgesellschaft (IABG) in Ottobrunn, FRG, belong to the first two categories. The analysis of a further concept of the second category was presented by *Dr. David P. Dare* of the Defense Operational Analysis Establishment (DOAE). However, no paper was available for publication.

Weiner's analyses use a theater level, expected value, piston-type force ratio model which divided the geographical area of the Federal Republic of Germany into 40 regions consisting of eight Corps areas with five zones each. However, for the analysis of the Distributed Area Defense Concept the theater level model was supplemented by a computer-assisted manual game on a three-dimensional terrain board.

The evaluations at the Institute for Applied Systems Sciences and Operations Research of the German Armed Forces University Munich are based on a series of combat experiments by means of a detailed Btl/Rgt level closed Monte Carlo-type simulations in digitized terrain sectors of West Germany.

IABG's study approach examplifies the process of an iterative model application. The results of deterministic Corps level interactive simulations (war games) represent the input for an optimization model which, using different objective functions and sets of restrictions, generates brigade structures that are subsequently validated in war gaming experiments. The inputs for the war games are to a large part generated from a company level closed simulation model.

The assessment reports compiled in part IV of this book resulted from the discussions of the concepts and proposals in five assessment groups on:

- political implications
- military rationale and operational robustness
- technological prerequisites and growth potential
- resource implications
- operational effectiveness and its assessment.

Considering these assessments, the general conclusion was reached that the introduction of reactive defense elements into the present force structure holds the potential for significantly strengthening NATO's defensive capabilities. However, while providing some valuable insights with regard to long-range trends for force structuring, none of the analysis results presented were regarded as providing sufficient information for the discussion and formulation of more or less comprehensive improvement objectives. To this end, the rather limited set of circumstances included in the analyses needs to be extended as well as the set of improvement options themselves.

For example, all studies implicitly assumed sufficient warning for a full deployment of the defense forces and a more or less intact command and control structure. Depending primarily on the manning and peacetime deployment, the former assumption might, under certain circumstances, indeed be justified for some of the reactive defense modules but not for others. And there should be considerable margins with regard to the various proposals' sensitivities toward disruption of the command and control system. Similarily, susceptability to non-conventional threats might differ widely.

While raising such questions was generally considered to be one of the important functions of a workshop like this, providing more or less comprehensive answers was not. Rather, it should stipulate an in-depth study, by interested institutions and individuals, of ideas and concepts which the workshop participants identify as promising based upon the presented evidence and the ad-hoc assessment of the group. It should also act as a catalyst for the stimulation of cooperative or joint studies the results of which might be put forward for debate at further meetings.

There was unanimous agreement that the institutionalization of such workshops might be a worthwhile effort in order to not only stimulate new ideas and innovation, but also to promote a better understanding of mutual perceptions essential for a viable assessment of long-range options that need the common support of all NATO nations for their eventual adoption.

Part I

BASIC PREMISES FOR THE EVALUATION

THE NUCLEAR RELATIONSHIP: CONVENTIONAL DEFENSE AND NUCLEAR POSTURE IN THE

STRATEGY OF DETERRENCE

K.-Peter Stratmann

Stiftung Wissenschaft und Politik

8026 Ebenhausen, Federal Republic of Germany

The aim of this symposium is to analyse alternative approaches and concepts for the improvement of Western conventional defense capabilities. There is a broad consensus that NATO ought to reduce its current over-reliance on potential early use of nuclear weapons. This objective should not, however, lead us to assume that all strategic functions of NATO's nuclear options could be replaced or compensated for by a stronger or better organized conventional defense. Consequently, the following remarks focus on the political-strategic frame of reference, i.e., on such parameters that define the direction and latitude for the endeavor of this conference: modelling alternative force structures and operational concepts for conventional defense. Unfortunately, this subject cannot be left to the "non-political technical experts", but must be addressed in a wider perspective. It cannot be analysed separately from the highly politicized nuclear dimension and from other structural aspects of NATO's strategy of "flexible response".

Nuclear weapons are here to stay. Therefore, they must be dealt with conceptually. Conventional combat will have to be conducted under conditions of a nuclear threat and the employment of nuclear weapons may have decisive influence on the outcome of operations. This conventional-nuclear interface can be systematically exploited to enhance the stability of NATO's conventional defense. In addition, it must be taken into consideration in designing effective countervailing force capabilities against Warsaw Pact combined offensive operations. For these reasons we must not obscure the importance of dealing with the intricate and controversial problems of coordinating and integrating NATO's conventional and nuclear force components in the modeling and design of future structures for conventional forces and their operational and tactical doctrine. Generally speaking, we must base our research on an integrative approach that is conducive to assessing the comparative vulnerability of alternative conventional postures to enemy nuclear (and chemical) attack. By the same token, such an approach will help us to decide which postures are most suitable for attaining the synergistic effect of combined options on NATO's part that reinforces the combat potential of its conventional forward defense.

Let me start by briefly illustrating how NATO's current strategy and operational concept intend to exploit this synergistic interrelationship. Subsequently, I will describe how the viability of this crucial link is being challenged by developments in the Warsaw Pact threat potential: specifically, the improvement of both its conventional capabilities and the flexibility of its operational and tactical nuclear potential. No attempt will be made to systematically explore the total range of possible NATO responses to this double challenge. I will content myself to sharing some observations and raising some questions in order to stimulate discussion, rather than propose any ready answers or concepts.

The first priority objective of NATO strategy is to help prevent aggression by means of deterrence. This presupposes the political will and, of course, adequate military capabilities on the part of NATO countries to burden any possible aggressor countries with the risk of military failure or escalation, which would deter such an act. Nevertheless, in the event that the Warsaw Pact attacked, NATO would have to be able to make effective use of its military capabilities in order to demonstrate these operational and political risks so unambiguously that the political and military leaders of the other side would be compelled to discontinue their aggression. NATO's political objective would be to force the termination of hostilities on conditions acceptable to the Alliance. One of the relevant criteria would be the restoration of the territorial integrity of the Alliance by either voluntary withdrawal or forced retreat of the aggressor's forces. Another criterion demands that this objective be accomplished as quickly as possible and at the lowest possible level of force and destruction. Whether, and to what extent, NATO would be able to achieve these objectives and implement these principles would, of course, depend on the prevailing circumstances: above all, on the Warsaw Pact leaders' political motives for attacking in the first place and on the inherent risks they anticipated and were prepared to bear.

In any case, NATO strategy would have to try to meet three conditions requisite to success. These conditions are: 1) to achieve denial by effective defense, 2) to maintain intra-war deterrence, which is a very important prerequisite for military denial, and 3) to try to coerce the opponent, by means of controlled escalation, into terminating the war. Let me just briefly outline these three requirements.

In an initial successful operation, defensive measures would have to be able to disrupt the enemy's offensive concept to be effective. I stress this point, because there are those who would like to see NATO's strategy based mainly on the mechanism of attrition. To what extent could NATO hope to achieve its political and strategic objectives in a war by simply attritting Warsaw Pact forces in defensive operations on its own territory? If we decide in favor of such a strategy, then, of course, we must decide to base our own thinking, in terms of war termination, mainly on nuclear escalation. Such a strategy could have a certain plausibility, but without a strong reliance on the mechanism of nuclear escalation, I have doubts that such an "alternative strategy" would work. In any case, from the beginning effective defense measures would have to break the momentum of the enemy's offensive and thus deny him any prospect of winning a military victory within the timeframe and on the scale of violence he envisaged. This would confront the adversary's political leadership with the alternative of either accepting failure of their offensive or intensifying or expanding hostilities in order to crush or to overcome NATO's resistance by escalation.

This possibility would have to be blocked by NATO with the aid of effective countervailing options. Bringing its capabilities of counter-escalation, retaliation, and neutralization of stepped-up enemy operations to bear, NATO's strategy and posture would seek to persuade the Warsaw Pact to impose restrictions on the use of its forces and to control escalation. This is denial by intra-war deterrence, which from everyone's point of view is important, but which from the German perspective is absolutely essential in terms of keeping damage to limits that can be tolerated. In addition, NATO envisages employing coercion in the form of various steps of controlled escalation in order to influence enemy leaders' awareness of the risks they are running and to try to induce them to terminate the conflict.

The relative weight that would have to be accorded to these three components in a synergistically combined strategy for NATO would be determined, on a case by case basis, by the attack scenario and the cause of the war. The same applies to the proportions and types of non-nuclear and nuclear NATO forces employed to perform these tasks. If such employment were governed by the theoretical preferences of the NATO nations, nuclear options would be reserved for the roles of intra-war deterrence and coercion, if possible, while NATO would strive to deny the enemy successful offensive operations on the battlefield by conventional forces alone. Such a distinct separation of functions would largely eliminate military operational constraints on the use of nuclear weapons. Their employment could then be planned and implemented primarily as a means of exercising a direct influence upon the enemy's awareness of the risk of escalation. One will recognize that this interpretation of NATO's nuclear doctrine is the familiar German one.

Unfortunately, however, the strategic concepts, the military capabilities and the operational options of the Warsaw Pact may preclude any such clear cut conventional/nuclear division of functions and missions. NATO's conventional forces alone are inadequate to successfully deny the enemy every available variant of conventional offensive operations. There is a significant defense capability residing in NATO's conventional forces, but, according to most experts' judgements, it is not sufficient to fend off a major sustained conventional offensive by the Warsaw Pact in Central Europe. Moreover, Warsaw Pact forces would be able, with the aid of selective use of nuclear and chemical weapons, to quickly breach and crush any NATO defense conducted exclusively with conventional forces.

These last two assertions may, of course, be contested. There are those who maintain that the conventional stability of NATO's defense could be decisively enhanced by adopting alternative structures and modes of operation. They maintain that, by restructuring NATO's conventional defenses, incentives for the Soviet Union to employ nuclear weapons could be reduced. (However, whether this means that we could, in fact, hope to control Soviet behavior in a wartime situation by changing our own force structure is an open question.)

It follows that NATO planning for the contingency employment of nuclear weapons in Europe cannot confine itself to the objective functions of deterring Warsaw Pact nuclear use and coercion by controlled escalation. It also must be geared to the objective of denying military success by defense, and, with this purpose in mind, it must be governed by the principles of selective employment: meaning that such principles of employment would have to be implemented under strict political control and within the limits of clearly recognizable restrictions that, of course, may conflict with the requirement of military effectiveness. In any case, NATO would continue to try to stabilize its conventional capability in order to reduce its dependence on an early nuclear use, dictated by military necessities.

The strategic configuration outlined earlier appears to be ideal for NATO in terms of political acceptability. Enemy aggression on a limited scale could be deterred and, if this failed, could be warded off by NATO's nuclear reinforced conventional capability. The onus of further escalation to the level of massive use of nuclear or chemical weapons would fall upon the Warsaw Pact. This could be effectively deterred by NATO with threats of controlled escalation to the level of strategic employment in conjunction with the possibility of general nuclear response. This massive nuclear employment could be withheld on the part of NATO as a means of limiting war by deterring enemy ecalation. However, as mentioned earlier, the strategic realities of NATO are moving more and more away from this ideal.

NATO's conventional denial capabilities and its options for nuclear support have long suffered considerable weaknesses and problems whose weight is increasing in critical measure, owing to improvements in the conventional and nuclear offensive capabilities of the Warsaw Pact. There is no need to explain how the negative, in NATO's perspective, development of the balance of nuclear power in the intercontinental strategic, regional strategic, and operative and tactical spheres have in general complicated the tasks and limited the options of the Alliance's nuclear doctrine. Given strategic parity (or equivalence or rough equivalence or whatever you will) and the regional superiority of the adversary in Europe, NATO can no longer expect to have any natural advantage from nuclear employments. The risk of escalation would be about equal for both sides and, as regards military operations, assuming symmetrical employments by both sides, the Warsaw Pact would have an advantage. Against this general background of a changed perception of the risks involved and of the declining dependability of the nuclear component of NATO's strategy, developments in the adversary's threat potential are taking place that are aimed directly against the conventional defense of Western Alliance. They are obviously intended to block NATO's escape route from the growing and politically burdensome nuclear dilemma into a better non-nuclear defense and deterrence capability. At the same time, they represent further radical attempts to undercut NATO's nuclear response capability.

Thus, the Soviet Union presents a two pronged attack on the structure of NATO's current strategy. It is seeking to take strategic advantage of the fact that the capability to establish an effective conventional defense in the event of war is absolutely essential for the West's nuclear flexibility and scope of action. Only if NATO were able to ensure the cohesion of its forward defense by conventional means and maintain it, at least for a few days, would it have the time that its notion of deliberate escalation through selective nuclear employment requires. Otherwise, it would find itself in the nightmare of being compelled to employ nuclear weapons, possibly even without prior political consultation, almost as a reflex action. As a precaution, it would probably have to alter its request and release procedures accordingly and make provision for the conditional predelegation of nuclear release and employment authority to military commanders. For perfectly good reasons, all NATO governments have consistently refused to accept such a notion and will no doubt continue to do so.

Thus, in this case, the principle of strict political control would have to be compromised. Moreover, the spectrum of available nuclear options would be considerably narrowed. The prospects for limited coercive options, on which some European nations seem to place their hopes, would be slim because, in a situation where NATO's forward defense were about to collapse, the leadership of the Warsaw Pact might see the chance of a decisive military victory right before its very eyes. NATO would not have sufficient time to assess the effects of escalatory employment on the actions of the other side before suffering a perhaps irreversible defeat which would predetermine the outcome of negotiations for a cease fire and a termination of the war.

Moreover, and this is important, the military impact of selected nuclear employments in support of defense on the immediate or on the extended battlefield would be inadequate if there were no longer any organized, coherent defenses that could be stabilized by such employments. Thus, a speedy collapse of forward defense would leave NATO with only two alternatives to capitulation: it would have to initiate a highly dramatic escalatory nuclear employment that would confront the Soviet leadership directly with the danger of strategic war in such a way that it might immediately order the cessation of hostilities, or NATO would have to try to make up for its lack of conventional operational capabilities with nuclear battlefield and interdiction employments.

If possible at all, this would require massive, militarily determined employments. The preconditions for politically controlled selection and restriction of nuclear employments would no longer be applicable. Consequently, NATO would find itself in the acute dilemma of having, with even its first use of nuclear weapons, to unleash an intensified and self-destructive battlefield nuclear employment, theater nuclear war, or perhaps even uncontrolled escalation to general nuclear war. In any event, it would no longer have at its disposal that spectrum of limited and probably controllable escalatory and militarily supportive employment options, the use of which NATO governments could consider and agree upon through consultations in a crisis.

In short, the onus of nuclear escalation would be on NATO and the options available would probably be unacceptable to either the United States or the Western European countries under attack. NATO's ability to take unified nuclear action would be paralyzed while unilateral actions would create the danger of political disintegration of the Alliance. This is not a very comforting prospect, but it summarizes the features of a real threat. What is especially alarming is the growth in Warsaw Pact capabilities for a conventional offensive after only a short preparation period. Due to the much improved Warsaw Pact offensive air assets and to the growth in mobility, firepower, and sustainability of the first echelon ground forces, these forces are now in a much better position to achieve operational surprise (to be distinguished from strategic or political surprise). However, in terms of results, this may, under certain conditions, be as effective as strategic surprise.

This has a two-fold impact on the synergism of NATO's forward defense. Firstly, this conventional attack capability could interfere directly with NATO's nuclear support assets, either by preempting the operational availability of those assets, or by directly attacking nuclear systems and their associated command, control, and support components. Secondly, this conventional attack may significantly degrade the synergism of NATO's conventional/nuclear operations by significantly reducing NATO's conventional capability. The effectiveness of nuclear support would be crucially diminished, once again, in a two-fold manner. NATO would lose its ability to develop nuclear targets by means of conventional fire and maneuver. This, in turn, would reduce NATO's effectiveness in target acquisition and target engagement, as well as the military effectiveness of such employments, because targets could not be slowed down and congested to the same degree. Equally important, NATO would lose its capability to tactically or operationally exploit the immediate effect of a nuclear use - a quality that must be regarded as an essential prerequisite for the military effectiveness of any selective nuclear battlefield use.

The crucial nature of this multiple challenge presented by the Warsaw Pact's conventional capability is enhanced by the Pact's growing nuclear employment flexibility. Both the indirect and the direct method of disrupting NATO's nuclear support capability could be applied with a much more rapid and devastating effect if the Warsaw Pact were to employ chemical or nuclear weapons to neutralize NATO's organic nuclear assets and C^3I components by simultaneously attacking front line forces and their operational reserves in the envisaged breakthrough areas.

Let us turn to a few observations and questions that relate to important structural problems of modelling conventional force concepts.

The most fundamental issue is, of course, whether we should retain or, if we think it has been lost, reestablish the conventional/nuclear synergism of NATO's strategy and how we can go about it. The questions I pose here concern the terms of reference: the political strategic parameters that we either have to accept as premises or change as we debate the issues according to our own views and concepts.

One important set of parameters is affected by tendencies in the Western debate, and particularly in the FRG, that stress the necessity of restraint in further developing NATO's military posture as a contributing factor to crisis stability. As nobody attributes any inclination to provoke a major war to the current Soviet leadership, most people view the potential causes for war in Europe as stemming from a crisis situation that has gotten out of hand. It then follows, so the argument goes, that

NATO must posture for its defense in a non-provocative way. Just what constitutes a "non-provocative" posture is, of course, subject to broad interpretation.

Some, for instance, argue against the organic integration of nuclear weapons into the ground forces' structure, as currently practiced with the so called tactical or battlefield nuclear systems. In the view of those who make this argument, the presence of such short range systems in Central Europe poses the grave danger that a crisis may not only turn into war, but escalate to virtually instant nuclear use. In order to avert that risk they propose a "nuclear-free zone". So one key question is: Do we want to keep battlefield nuclear systems (and nuclear systems for operational employment) as instruments of a nuclear-use strategy that has a significant specific deterrent effect because of their potential for military denial or do we decide to compensate for their removal by conventional capabilities only and/or by relying on the escalatory use of nuclear weapons in the extended geographical area?

Furthermore, some proponents of military restraint on NATO's part would like the alliance to complement the denuclearization of its forward defense by adopting a "purely defensive" concept of operations for NATO ground forces. In its most radical and purest form, the model of a distributed area defense, such a notion would even exclude the capability to maneuver in counter-attack, exploitation, or delaying operations at the tactical level. Combat functions of the defense would thus be limited to engaging and waring down advancing enemy units through firepower, barriers, etc. In the view of its adherents, this posture, in addition to its hoped for confidence building political effect, offers two significant advantages as compared to NATO's current defense set-up: First, because of its extended depth, such a system would preclude rapid breakthroughs. This increase of defense stability would relieve NATO of the burdensome prospect of having to use nuclear weapons early. Secondly, a distributed area defense system allegedly would not offer sufficently rewarding targets for hostile nuclear or chemical attack. In addition, it would be less susceptible to the damage effects of such attacks.

In total opposition to these views the U.S. Army's AirLand Battle doctrine puts special emphasis on major offensive operations of the combined arms and services ("extended battlefield") and on the total integration of conventional, chemical, and nuclear fires in support of maneuvering NATO forces ("integrated battlefield"). Consequently, the principles of this national American doctrine also appear to deviate from NATO's established strategic doctrine in following respects: They tend to blur the clear distinction between the employment of conventional and nuclear weapons and they seem to transcend the latitude allowed for counter-offensive operations in NATO's defensive concept of "forward defense".

I do not intend to elaborate on these rivalling quests for alternative doctrines and force structures that fundamentally challenge NATO's existing policy and force posture. It is, however, safe to assume that far reaching changes will remain very unlikely for the foreseeable future. Attempts to turn the current posture of forward defense into a more offensive concept that would envisage major border crossing operations into the depths of Warsaw Pact territory will probably remain futile and merely theoretical for many reasons. First and foremost, current and programmed levels of conventional NATO forces will not suffice to realize such a concept. In addition, political resistance in most NATO countries against any shift towards a stance that could be perceived and attacked as potentially aggressive and destabilizing is bound to be prohibitively effective. As regards all notions of a "defense in depth" that would jeopardize NATO's coherent close-to-the-border defense, they seem to be flawed on both military and political grounds. Yielding major portions of West German territory would deprive NATO's defense of indispensable assets of military infrastructure, of terrain particularly suitable for the defense, of essential mobilization potential, etc. Furthermore, and equally important, the government of the FRG must oppose any proposals that envisage use of large areas of its small, heavily populated and industrialized country as delaying and killing zones. The German (and other frontline countries') reading of NATO's political rationale and war aims would certainly preclude such concepts.

With regard to the structure of NATO's nuclear posture, we are already witnessing changes in the composition of the overall stockpile. Still, it seems likely that the structure of NATO's nuclear employment options, which currently encompasses the whole range from battlefield support options to deep interdiction by means of INF, will basically remain unchanged.

Excluding the possibility of revolutionary discontinuity with regard to the structural parameters of NATO's doctrine and posture does not, of course, rule out future changes at the operational and tactical level. In fact, the challenges posed by the Warsaw Pact military build-up, tightening Western political and resource constraints and the appearance of new technologies do call for innovative efforts in analysis and planning. In order to make the most effective use of limited assets against a growing military threat, NATO must strive to determine its priorities properly and to carefully match missions and tactical concepts, technological opportunities and force structure development. It is, of course, rather easy to state the desired outcome of such a process in general terms. NATO's force posture should effect maximum robustness vis-à-vis the total spectrum of Warsaw Pact options - conventional, chemical and nuclear. In order to meet this objective, force structures and employment concepts must be designed for maximum flexibility, redundancy and coordination of effort (interoperability, commonality and integration) at all levels. It is, however, much more difficult to translate these laudable postulates into specific concepts and programs.

Focusing on the theme of this presentation, the problems of the conventional-nuclear interface, these difficulties can be demonstrated very clearly. Take for instance the complex question to what extent and by what organizational arrangements NATO's nuclear force components should either be kept separate from conventional forces as special units and weapons systems or, on the contrary, be closely integrated into, and in fact, indistinguishable from these forces.

Most people agree that NATO should have a fully independent conventional defense capability that is strong enough to at least assure i n i t i a l s u c c e s s against any type of c o n v e n t i o n a l Warsaw Pact attack. Accordingly NATO must be capable of successfully executing all time-critical missions with conventional means only. The range of such missions would pertain to the FEBA battle (troop air defense, emplacement of barriers, artillery support, counter battery fire etc.), to the air battle and to the "deep battle" in general (including the suppression of enemy air defense [SEAD], offensive counter air strikes [OCA], battlefield air interdiction [BAI] etc.).

To the extent that NATO conventional forces can meet these initial defense requirements for survival and mission execution, military pressure for early initial use of nuclear weapons would recede. Nuclear options could then be withheld for the purposes of deterring Warsaw Pact nuclear employment and for deliberate escalation. Emerging (and emerged) technologies hold great potential for significantly improving the effectiveness of conventional weapons systems. From this, many analysts have concluded that nuclear weapons can be replaced for many, if not all, missions by non-nuclear ones. This may indeed become possible for conventional combat conditions, provided that NATO forces are supplied with sufficient quantities of rather expensive delivery systems, smart munitions, target acquisition and engagement assets etc. Unless this condition is met, NATO must definitely remain capable of hedging against conventional attrition and unexpected failures and crises by means of nuclear back-up options. This becomes, of course, even more compelling when we acknowledge the possibility that the Warsaw Pact could initiate battlefield employment of chemical and nuclear weapons. There would be little hope that NATO forces could successfully defeat Warsaw Pakt breakthrough and exploitation operations that were supported by selected nuclear and chemical attacks by conventional means alone.

One particularly difficult problem results from the fact that those delivery systems that are the prime candidates for enhancing the effectiveness of conventional weapons delivery over larger distances, i.e., terminally guided cruise missiles and ballistic missiles in addition to aircraft, also have a nuclear role. As these systems have variable range capability (depending, i.a., on payload), short flight times or signatures that can make detection and identification of flight paths very difficult, time and confidence for strike warning and attack assessment would diminish. Because it would be impossible to discriminate between nuclear armed systems and conventional ones, conventional attacks could be misperceived as being nuclear. A large conventional "holding at risk" potential, consisting of large numbers of dual-capable medium and longer range missile systems, would be virtually indistinguishable from a powerful nuclear deep strike force. Consequently, fear of enemy nuclear preemption or launch on warning may inhibit any time critical massive employment of conventionally armed missiles and cruise missiles, although this employment could become essential for the initial success of NATO's defense. Moreover, such fears would also keep NATO from employing these systems as means for selective nuclear options in line with deliberate escalation. Therefore, NATO must think hard about how to establish observable distinctions in terms of hardware, deployment, organization, command and control procedures, etc. that could be used to establish verifiable limitations and to allow for crisis and wartime communication with the enemy in order to clarify and demonstrate the meaning and intent of the respective military actions. On the other hand, dual capable systems obviously are attractive in terms of survivability, flexibility and costs.

As far as command and control, intelligence and target engagement functions are concerned, it would be sensible to strive for the greatest possible commonality of assets and integration of functions with regard to conventional and combined conventional nuclear operations in order to minimize the problems of transition.

Another field of inquiry pertains to the suitability of different types of conventional operational concepts and force structures for effectively coping with conditions of nuclear combat, i.e., their vulnerability to enemy use and their amenability to effective integration and exploitation of one's own use of nuclear weapons on the battlefield. These issues are, of course, to be seen in close relation to the objective function of maximizing the pay-off of force models for conventional combat conditions. Taking a closer look at the two contrary alternative models mentioned before, the distributed area defense and the AirLand Battledoctrine's integrated and extended battlefield, it becomes obvious that trade-off relationships are very complex. Both models exhibit particular strengths and weaknesses, whose relative weight must be assessed against a range of contingencies, combat objectives and constraints.

Homogeneously s t a t i c   t y p e s   o f   d e f e n s e that are predicated upon holding lines or strongpoints are very vulnerable to nuclear attack, because they facilitate enemy targeting and lack the protective quality of mobility of forces. Distributed area or checkerboard defenses, however, are less vulnerable. They profit from dispersal, prepared positions, concealment and a robust command and control system. Within such a structure, attacking enemy units can be engaged effectively by observer directed responsive and discriminate fire, conventional and nuclear. But there are conspicuous drawbacks, too. In the frame of distributed area defense, enemy units cannot be canalized and congested by the maneuvers of one's own troops. Therefore, many small units must be attacked with high numbers of low yield nuclear weapons. In addition, the immediate effects of such employments cannot be exploited for counterattacks. Thus, the enemy can retain the operational initiative. NATO would have to rely exclusively on attrition by nuclear fire. This process would take place on its own territory, not a very palatable solution, although battlefield support employment could, of course, be complemented by nuclear battlefield interdiction and other employment options.

M o b i l e   t y p e   d e f e n s e s , that are designed for combined arms combat and maneuver, can apply tactics that reduce their exposure to the enemy nuclear threat. Surprise, continuous movement, hugging and interspersal with enemy forces, can all provide a degree of protection. Maneuver can also be used to develop valuable nuclear targets on the opposite side and to exploit their destruction for counterattacks that could perhaps be expanded to a counter-offensive. Thus, a mobile type defense holds the opportunity for combined conventional-nuclear operations that can attain decisive results, even if the number of nuclear weapons used is comparatively small. It is clearly an advantage that suitable maneuvers can multiply the overall impact of selective nuclear employment on the battle. On the other hand, there are conspicuous risks. Timely and reliable target acquisition and engagement in a fluent battlefield environment is very difficult and success is by no means assured. This assessment pertains as well to the general task of integrating conventional and nuclear fire with the operations of one's own combat forces. Furthermore, NATO's attacking units may run into prepared defenses and be effectively targeted and destroyed by enemy nuclear weapons. Given the deep echelonment of Warsaw Pact forces and their defensive strength as well as the scarcity of operational reserves on NATO's part, such attacks could fail totally and lead to Warsaw Pact counterattacks - with devastating effects on the stability of NATO's defense. In short, Warsaw Pact forces can turn the tables of mobile combined conventional-nuclear operations against the West.

It seems common-sensical to submit that NATO's defense posture should not be redesigned on the line of pure types of either "reactive defense" or "maneuver warfare". Rather, it should retain a mixed structure that combines static and dynamic force components and modes of combat. This complementary relation helps to make maximum use of flexibility in adapting to varying physical environments, enemy tactics and to other operational parameters of the particular military situation. In this way, strengths can be mutually reinforced and weaknesses can be compensated for. Consequently, the opposing military planners face the difficult task of preparing for multiple forms of possible NATO reactions. Most remarkably, the assessment that a mixed structure will yield the maximum pay-off is probably valid for all combat conditions, conventional and nuclear. The employment of nuclear weapons would, however, magnify the scope and the pace of combat events (attrition, surprise, etc.) and the chances and risks associated with them.

Finally, let us return to a basic strategic point raised earlier. What nature, scope, and timing of operational effects do NATO planners have to envisage in order to realize the professed political aims of Western defense against a major attack; to wit, terminating the war as quickly as possible and under acceptable (if not favorable) conditions? It seems doubtful that NATO can expect to attain these objectives solely by holding and drawing down attacking hostile forces in the hope of establishing a reinforcement ratio over time that would be sufficient to sustain protracted attrition warfare. Wouldn't it be preferable (if not mandatory) to blunt the attack and to subsequently make every effort to rapidly upset the structure of the Warsaw Pact attack plan and reinforcement schemes by counter-offensive action? Are there any other operational approaches that could force the political and military leadership of the Warsaw Pact to rapidly reassess their risks and reconsider their decision to attack? If NATO had to yield the operational initiative to the opponent, would it then be at all possible to effect a military setback of such a proportion to the Warsaw Pact, that its General Staff would have to refer back to the political leaders and require new strategic guidance, rather than leave the emerging problems to be handled by subordinate regional, front, army or divisional command levels? It is true that nuclear escalation is supposed to, and, in fact, may, work as a "war termination" mechanism and thus compensate for the absence of sufficient military operational leverage. But, as was mentioned before, the political acceptance and dependability of this option have suffered from the adverse shift in the military power equation. Consequently, addressing the issue of NATO's counter-offensive capability requirements should be part of the Western debate on reassessing NATO's strategy and force posture.

CRITERIA FOR THE EVALUATION OF CONVENTIONAL

FORCES AND QUANTIFICATION

>   John W. Gibson
>
>   Shape Technical Centre (STC)
>   The Hague
>   The Netherlands

DEFINITIONS

1. Evaluation of conventional military capability calls for definition of objective functions and where possible their translation into measures of effectiveness. Such evaluation may be aimed at assessing the totality of the conventional balance, or concerned with a sub-set of capabilities at the operational or tactical level.

2. Many decisions about future force design, in particular those concerning acquisition, are based on study of the latter and dependent on the development of "intermediate" measures of effectiveness. These may be related to:

    - enhancements of/trade-off between, major components of force design, eg forces that hold ground, forces that project firepower, "swing" assets that can reinforce where they are needed

    - the mix of mission area capabilities within each major component

    - solutions to mission area requirements, eg choice of weapon systems and sub-systems

3. A great deal of application over the past three decades has established that valid intermediate criteria can be derived based on constraining the domain of interaction to that which affects the issues to be decided. But the relationships and implications of these criteria to "higher level" factors must be understood. For example, a study of offensive counter-air (OCA) operations may be required to provide insight into a choice between candidate systems for the attack of air bases. The alternatives could to varying extent aim to destroy or damage the constituent air base components, and much can be learned from assessing the extent to which each system would degrade air base sortie generation over time. This is a simple and commonly used effectiveness measure. But it must be interpreted in relation to objectives that view OCA in a broader context : the attack of a group of airbases : the expected duration of hostilities : the fact that judgements about the level of investment in OCA must consider linkages and trade-offs within the overall domain of air defence : that decisions on air defence may need to be assessed in respect of the total interaction between opposing air forces.

4. The key to developing rational intermediate effectiveness measures relies therefore on the translation of overall force structure into an hier-

archical framework of functional areas, each representing a domain of military capability:

- within which it is valid to examine costed improvement options and trade-offs

- which permits trade-off and prioritisation with other areas.

This is no simple task but it is probably less intractable than seeking to develop analytical measures representative of the overall conventional balance.

5. Conventional forces, together with theatre nuclear (TNF) and strategic nuclear, form the three components of NATO's defensive capability, which collectively aim to provide a credible deterrence to aggression. The strategy of flexible response can be interpreted as providing for:

- effective conventional defence that would additionally force the burden of escalation onto the other side

- the capability for deliberate escalation (which pre-supposes that TNF assets would be survivable)

- general nuclear resonse, being the ultimate guarantor of deterrence

These capabilities and their ordering are not intended to imply that planning should be based on the single assumption that there would be a conventional phase of hostilities with the possibility of subsequent escalation. But it is proposed, and this can be argued, that the design of NATO's conventional forces may be based on that premise.

6. Criteria for conventional forces may then be related to possession of a credible capability to:

- prevent loss of NATO territory for "as long as necessary", implying the ability to retain viable command and control, reinforcement/resupply functions

- preserve TNF assets and posture

The aim of this paper is to examine these general criteria in relation to perceptions of threat developments and to translate them, where possible, into quantifiable measures descriptive of the aggregate of land/air forces in Allied Command Europe (ACE).

PERCEPTIONS OF THE THREAT

7. The above criteria convey an impression of relevance to a major aggression against the Alliance aimed at territorial acquisition, the "design contingency" which has largely dictated NATO's force posture and the bulk of its defence expenditure. Convincing arguments have been made* that highlight the essential need to consider a diversity of scenarios, variants of those related to a major aggession as well as other "off-design" contingencies involving more limited objectives, pre-cursor actions and out-of-area activities. Force assessments, other than those based on static indicators, eg numbers of men and equipment, are necessarily scenario-dependent; they are implicitly based on political factors and on questionable assumptions about why and how a conflict might start.

---
*"Conflict scenarios and basic military missions in the defense of Europe". Dr. P.K. Davis, RAND Corporation

However, the need to plan against this area of uncertainty points to an important aspect of conventional force effectiveness more related to flexibility of response (in space and time) than to notions of the balance or correlation of forces. This point is discussed later.

8. Perceptions of the future threat* can be developed from study of evolving Soviet strategic and operational concepts. There is consensus among the threat assessment community that in order to succeed in a major aggression against the Alliance, it would be necessary to neutralise NATO's military forces and politial institutions quickly to avoid a situation in which the US military industrial potential could be brought to bear and to avoid escalation into a massive nuclear exchange. The first requirement then is speed. Many analysts would argue however, that because of NATO's impressive arsenal of defensive weapons, albeit numerically smaller than that of the Warsaw Pact (WP), there would be uncertainty in Soviet eyes of an assurance of success if NATO forces were fully deployed and well prepared. This points to the need to pre-empt a quick success, and that surprise is another essential ingredient of Soviet strategy.

9. Other factors can be identified that could influence Soviet perceptions and calculations. Some are inherent in the structures of the respective alliances and the asymmetries between them. In NATO, national contributions and their potential employment have to be coordinated through collective discussion and agreement, a process that promotes a measure of democratic solidarity but one that can lead to protracted decision-making. In Soviet eyes, NATO's political-military structure could suggest hesitancy and indecision in all but the most unambiguous crises. Moreover, in respect of the conduct of military operations, it must be apparent that NATO forces are less controlled by standardised doctrines and concepts, which might be perceived as exploitable weaknesses but which could present problems to the WP due to the need to face a variety of countermeasures. A further asymmetry between the alliances stems from the relationships within each in respect of contribution, commitment and reliability. Given political developments in Eastern Europe, Soviet commanders must have serious doubts about the reliability of some of their allies and this could influence the deployment of Soviet occupation forces and present a weakness that could be exploited by NATO.

10. Perhaps the most evident differences between the two military postures relate to the lack of depth in NATO's defences, the commitment to forward defence, the uncertain position of France and the maldeployment in peacetime of a substantial part of NATO's forces. These are serious weaknesses that the structure and deployment of WP forces are fully tailored to exploit. NATO is seeking to minimise these weaknesses by measures designed to increase the readiness of "in-place" forces, the early arrival of reinforcements and to improve the detection and interpretation of "warning time".

11. The objectives of WP forces on the Central Front would clearly be to exploit these potential weaknesses and to choose the most advantageous time to attack. Studies are frequently made on the basis of three warning scenarios: surprise attack by Soviet in-place forces; an attack after partial mobilisation; or after full build-up. The first would seem attractive and well suited to Soviet force design and deployment, but it could be a high risk option if based on a misappreciation of NATO's ability to respond and if it failed to achieve operational surprise. It is this question of surprise that poses the most difficult problem for a defence analyst in respect of developing effectiveness criteria. Soviet preparations for war would provide indications to NATO unless, as they undoubtedly would be, they were ambiguous, involving various forms of deception. NATO's ability to counter

---

*The remainder of this section draws from "A threat assessment for the 1990s". Consultant report to STC coordinated by John Bell Defence Systems

surprise is generally seen to be related to its alert system and to political decision-making. But if it is a factor that could influence NATO force design, this should be given high priority.

12. The following discussion aimed at developing quantified evaluation criteria for conventional forces, is focused on consideration of a major aggression against the Central Region and Baltic. It is assumed that actions in the far north would be related to the preservation of Kola assets and the ability to project power from that area. Activities in the Southern Region would be aimed at tying up the US and NATO forces in that area, and preventing any strategic relocation to the Central Region, or counter threat to the Southern USSR. It is re-emphasised that this is but one scenario and should not be used as the sole basis for planning.

DEVELOPMENT OF NUMERICAL EVALUATION CRITERIA

13. In trying to suggest quantifiable evaluation criteria for land/air forces in ACE, the discussion will comment on:

- static measures and force ratio comparisons

- deterrence criteria that extend on force ratio comparisons to include the drawdown of forces over time - their applicability and limitations

- operational factors; speed and surprise; multiple objectives

- flexibility in future force design

14. Many people outside of the defence community are familiar with static indicators of NATO/WP relative force capability. Various institutes produce statistics of numbers of men, ground equipments, aeroplanes and ships which provide some estimates of relative strength or force ratio. In the case of ground equipments, attempts have been made to allow for qualitative differences in NATO and WP divisions, based on computing combat potential, expressed typically in armoured division equivalents (ADEs). For an individual weapon, a weighted effectiveness index (WEI) is a composite of firepower, mobility and vulnerability indexes. The WEIs are multiplied by the respective number of each weapon in a unit (eg a division) to give a weighted unit value (WUV), and these provide a common measure for the two opposing ground forces.

15. These indicators take no account of unquantifiable factors such as the quality of men, training, morale, readiness; they are unrelated to scenarios, to the projectability of forces and to the dynamics of combat. But they convey an impression of the likelihood of a force being able to deter an attack, and rules of thumb have been developed which relate perceptious of the chances of success to specified force ratio levels.

16. Opinions vary on whether possession of an effective conventional posture for deterrence differs in any significant respect from an effective war fighting/winning capability. It appears that the Soviets have never accepted such a difference, believing the former to be a by-product of the latter, Militarily, the idea of deterrence has evolved around nuclear weapons, long-range delivery means and massive destruction, the effects of which are amenable to comparable calculation by each side. Deterrence implies building up perceptions, assurances and risks, in the mind of an adversary on the basis of understood criteria. It may be viewed as a backcloth to detente and defence and not interpreted to apply to some stage of sequential process. It could be argued that a viable deterrent posture should be based more on an

assessment of demonstrable capabilities that would be involved in the development of a confrontation/contingency, than on the less predictable dynamics of action after war start.

17. Obvious parameters included in perceptions of deterrence, are the forces and their composition : (regional, in-theatre, mobilisation, reinforcement) : crisis management : the political and military responses affecting action and the build-up of forces. The NATO objective can be related to sustaining conventional operations to the extent that Soviet planning would fail to demonstrate with confidence a conflict development leading to successful termination. This argument can be exemplified by postulating evaluation criteria that relate to NATO's capability to:

- hold forward for a specified period in the main defence positions

- achieve after that time an improving ground force ratio development

These are simplistic criteria whose limitations will be discussed later. They give emphasis to the relative ground force ratio build-up, and its drawdown after war start (taking account of airforces contributions).

18. Studies have assessed the conventional balance in the various regions of ACE on the basis of these criteria, using an aggregated differential equation model, calibrated by the results of wargames, to examine a wide range of threat assumptions, parametric variations, and improvement options, ranging from low cost political factors to larger-scale force enhancements. The analytical measures of effectiveness (MOE) corresponding respectively with the two criteria listed above were:

- average penetration across the front after X days of combat, (D+X), by the Orange force

- average rate of change of the Orange/Blue ground force ratio from D+X onwards

19. It is not claimed that the first measure provides a realistic interpretation of force movement over time, a factor that is extremely difficult to estimate confidently with any analytical technique. Although the model was calibrated by war game results, which included the effects of a non-integral "forward edge of the battle area" (FEBA) and breakthroughs, the mathematical formulation in effect represents movement as a linear flow. It is an attrition model and more credence should be placed on the second MOE : ground force ratio development as displayed in Figure 1. This illustrates the results of two outcomes, marked by circles and crosses respectively. The curves start at Blue mobilisation, assumed to be some days after Orange mobilisation. In each case, the right hand fork traces force ratio in the build-up process with no hostilities. The left hand fork portrays force levels after war start (D-day), some days after Blue mobilisation and represents the effects of continuing build-up and attrition of the ground forces by opposing ground and air forces. The outcome marked by circles is one in which the force ratio moves in favour of Orange; in that marked by crosses, the force ratio develops steadily in favour of Blue. The Blue objectives, as related to the deterrence criteria are to prevent penetration, and to achieve no worse than a constant force ratio development as indicated by the dashed line.

20. This representation of the conventional balance based on combination of the two criteria is displayed in Figure 2. The two situations described by Figure 1 (circles and crosses) and here represented by points A and B respectively. The technique was used to examine the criticality of input assumptions such as the rate of build-up and reinforcement of each side. It

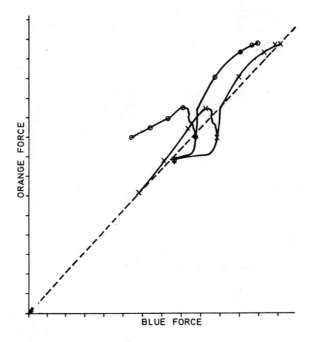

Fig. 1. Ground Force Ratio Build-Up/Drawdown

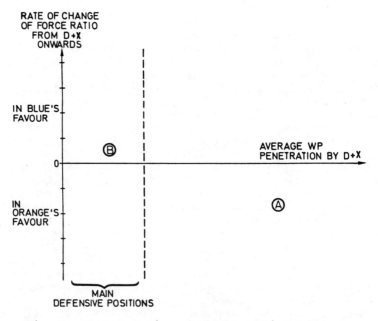

Fig. 2. Representation of the Conventional Balance

examined force enhancements that would transform a balance, unfavourable to Blue (point A in Figure 2), to a more favourable situation (point B). This could be achieved by having more forces in-place or by having more reinforcements; and there is a relationship between the size of a force enhancement and the timing of its arrival. For example, in this representation of the drawdown process, four additional in-place divisions available on D-day, either forward deployed or as theatre/army group reserves, would be equivalent to having six additional reinforcement divisions arriving later, say between D+3 and D+12. The technique can also be used to assess the value of other improvements to force posture or response, eg, the effects of having the capability to attrit and delay follow-on forces in the Orange build-up. It provides a means of quantifying the value of improved reaction time in mobilisation.

21. The technique provides for a simple and transparent means of comparing a range of quite disparate force enhancements or measures aimed at improving the "deterrent" posture of conventional forces. The criteria underlying the technique may be regarded as necessary conditions for an effective defence but they are not sufficient conditions. They do not take account of:

- operational and tactical concepts: the use of manoeuvre to breakthrough, fracture and envelop defensive deployments: surprise attacks

- linkages with tactical nuclear capabilities

22. Analytical studies of the former entail highly complex and often suspect simulations of combat or wargaming techniques that are driven by the judgements of the players. Figure 3 shows the results of a wargame for a scenario in which all of the opposing forces were assumed to be in theatre before war start. This depicts the drawdown of the two forces of combat and reflects the consequences of the sequence of operations that resulted in a successful outcome for the Orange force. It will be seen that during the initial period when Blue held in its main defensive positions the exchange ratio was clearly in favour of Blue. However, due to the employment of manoeuvre forces and airborne landings Orange achieved a breakthrough and during the following phase, exacted massive attrition against Blue. Later, a second line of defensive positions was established, the subsequent drawdown was near constant for some time, after which the defence was fractured and the Orange objective secured. This drawdown curve is typical of wargame outcomes in which breakthroughs succeed, but it is subject to considerable variability and dependence on player judgements.

23. The interesting point is that analysis of this scenario using the aggregated attrition model portrays an average drawdown that moves to some extent in Blue's favour. This would present the Orange commander with the perception of an insufficiently favourable balance in respect of wearing down the Blue force, and the realisation that confidence of success and risk of failure would be related to the unpredictable outcome of an operational plan. In this particular wargame, Orange succeeded because Blue failed to acquire timely intelligence about the deployment of the Orange second echelon forces and was unable to move his theatre reserve to counter the breakthrough.

24. This suggests that evaluation criteria descriptive of the balance or correlation of forces, and their translation into "quazi-dynamic" measures of effectiveness, as rehearsed earlier in this discussion are meaningful in relation to sizing force deficiency and assessing alternative prescriptive options. They imply that in order to deter aggression with conventional forces, NATO must first be seen to possess sufficient forces in respect of defensive and offensive firepower. However, the choice between various improvement options that would redress an imbalance, should be influenced by other factors, operational and political, that are difficult to study and

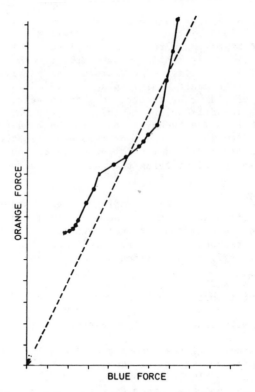

Fig. 3. Drawdown of Forces relating to Breakthrough Operations

measure analytically, but that could be seen by the Soviet Union to be critical at the onset of a conflict. This means that preferred solutions based on consideration of all relevant factors may not be the most cost-effective as judged by the more simplistic criteria.

FORCE IMPROVEMENT OPTIONS

25. Improvements to land-air forces can be related to three components:

   A. In-place Ground Forces

      o   corps organic units, theatre and mobilisable reserves

   B. Air-delivered Firepower

      o   counter-air : defensive and offensive

      o   offensive air : by aircraft (over target or stand-off) : tactical missiles

         - to support forward area combat

         - to attack follow-on forces

   C. Reinforcement and Re-supply

      o   air forces

      o   ground forces, by air, sea or prepositioned

26. This discussion has been focused on the extent to which balance assessments, based on relatively simple criteria, can influence procurement decisions, and it is argued that account must be taken of many operational factors that are difficult to quantify. The wargame outcome (para 22) exemplified the importance of having timely information on threat developments across the front in order to attack follow-on forces and make effective use of theatre reserves. The simple balance assessments omit other factors. They relate the total interaction between airpower (item B above) to the ground force ratio drawdown and average movement of the FEBA. They do not include the measures needed to retain, or degrade opposing, command and control capabilities and TNF assets; the implications of this omission have to be examined in more specific studies and included in the overall appreciation.

27. They do not assess the consequences of an attack achieving operational surprise. The studies discussed earlier examined various warning scenarios; short warning, partial build-up, full build-up : that refer to war start in relation to numbers of days after WP and NATO mobilisation respectively. But even in the short warning cases, it is assumed that the in-place forces are deployed in their defensive positions on D-day, albeit having had relatively little time for preparation and fortification. While accepting that strategic surprise would be most unlikely in a future conflict, strong arguments are advanced by informed analysts (Ref. 2) that the initiation of a conventional attack would be dependent on achieving a high degree of surprise in respect of its timing. This would imply a scenario involving a pre-emptive air and/or ground attack against a defence that is not fully deployed, and it suggests that in assessing force improvement options, weight should be given to those that could provide a high degree of readiness.

28. Indicators of response and resolve in a crisis involve measures and military actions which, to varying extent, require political concurrence and decision. Such decisions when taken, entail implementation procedures which, to varying extent, require action by national authorities and NATO commanders, and the subsequent times to implement action vary, depending on the forces involved. Air forces can provide reinforcement much more quickly than ground forces. Manned assets, in theatre, that could be brought to the ready by a centralised command would offer the highest degree of responsiveness and counter to surprise.

29. Mention has been made of linkages between conventional and TNF forces, the requirement on both sides to deploy the former under the threat of escalation, and the need to retain a viable option for deliberate escalation. It is argued that possession of effective conventional weapons for deep attack can affect the nuclear "threshold" and influence the decision to escalate. These are factors that could have an important bearing on force acquisition and they are not easily related to cost-effectiveness criteria, or amenable to simple analysis.

30. It should never be claimed that operational analysis can provide solutions to problems, but the process of defence planning, involving decisions and interactions between political, military and scientific judgement, can be supported by analytical methods which attempt to quantify alternative choices and focus attention on critical issues. This discussion at best exposes the difficulty of defining evaluation criteria for conventional forces, let alone attempting to quantify them.

31. It has been argued that notions and measures relating to the balance of forces are meaningful in respect of a credible deterrent posture, but that they give emphasis to weapon systems and firepower. In a strategy of forward defence, there will be a continuing need for effective in-place ground forces, and air defences, and there is room for improvement. But the dis-

cussion has pointed to attributes of force design that appear to be of increasing importance related to strategic and operational flexibility. In combination with a capability for intelligence and real-time information on threat developments, there appears to be need for enhanced firepower, that could respond in time and space (deep or shallow) to counter threat variability and evolving WP deployment doctrines, that could be rapidly deployed in tension, providing a credible counter to surprise, and that would be survivable in war. Solutions that meet this need in part have been the subject of wide scale debate.

Part II

CONCEPTUAL APPROACHES TO THE ASSESSMENT OF ALTERNATIVES

GAME-STRUCTURED ANALYSIS AS A FRAMEWORK

FOR DEFENSE PLANNING

        Paul K. Davis

        The Rand Corporation
        1700 Main Street, P.O. Box 2138
        Santa Monica, CA 90406-2138

SUMMARY

    The debate about NATO'S defense options has changed little in more than twenty years, with even less convergence of views. This nonconvergence has its principal origins in politics, economics, and the sociology of democracies, but the problem has been exacerbated by the absence of a coherent analytic framework within which to force issues toward resolution. Indeed, specialists in NATO defense issues fall into several disjoint groups with little intergroup communication--and few serious efforts to resolve differences, coalesce on recommendations, and advocate actions with the weight of consensus. It is then not surprising that it has been difficult to formulate, agree on, and maintain continuity in NATO's improvement programs. It is also not surprising that proposed initiatives all too often lack coherence and balance.

    Fortunately, the environment is now changing and the prospect exists for a more enlightened approach that would regularly bring together military officers, historians, technologists, and quantitative analysts-- both those concerned primarily with simple models and resource issues and those concerned primarily with the phenomena of warfare and simulation models. The improved environment includes increased interest in analytic realism, operational relevance, combined-arms planning, and in actually *solving* military problems.

    With this background, then, *the major point of this paper is that defense planning in the new environment should increasingly make use of conceptual structures akin to global political-military war gaming*. Such planning--whether for evaluating future force-structure options or near-term operations plans--should represent faithfully the asymmetric capabilities, operational strategies, and objectives of the two sides; it should also emphasize beginning-to-end global scenarios, taking into account possible mechanisms of escalation and termination and reflecting the nuclear shadow's effect on conventional operations. The concepts and techniques for such analysis are now becoming available.

    Some of the consequences of game-structured analysis with modern analytic models will be: (1) *multiscenario analysis*, to better account for the uncertainties attending any discussion of possible conflict, and (2) the development of *diverse and complex strategies*--strategies with branches for different circumstances and with explicit recognition of the need to exploit opportunities as well as cope with difficulties. The possibility exists that game-structured analysis could become a unifying framework within which many chronically unresolved debates could be joined and in which strategic thinking and a more aggressive approach to practical problem solving would be encouraged.

If there is indeed to be a convergence of strategic thinking, however, there are numerous necessary conditions. In particular, quantitatively inclined analysts must make their models more relevant to the issues being debated by strategists. Their models must be unequivocally strategic in perspective, flexible enough to address a vast range of "What if?" questions, transparent enough to establish credibility, and interactive enough to allow people other than inveterate modeler-analysts to use the models directly. Finally, there must be progress on what has long been promised but never truly delivered: relating assumptions in the aggregated strategic-level models to insights gained from empirical experience and detailed studies. This paper describes recent progress on many of these issues in the Rand Strategy Assessment Center (RSAC). It also proposes a cross-national cross-cultural effort to develop an improved analytic framework that could be used throughout the NATO community.

INTRODUCTION

A Context of Nonconvergence

One remarkable feature about the continuing debate on how best to defend Western Europe is the constancy of the issues. Another remarkable feature is the lack of convergence over a period of twenty years or so. Figure 1 reminds us of some of those enduring issues.

o Nuclear deterrence is not (or is) sufficiently credible

o Conventional defense is (or is not) feasible given the modest (or large) quantitative superiority of the Warsaw Pact forces

o Increasing reliance on conventional defenses would raise (or lower) overall deterrence while raising the nuclear threshold

o Improving conventional defenses is (or is not) feasible given realistic estimates of the requirements and the implications for budgets and manpower

o Europeans already shoulder (or should shoulder) most of the burden for defense of Europe

o NATO's air forces would (or would not) compensate significantly for Pact advantages in numbers of divisions

o The real threat is from a lengthy war in which the Soviets can exploit the sheer magnitude of their land army (or a blitzkrieg with minimal warning)

o In time of multifront crises the United States would (or would not) have to focus its attention solely on Europe, to the exclusion of the other fronts

Fig. 1. Persistent themes in the debate about defense of Europe

Even when we get past the larger themes of Fig. 1, there remain many issues and disputes about down-to-earth defense programs and operational strategies (Fig. 2). Although neither complete nor entirely fair-minded, Fig. 2 is valid insofar as it conveys a sense of continuing confusion and a sense that the landscape of options is broad.*

Given the continuing arguments about fundamentals as well as improvement options, it is surprising that there has been any progress at all. Still, in spite of the massive Soviet buildups throughout the 1970s and into the current era, now is a reasonably good period for NATO in some respects because the fruits of modernization programs are becoming felt. It is also a period in which the United States has taken substantial measures to improve readiness across the board and to raise the status of the military in public eyes. Morale in the military is good and there is a sense that problems can be solved and needed improvements achieved.** Another good development has been the increased attention paid to operational commanders--even to the extent of providing them directly with funds for miscellaneous problem-solving best done in the field. Finally, some of the new technology is here and impressive. Over the next decade it should be possible to field defensive systems with extraordinary capabilities.

o Forward defense is the best (or worst) use of NATO's limited forces

o We should not (or should) consider alternatives such as defense in depth and mobile defense

o Modernization should (or should not) focus on "heavying up" NATO's divisions; ultimately, firepower and mobility dominate (or are only one factor)

o The focus of improvements in conventional defense should be:

   -- additional operational reserves
   -- (or heavier divisions)
   -- (or smart munitions for second-echelon interdiction)
   -- (or smart munitions for use on the front and in battlefield interdiction)
   -- (or systems for advanced command and control, including theaterwide situation assessment)
   -- (or preparations for a long war with increased buys of munitions and spare parts, and plans for mobilization)

o The focus of thinking in conventional defense should be on deterring the short war (or the long war)

o The biggest threat is a short-warning (or full-mobilization) attack

o NATO partners should (or should not) plan for defense actions outside the NATO area per se, particularly in Southwest Asia

Fig. 2. Enduring disagreements about NATO options

---

*See, for example, Levine et al. (1982).
**Two examples stand out: the buildup from virtually nothing of an operational capability to deter or deal with a Soviet invasion of the Persian Gulf (see Davis, 1982a, for an account of what made that buildup possible), and the buildup of the U.S. Navy under Navy Secretary John Lehman.

In spite of these optimistic comments, there has not yet emerged a consensus among NATO members about how best to proceed toward an adequate conventional defense in the course of a finite number of years; nor is there adequate attention at the policy level to the kinds of problems that money will not solve--e.g., problems of multinational operations in the presence of Soviet blitzkrieg tactics. Indeed, far short of that, *there is still no consensus on the most fundamental of issues: the importance of NATO's being able to defend itself conventionally, with some confidence-- not just for a matter of days, but indefinitely.* As a result, it is hardly surprising that NATO improvement programs appear to be largely business as usual--important business to be sure, but not very impressive by comparison with the problems to be solved.

One reason that more convergence has not occurred is that those interested in improvements live in different professional communities with minimal communication. As a result, potential natural allies have often worked at cross purposes. Figure 3 summarizes some of these groups and their natural predilections. Although stereotyped, these characterizations are legitimate for present purposes: the groups exist (in the military services and in civilian organizations), they are remarkably disjoint, and

Policymakers: concerned primarily about excessive reliance on the nuclear deterrent, about obtaining adequate budget levels for defense, and about peacetime alliance cohesion; language: forward defense, flexible response, reestablishing deterrence; models: primarily, those of the program analysts or the bean-counting models of balance assessments

Program Analysts: concerned with making reasonable resources available to military commanders; language: force ratios and FLOT locations versus time, mobility forces, prepositioning programs, days of supply in theater, programs for improving the survivability of air bases; models: stereotyped attrition warfare under a few short-war scenarios differing primarily in warning time

Military Historians and Strategists: concerned with grand strategy and operational strategy in conflict; language: maneuver warfare, daring thrusts, breakthroughs, attacks on rear-area targets, cohesion, quality, initiative, possibility of stalemates or protracted wars requiring national mobilization, surprise attack; models: none (partial exceptions: Dupuy's QJM model and some manual games)

Simulation Modelers: concerned with modeling selected phenomena of an idealized war (while deferring other phenomena to later studies) and adding complexity; language: data bases, subroutines, Lanchester equations; models: many, at several levels of detail further distinguishing among cultures (strategic-level, theater-level, corps-level, battalion-level, and weapons-level)

Technologists: concerned with finding ways to solve problems with modern technology weapons; language: PGMs, cluster munitions, sensors, fusion, centralized C^3I, capability multipliers; models: many, almost always at the weapon vs. target level

Fig. 3. Distinguishable analytic communities interested in conventional defense

none of them seems to feel--at present--an obligation or burning desire to
resolve the various problems among groups. To make things worse, there is
little tradition for integrated analysis of air and land issues (although the
climate exists for doing so). If there is to be a period of convergence, there
will have to be some unprecedented cross-cultural efforts. More on this later.

The Role of Analysis in Achieving Convergence

With this background, then, the present paper is concerned not with the
full range of issues raised, but with the potential role of quantitative (or
at least formal) analysis. It seems appropriate at the outset to ask why one
might expect there to be *any* role. After all, if the problems stem from
economics, politics, and the short-sightedness of democracies with regard
to defense, then what can analysis really contribute? First, some general
observations:

- Problem solving occurs when people believe the problems are
  solvable (even if with difficulty)

- Analytic models and balance assessments affect what comes to be
  conventional wisdom about the seriousness and solvability of
  military problems

- When there have been periods of rapid and focused progress in
  solving defense problems or fielding new capabilities, there has
  often been strong analysis behind the effort--analysis that could
  be explained at several levels of sophistication and communicated
  all the way from the top leadership to the officers in the field*

Second, consider two of this paper's premises:

- Some of the most important problems in NATO's defense posture have
  to do with operational issues that cannot easily be understood and
  explained without analytic models

- If convergence is to occur on such complex issues as the interrelationship of conventional and nuclear capabilities, the airland battle, the role of effective but expensive munitions, and
  the complementarity of what are now seen as opposing operational
  strategies, there must be an analytic framework within which to
  have the associated debate; otherwise, we shall continue to see
  competing essays and a failure of proponents to make their ideas
  "stick" when it comes time--not just once, but continually over a
  period of years--to convince policymakers, budgeteers, and
  bureaucracies

These, then, are the articles of faith. It remains to add some details.

FRAMEWORK PROBLEMS FOR CURRENT ANALYSIS

The Role of Simple Models

One might naively think that operations research and simulation
modeling would have had an enormous impact on policy-level thinking about
the military balance and appropriate Western strategies. In practice,
however, it seems that the most influential quantitative analyses have been

---

*Examples here include U.S. programs to improve strategic mobility,
basing, and support capabilities for the CENTCOM mission in Southwest Asia.

simple and essentially constant in form. So, for example, one can find similar analysis in studies by Enthoven and Smith (1971), the Congressional Budget Office (1980), Kaufmann (1983), Posen et al. (1984), Mearsheimer (1983), Mako (1983), and unpublished work by Richard Kugler of the Department of Defense. These analyses focus on a highly aggregated view deemed appropriate to civilian planners attempting to make adequate resources available rather than attempting to assure good operational planning or clever generalship. The continuing themes of that school include:

- The NATO balance is driven by assumptions about which nations will commit forces, which forces of each nation to include, how to count forces of different quality and composition, and *timing*

- NATO's chances for success should be reasonably good for theater force ratios less than about 1.5, with force ratios of 2.0 being quite worrisome*

- The principal problem, then, is for NATO to assure that theater force ratios be kept as low as possible at all times--thus implying a need not only for forces but also for rapid mobilization and deployment

- High-leverage measures include: (a) maintaining European reserves at a high state of readiness; (b) prepositioning equipment for U.S. forces so that fully equipped divisions would be available as quickly as the men could be flown in from the CONUS (POMCUS programs); (c) starting NATO mobilization early; and (d) obtaining substantial early French participation

In their simplest form, these arguments require little more in the way of modeling than a method for normalizing divisions to a standard measure (e.g., Armored Division Equivalents, ADE) and a model for predicting the rates at which various forces can be mobilized and deployed to the front. Such "models" can be back-of-the-envelope constructs plus some data tables.

These simple models have been influential because they are understandable, dealing with issues at only the most aggregated of levels. Also, the principal conclusions drawn from these models have been almost obviously valid: strategic mobility is good; rapid mobilization is good; operational reserves are good; and providing divisions in Europe with substantial firepower and mobility is good (although overemphasis on ADE score alone has been a chronic problem in cost-effectiveness studies, especially those involving combat in mountains, forests, and urban areas).

Users of the simple models have also had an impact on notions about what is *feasible*. It is difficult to read papers by such an experienced figure as William Kaufmann and not conclude that in theory the resources are there for NATO to be successful--the issue is how and with what

---

*Roughly speaking, these rules of thumb relate to the famous 3:1 criterion of local concentration as follows: imagine, say, 40 NATO and 60 Pact divisions scattered evenly among 8 corps sectors (5 and 7.5 divisions per corps sector, respectively, for an overall ratio of 1.5). The Pact could take its excess 20 divisions and concentrate them on main axes. With, for example, 2-3 main axes, the Pact could achieve local force ratios of 2.8-3.5 if NATO failed to detect and react to the concentrations. Concentrating on a single axis would be possible in principle, but more difficult to achieve without NATO observing and concentrating its defenses quickly as well.

efficiency we *allocate* those resources (dollars, manpower, etc.)--and how well our generals use them. That is, one can argue that the problem is one of outputs rather than inputs. This is especially so now with the sustained real growth in U.S. defense budgets.

In summary, there is much to applaud about simple transparent models. Moreover, they have been and will continue to be the first line of advocacy and analysis. Nonetheless, it seems to me that the simple models have already accomplished what they can--although continual reminders of their lessons are necessary. The serious problems preventing the convergence discussed above cannot be solved by analysis with simple models because:

- They lack *credibility* among those who rightly expect that there "must" be more to the balance than theater force ratio and those who note that the simple models have not been "validated" as approximations to more complex treatments

- Because they are so aggregated, they have no potential for unifying such disparate communities as the technologists, historians, maneuver warfare advocates, and resource managers

- They have little to say about matters of command and control, military organization, and the doctrines behind decisions

- Finally, they often fail to convey a sense of interrelationships and provide only a modest sense of operational strategy*

It follows, then, that there is need for a more profound analytic framework than is possible with the simple models. The search for such a framework has begun but will not be completed soon.

Balance Comparisons by Bean Counts

There is another form of simple analysis that is usually associated with the name "static measures" (or, less formally, "bean counts"). Over the last two decades, the effort to count weapons and divisions and to deal in other miscellaneous static measures has become somewhat of a cottage industry. There must be a dozen organizations in Washington alone that consider themselves as doing analysis because they can generate bar charts displaying such comparisons. Such "analyses" have had a profound effect on the thinking of the American man in the street, albeit indirectly. The vague impression that slowly turns into a conviction that more money should be spent on defense, and that more should be done to modernize our forces, comes in significant measure from ten-second news spots reflecting defense reports and other studies of the "bean-count" variety.

Interestingly enough, the most expert producers of balance studies are less than enthusiastic about the state of the art. Indeed, more than anyone else they have argued for more intellectually respectable analysis

---

*The problem here is not the authors but the medium: the effort to reduce issues to an analytic framework oriented toward resource allocation tends to produce a cold product, with the richness of strategic thinking to be found only in the essays that accompany the quantitative analysis (see, for example, Kaufmann, 1983). The essays, however, tend often to be brief and subjective. Furthermore, the linear nature of essays makes it difficult for readers properly to integrate their content. This is why human war games have had so much effect on many peoples' thinking: they have the right format, including a sense of drama, to exploit uniquely human capabilities for integration (e.g., capabilities to learn from argumentation and debate).

(see, for example, Marshall, 1982). Nonetheless, it is likely we shall continue to see bean-count comparisons indefinitely--they have a place, they do convey some information, and they are simple. Unfortunately, they also lend themselves to simplistic thinking and tend to focus attention *too exclusively* on objects such as tanks or ICBMs rather than on more complex matters such as flexibility and command-control.*

The Role of More Complex Models

Complexity is a matter of degree and a matter for the eyes of the beholder to discern. Here, however, I shall consider models to be either simple or complex, with simple models being those discussed above. By complex models I shall mean the full range of models for which computers are needed. Later, I shall introduce some distinctions.

Given the many years of experience with combat simulation models, one might expect that such models would have had a significant impact on policymaking. I would argue, however, that simulations of NATO/Pact conflict have had very little influence on policymakers (although they have certainly affected logistics, weapon-level, and doctrinal planning within the individual military services. The point is arguable, but I will assert that I have *seldom* heard a senior or mid-level official of the U.S. government base policy-level conclusions on the results of a theater combat simulation. To the contrary, I have *often* heard such simulations derided and arguments based on them dismissed out of hand.

The reasons for this lack of influence are many and varied. The most fundamental reason is that the combat simulations lack *credibility* among experienced policymakers, just as the simpler models lack credibility among those familiar with details. A common impression is that the complexity of simulations does not help. Ultimately, model results are still driven by *assumptions* about: (a) which forces are counted; (b) buildup rates, (c) the scores given to each force (a function of equipment quality and quantity); (d) various attrition rates (by killer-victim pair, reflecting weapon capabilities); and (e) the rates of advance. There are really two points here: first, it often seems that the simulations are not really adding anything of first-order importance; and second, the simulations often seem to bury key assumptions.

There are other problems as well: most combat simulations have been perceived to be (a) opaque; (b) unmaintainable (everyone has seen results that had to be withdrawn because some deeply buried data element was wrong); (c) slow; and (d) anti-intellectual by virtue of their opacity. Modeling organizations have not generally been eager to participate in detailed comparisons of models and assumptions.

I mention item (d) because senior officials tend to believe that most problems can be understood with a few variables, and to ask how outcomes change with those variables. Answering them is often more successful with simple models and graphs than with piles of computer output and grimaces in reaction to questions.

Finally, let me mention a drawback of the complex models that may in some respects be the most compelling of all: they are "beyond touch"-- not only is it impossible for a policymaker to get into them personally, it

---

*Blaker and Hamilton (1977), themselves well experienced in balance assessments, predicted some seven years ago that the U.S. Congress would begin to hear more about these matters and less about bean counts. That prediction seems to have been premature but was certainly in the same spirit as the present paper's suggestions.

is often impossible for his aides to do so. The complex models are in the province of contractors or separate agencies and are simply too far away and inscrutable to be trusted.*

If big policy-relevant simulations are so bad, why do I even raise the issue? The answer, of course, is that I think their time is coming. Much is possible now that was not possible twenty years ago when technology was more primitive and experience more limited. In particular, complex analyses can now be controlled better and presented more clearly. Moreover, *the more complex models are essential to our understanding of the phenomenology of war*--and the associated analysis of defense options. Figure 4 cites some examples of problem areas for which the truly simple models (and *current* complex models) are not adequate.

Requirements for a New Analytic Framework

Let us now turn to the future: What kind of framework is needed to go beyond where we now stand? Clearly, there will be a role for both simple and complex models, but let us focus primarily on the latter. What characteristics should they have?

Strategic Breadth: A Global Framework   One enduring difficulty in discussing NATO defense issues is that so many problems are dealt with by separate organizations. For example, the U.S. Department of Defense has independent offices that seldom interact for strategic nuclear, theater nuclear, and conventional defense issues; similarly, NATO governments

o   Command and control

   -- technical (e.g., situation assessment)
   -- operational (e.g., air-land coordination and cross-national maneuver)

o   Logistics (including cross-national problems and implications of interdiction)

o   High-technology weapons

o   Employment options for airpower

o   Barrier defenses

o   Responses to operational maneuver groups and early breakthroughs

o   Interrelationship of conventional and nuclear planning

o   Multitheater conflict under a range of scenarios

o   Deterrence and escalation control once conflict has begun

o   Alternative operational strategies (e.g., mobile defenses)

Fig. 4. Representative subject areas for which more complex models and games are needed

---

*There are some exceptions to this in strategic nuclear analysis and strategic mobility analysis. In both cases, the Office of the Secretary of Defense and the Office of the Joint Chiefs of Staff routinely use complex in-house models. However, there are special circumstances. The quality of analysis is high in both areas--with the analytic assumptions being generally understood by a considerable community. Also, both subjects are in many respects more intuitively understandable, and even simpler, than theater warfare. Thus, policymakers can feel they understand what the models are doing even if the details of number crunching are obscure.

typically have different offices for different regions (Europe, South Asia, East Asia, etc.). An improved framework for strategic analysis should attempt to cut across such boundaries.

Integrated Planning

The next issue is more controversial. In my view, *if a new analytic framework is to be unifying rather than divisive, it must start by bringing together what are sometimes referred to as (a) declaratory policy, (b) program planning, and (c) employment planning*. These terms are most familiar in strategic nuclear problems but they apply in the NATO context as well. Note, for example:

- NATO's *declaratory policy* has generally emphasized the potential use of nuclear weapons, with conventional defense being characterized more as a means for avoiding quick and easy conquest, and for providing an opportunity to reestablish deterrence should war begin, than as an end in itself.

- NATO's *defense programs*, however, have generally emphasized conventional modernization (with the exception of some highly publicized items such as the GLCM and Pershing II). The related program analysis has generally been conducted at the DoD level with simple models focused on trends in various static measures and goals for the ability to build up Armored Division Equivalents in the European theater as a function of time after mobilization. There has been minimal discussion of maneuver and operational issues, although that is beginning to change (Kugler, unpublished).

- NATO's operational commanders, by contrast, have had to concern themselves with *employing* the forces available to them. The language of force employment, especially as there has been renewed interest in maneuver warfare and a more generally active defense effort, is fundamentally different from that in either declaratory policy or programming analysis. Also--at least in theory, *operational commanders cannot, or should not, allow their thinking to be constrained by standardized planning scenarios*.

It is apparent that declaratory policy is often just that, a product of peacetime pressures and compromise as much as strategy. The traditional program planner's point of view is often more nearly to the point, but not very rich. If we seek something more profound, we should take the viewpoint of force *employment* to uncover problems and solutions going beyond "more is better." Only in this way can we hope to bring together in one framework specialists from the military, technological, and resource allocation worlds. Why? Because only here is there enough specificity, depth, and military content to provide the tangible examples that are the stuff of integration across cultures.

A Strategic Perspective   There is at the same time a conflicting requirement. If the framework is to be relevant to *strategy*, it must somehow remain above the clouds--i.e., we must not lose sight of the forest among the trees. This, of course, has been the fundamental problem from the beginning of analysis: the clamor is always for more detail from those who are concerned with the pieces, but for those addressing issues of strategy, the details must *ultimately* be scrupulously suppressed except by reflecting them implicitly in more integrated concepts.

All of this is old stuff--going by the rubric of top-down analysis-- and is understood by strategists and managers in all walks of life. The trick is to pull it off: if one ignores the wrong details or interrelationships, the impression at the top is seriously flawed; if one includes all the details and interrelationships, the effort sinks of its own weight. In fact, there is no general solution other than putting smart people on the task--some with interest in details, some with interest in integration, and yet others interested in the final communication of results.

Political-Military Structure   Credibility involves more than building good combat models; it also requires addressing--in a single structure if we are to achieve integration--the more important political-military issues such as alliance cohesiveness (NATO's and the Pact's), constraints on actions, and escalation control.

Reflecting National Doctrines and Propensities   In attempting to treat political as well as military issues it is essential to be concerned with the asymmetries between the Western and Soviet views of almost everything. This can be overdone because Soviet doctrine is written for an "ideal war" very different from that we would regard plausible (e.g., the Soviet doctrine tends to assume a context of aggression by NATO under circumstances where a fight to the finish is inevitable). Nonetheless, it is ignored at our peril, since Soviet concepts of warfighting differ markedly from the image implicit in most Western combat models, and Soviet concepts of escalation control tend to be dangerously dissonant with those of NATO (see, for example, Davis and Stan, 1984).

Transparency and Comprehensibility   As noted earlier, any modeling framework should be as transparent and comprehensible as possible (I distinguish transparency of a particular algorithm or rule from comprehensibility of an overall model). There is little here to engender quarrels--only when one asks what these terms mean will there be arguments, as one discovers that what is transparent to one person is opaque to another; and, indeed, what is top-down to modelers and programmers is often bottom-up or sideways-in to a strategist.

What then does the requirement mean? It means, for example, that one can find where all the important issues are treated (good modularity). Less trivially, it means that the various modules are the "right ones"-- i.e., that the model's parts (and names) correspond with the objects of the strategist's attention. Also, of course, it means that one can find the important data, properly formatted and maintained in terms understandable to the strategist. It may also mean that key elements of the computer code itself are understandable to people with only modest programming skills.

Flexibility and Ability to Address Soft Issues   Extremely important in any model framework purporting to be the basis for integration and synthesis is the capability to consider a wide range of assumptions--to respond to queries about "But what if ...?" Without this capability there would be no way to achieve the convergence discussed earlier: individuals could continue to wander off saying "Yes, but they didn't consider ...." One subtlety is worth noting here: it is not sufficient for the clever modeler-analyst to wave his hands and say "Yes, but that washes out"-- even if it is trivially obvious (to him). The point will not be communicated and made to stick unless the models have knobs and switches allowing others to test the assertion directly. In practice, moreover, the "clever" modeler-analyst has often been wrong on such matters.

Examples of "What if?" questions are legion and involve many "soft" issues. Military historians, for instance, regularly deride modeler-analysts for their failure to account for differences in the *quality* of different national forces, the Arabs and Israelis being the most obvious example, and for their failure to account for effects such as surprise, the chaos resulting from having been attacked in the rear, "Fog of War," and "Friction" (Dupuy, 1979).

Responding to such requirements is not so difficult technically as it is paradigmatically. Many modeler-analysts have an emotional reluctance to treat issues that do not lend themselves well to quantification or algorithmic solutions. They also have good arguments. After all, they point out, it is one thing to create a new parameter, but who is going to provide the parameter value? The other traditional concern is that along with flexibility come more degrees of freedom and the *curse of dimensionality* when it comes time to sensitivity analysis. Such concerns are valid, but *if models of combat are to be more relevant and credible they must reflect both soft and hard issues.*

Interactivity Finally, let me mention a requirement that makes far more sense in today's world than the world of ten or fifteen years ago. Recall the assertion that a major problem in the use of complex models is that they have been inaccessible to policymakers and their aides. The answer must be greater interactiveness--for both an admiral's test and routine analysis. Flexibility is of little value if answering a "What if?" question requires hours by a group in another building. *Ideally, the response should come in seconds, but certainly in a matter of minutes-- i.e., within a cognitive cycle.* All of this implies speed and efficiency.

Interactiveness also means having what computer scientists sometimes call a "friendly interface." That is, the outputs should be natural and have almost self-evident meanings. In particular, it should not be necessary to wade through computer printout to hand-draw curves or fill out tables.

The Rand Strategy Assessment Center

Background The requirements levied in the previous subsection have a deliberately close relationship with those stated by the Department of Defense in 1979 in its search for fundamentally new concepts and capabilities in strategic analysis. After a series of committee efforts, competitions, and proposals, there emerged in 1980 an effort imbedded in the Rand Strategy Assessment Center (RSAC). Although originally focused almost exclusively on nuclear issues, the RSAC's work has come to be as relevant to global military planning in general as to nuclear planning in particular--primarily because one of the biggest challenges was to develop the capability to follow scenarios from beginning to end, with considerable attention on events during conventional phases of what might become general nuclear war.* Many of the RSAC's paradigms and structures appear relevant to the problem of developing an analytic framework for studying NATO's options. Before discussing this, let us first review some of the RSAC's characteristic features.

Automated War Gaming Because of precisely the same problems discussed previously (e.g., the poverty of bean-count "analysis" and the need for analysts to address issues of command-control and interconnections among the elements of combined arms forces), the DoD concluded in 1979 that the new methods of strategic analysis should combine the best features of human war gaming and analytic modeling (Marshall, 1982). From war gaming would come the strategic perspective, the interrelationships, the richness

---

*For the RSAC's general objectives and history, see Davis and Winnefeld (1983), a report written before the current development work. See also Davis (forthcoming), Davis (1984), and Davis and Stan (1984).

of context, and the asymmetries between West and East; from analytic modeling would come rigor, reproducibility, and the capability to draw conclusions reasonably.

In taking on this challenge, Rand concluded early that it was necessary to *automate* the war game (Fig. 5) to gain control over the many variables (Graubard and Builder, 1982). This meant building not only flexible and efficient combat models, but also building decision models to represent the various nations. Note in Fig. 5 that humans can play at any position (Red, Blue, or Control) or can use the system as a closed simulation model with which to do experiments. Both open and closed modes are important.

The essential features of the RSAC's conceptual approach can be summarized as follows (Davis, 1984, and Davis, forthcoming), starting with the description of fully automated play:

1. The structure is roughly that of a two-player game (Red = Soviet Union/Warsaw Pact; Blue = U.S./NATO), but with modeling of *political* decisions by *all* relevant countries. All decision models are "parametric," allowing for alternative decision patterns.

2. At any time in the war game, each side is following an *analytic war plan*, which represents to some degree the features of real-world war plans *plus* the adaptations made by military commanders as the scenario unfolds. The plans are adapted and executed in a hierarchical process related to command structure.

3. The analytic war plans contain rules calling for reconsideration of concepts when events arise for which the plans were not designed (e.g., opponent escalation). When these rules, or "bounds," are triggered, it is time for special national-command-level models (or human teams) to decide whether to pick new plans, modify the current ones, or continue the new plans without change.

4. The Force Agent is a large simulation model with a global strategic-level view. In Europe, the Force Agent's resolution is basically that of a theater commander rather than, for example, a

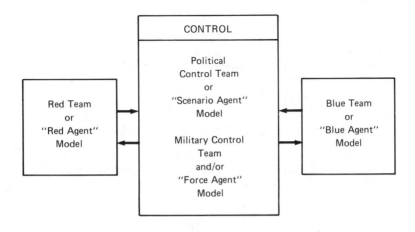

Fig. 5. Man-machine relationships in Rand's automated war gaming

corps commander. The various component models are extremely parametric and interactive to permit the analyst or human teams to explore changes in strategy or changes in analytic assumptions.

5. It is possible for humans to work with the whole system *or* with particular portions of special interest. So, for example, there is a *Force Standalone* capability allowing analysts or human teams to focus on "sandtabling" (with some expert-system models for certain command-control functions); there is also a capability to build or modify new analytic war plans to be tested against the automated opponent; and there is a capability to bypass the simulations of combat and third-country decisions while focusing on the decision rules of the national command level models.

Figures 6 and 7 summarize key features of the conceptual architecture, which is reflected faithfully in the system architecture. Figure 7 elaborates on part of the hierarchical structuring of military command levels. As Figure 7 indicates, the RSAC simulation is based on the U.S. point of view, so that Blue is primarily the United States and secondarily the NATO alliance.

<u>Program Status</u> The RSAC program has recently completed two years of full development activity (using some concepts and tools developed over a longer period). We now possess a *prototype* system with a wide range of capabilities. There remain many loose ends, including empty holes for undeveloped models and data bases of varying quality. Also, we have a great deal to learn about how to achieve transparency, flexibility, and all those other virtues. Nonetheless, the prototype system is a reality, applications are under way, and I can speak with some confidence about what is possible. For example:

- The decision rules are written in an English-like computer language allowing individuals with only modest knowledge of programming to understand the rules and make substantial (although constrained) changes.

- The force models can be run by a single analyst and are fast (e.g., 10 minutes on a VAX 11-780 for a 30-day European war testing sensitivity to some change in force structure or modeling parameter).

- A full-system automated war game (crisis through general nuclear war) takes about 1-2 hours.

- The National Command Level (NCL) and Scenario Agent models have proved powerful in organizing both "hard" and "soft" information and logic on national decisions. Research with NCL models has already been illuminating on how to think about deterrence and escalation control.

So much for a quick once-over of current RSAC capabilities. Let us turn next to how such techniques can be used to address issues of NATO strategy. The next two sections deal with treatment of uncertainty in balance assessments and with developing more complex strategies. A major theme is the importance of multiscenario analysis.

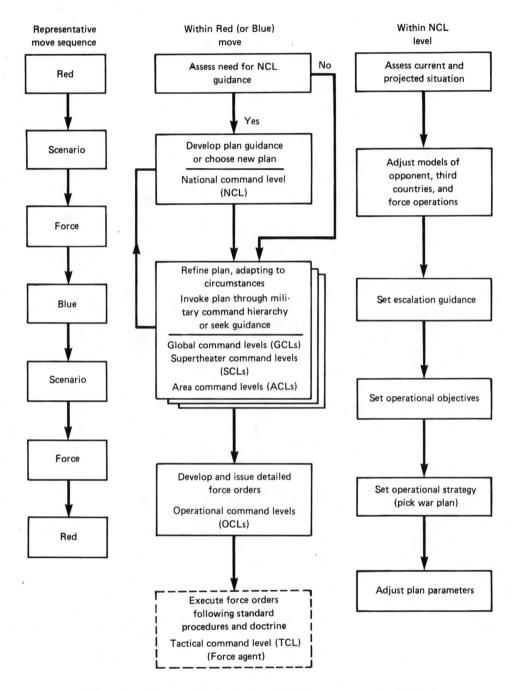

Fig. 6. Hierarchical view of RSAC war-game simulation

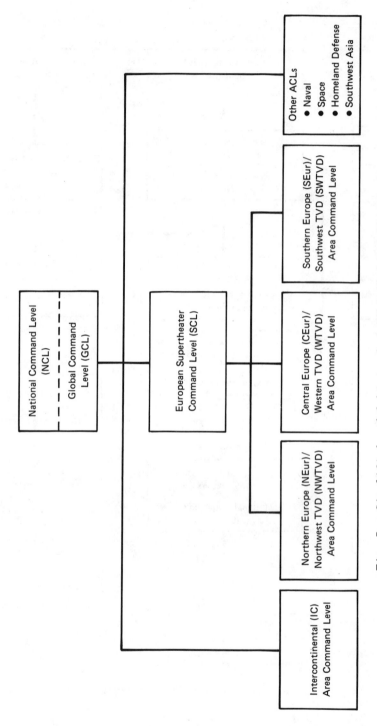

Fig. 7. Simplified model hierarchy within Red and Blue Agents

THE CONCEPT OF MULTISCENARIO ANALYSIS

Definitions

The problems with single-scenario assessments* are well known in the abstract, but we have lived with them so long it is useful to remind ourselves of their consequences (Fig. 8).

In principle, "standard scenarios" are used only for limited purposes such as developing total force requirements on a coordinated basis (e.g., with the Navy, Army, and Air Force buying munitions for the same type of war). In practice, the standard scenarios and standard planning assumptions are used for virtually everything. They even infect operations planning. Why? The reasons are many and varied but start with the desire in large organizations to avoid friction by following conventional procedures.

Many people would rightly argue that these problems have always been recognized and that even the fathers of system analysis emphasized the need to conduct multiple scenarios (see, for example, Madansky, 1968). However, this is all a matter of degree. For example, many articles treating a wide range of NATO defense scenarios turn out ultimately to be varying only warning time. Admittedly, warning time is a big issue, but if one wants to get in the spirit of adaptive thinking and into a mode of appreciating problems of command-control and flexibility more generally, there are many other uncertainties, such as those in Fig. 9. To elaborate on just one example--grand strategy--should not NATO's conventional-defense strategy at the time of conflict depend on whether the Pact is apparently seeking a short war for limited gains or a war of indefinite length for ultimate aims? It is this type of issue that leads me to emphasize the need for complex and adaptive strategies.

o Encourages organizations and planners to focus on rigid scenarios unlikely to be seen in the real world

o Discourages focus on adaptation and contingency planning

o Conveys an excessively firm impression about the military balance--one that can be unduly pessimistic in some respects while being unduly optimistic in others (i.e., creates bad intuition)

o Discourages certain types of initiative and daring actions (e.g., avoidance of battle at moderately adverse force ratios; excessive emphasis on static tactics)

o Tends to submerge important but non-best-estimate possibilities (e.g., early breakthroughs or the catastrophic failure of some weapon system)

o Provides little useful to operational commanders, who tend to look elsewhere (e.g., to intuition) for assistance

Fig. 8. Side effects of single-scenario analysis

---

*In this paper I consider multiscenario analysis to include variations in context, timelines, forces, strategies, and technical parameters--not merely basic timelines. A better terminology might be uncertainty analysis.

- Initiating political-
  military scenario
  - context
  - alliances
  - timing of events worldwide

- National temperaments and grand strategies

- Military strategies

- Force structures

- Operational-level strategies

- Technical assumptions about "laws" of combat

- Qualities of forces by nationality, unit, and region

- Effectiveness of various weapon systems and tactics

- Rolls of the dice in regard to particular battle outcomes, etc.

Fig. 9. Representative classes of uncertainty

Unfortunately, so long as analysts limit themselves to back-of-the-envelope calculations or to large and ponderous detailed models (e.g., weapons-level models designed primarily for use by the individual military services), it will be impossible to examine any great range of the variables in Fig. 9 intelligently. The result will be to maintain the schisms between classes of analysts.

Why is this so terrible? Because, for example:

- Standard NATO balance assessments provide a sense of doom and gloom even though the uncertainties involved suggest that NATO *might* actually do well were the Soviets to attempt a conventional invasion, even today (i.e, the attitude should be one of a distinct underdog, but with a significant chance of success).

- There are in fact many classes of plausible scenarios, some of them favorable to NATO and--as we all recognize--many that are quite worrisome. The trick, in part, should be to create a mind-set that NATO is not a passive actor--that with appropriate actions it can control to a considerable extent the scenario and the likelihood of successful defense.

- The opening days of a real conflict would probably bring some dramatic surprises: e.g., tactics or weapons that work or do not work. Without prior thought about how to adapt--exploiting opportunities as well as coping with problems--opportunities will be lost, the initiative sacrificed, and, quite possibly, the war lost.

- The single-scenario approach and its usual variants obscure many of the problems that would be most dangerous to NATO should war occur--problems of flexibility, reaction time, surprise failures of particular systems or forces, and cross-national operations, all of which tend to be assumed away in ordinary studies.

Principles of Uncertainty Analysis

Now that we are gaining some experience with multiscenario analysis, we are beginning also to formulate principles. Some of them will look familiar to system analysts with careers dating back to the 1960s or earlier. Figure 10 lists the principles I currently urge on my colleagues.

Philosophy	o Use complex measures relevant to commanders in preference to "analyst measures of effectiveness (MOEs)" (e.g., use maps or graphs in terms of variables the commander can control, charts showing critical windows in time)
	o Examine *all* classes of uncertainty, both hard and soft, then filter
	o Look for good cases as well as bad; seek opportunities as well as disaster
	o Consider less-than-optimal opponent (and own) actions as well as ideal responses
	o Remember objectives: improve odds, hedge bets, exploit opponent's problems, identify high-leverage measures
	o Reflect actual operational considerations rather than analytic simplifications
Techniques	o Eschew mechanical one-variable-at-a-time sensitivity testing, since correlations and analytic aggregations are important
	o Ultimately, focus on "cases" and alternative paths to them
	o Use multiple baselines, since model sensitivities are often sensitive to the assumed baseline
	o Resist the allure of Monte Carlo techniques or more detail

Fig. 10. Principles of uncertainty analysis

Let me comment upon only a few items from Fig. 10. First, the matter of looking for the good as well as the bad. The point here is not to obscure miserable features of the current military balance in Europe--I am sure that most readers are in no mood for that in 1984. Rather, the point is that if we are to be good competitors in peacetime and successful warriors should conflict occur, it is essential that we know where our opportunities lie. It is striking in this regard to speak with Israeli general officers about their contemptuous views of Soviet doctrine--not just as practiced by Arab forces, but as formulated by Soviets for Soviets. On the other hand, I am less impressed with the much-vaunted Western capability for innovativeness when I realize that contingency planning across a broad range of war situations is not a basic part of Western military training.

The second point I will touch upon briefly pertains to the last item, that about Monte Carlo analysis and the addition of detail. In our experience at Rand, it has been a constant effort to maintain comprehensibility in our force models: the pressure has almost invariably been to add details (but only details of interest to the particular suggester); and, from many analysts, to add Monte Carlo features. With respect to the former, I can only assert that it is extremely difficult to maintain comprehensibility, and that once that is lost, everything is lost. Furthermore, there are straightforward analytic tests to see whether certain details are worth inserting--with the answers dependent, of course, on the problems of interest. Merely because modelers love to include new phenomena, which they insist are "important," does not make the phenomena important for the purposes at hand; nor does it mean that the phenomena cannot be reflected adequately by some simple relationships.

With respect to Monte Carlo analysis, which can be extremely valuable when properly conducted, my experience has been that relatively few Monte Carlo models are exercised long enough to produce valid results. There is even a marvelous term, "one-pass Monte Carlo," that refers to the practice of using the model with precisely one sampling of all the random variables. It seems to me that the users of such models are either doing their sponsors a disservice or fudging the distribution functions to assure that the one sample will give something close to the expected value. In a war game or simulation as complex as the RSAC's, it is hopeless to think of extensive probabilistic analysis *except* on specific issues. And, indeed, we intend *sometimes* to insert stochastic features to treat some of those specific issues (also, to prevent human teams from being complacent about uncertainty).

Finally, a comment about the history of large-scale simulations when applied to policy problems. The most striking single observation is the number of sheer blunders that have been committed by people who became too obsessed with their simulation to step back for some thinking and consultation. Running big simulation models is *not* the same as running "experiments." It is with such examples in mind from other efforts that I urge people to avoid "mechanical" operations and sensitivity testing.

An Illustrative Discussion of Multiscenario Analysis in a NATO Context

   Background   Having discussed principles, let us now consider some examples. Consider a class of wars originating in some third area such as the Persian Gulf and then spreading to Europe. Suppose further that the war remains conventional. And, just to narrow our focus even more, suppose that unlike many studies, ours are concerned with measures other than force building. What, then, might we address as part of a balance study with recommendations for correctives? Figure 11 suggests one such list.

This list is neither detailed nor comprehensive, but rather illustrative. However, note the *range* of uncertainties it mentions. Assuredly, we would want to consider different basic timelines. In addition, however, we would want to look at uncertainties about the behavior of individual Pact states, about the effectiveness of certain key weapon systems, about the fungibility of operational reserves across corps sectors in a multinational environment, about strategic and tactical surprise, and about various analytic assumptions usually buried deep within models.

   Modeling Adaptations and Scripted Models   A characteristic of multiscenario studies is that the original models never incorporate all the sensitivities we are interested in. Thus, we must modify the models. An article of philosophy here is that when we encounter a phenomenon important to strategic-level discussions we make every effort to reflect its *effects* in our simulations--whether or not the *mechanisms* of the phenomenon can be adequately modeled. So, for example, there is considerable current interest in Soviet Operational Maneuver Groups (OMGs). It is not possible at our level of aggregation to follow the actions of such units individually (we work with effective equivalent divisions labeled by nationality, strength, location, and type). Moreover, even with high-resolution models, the

- o   The time gap between conflicts on the various fronts

- o   Pact and NATO preparations *before* formal mobilization in Europe (including development of barrier defenses during a prolonged period of cold war)

- o   Pact and NATO mobilization rates for different classes of unit

- o   Pact (and NATO) coalition problems: delays in mobilization, unenthusiastic participation, LOC problems

- o   Use and effectiveness of airpower and helicopters

- o   Stocks of "high-tech" weapons

- o   Use and effectiveness of chemicals and operational maneuver groups

- o   French participation and entry time

- o   Cross-national command-control problems

- o   Operational-level choices (e.g., Soviet decisions about the intensity of conflict; both sides' criteria for offensive operations; flank exposure)

- o   Effects of surprise and/or early breakthroughs

- o   Effects of assumptions regarding the mechanism of FLOT movement (e.g., dependence on force ratio, density, and/or attrition)

Fig. 11. Illustrative sensitivities to be addressed in a NATO balance study for fixed force levels and weapon capabilities

uncertainties attending any effort to simulate in detail the consequences of an OMG insertion would be legion. It would therefore be easy to rationalize dropping the issue altogether. However, in the spirit of human war gaming and consistent with an overall philosophy, we instead build a *scripted model* (Davis, 1982) by asking:

- •   If OMGs were used successfully, what would the results look like at the level of resolution of our model? That is, we do not "see" rear-area disruption, but if it occurred, what would be the consequences for the variables we do follow?

- •   If OMGs were used unsuccessfully, what would the results look like?

- •   To first order, what are the circumstances under which OMGs might plausibly be used with some likelihood of success, and what are the circumstances under which we might expect them to be largely annihilated if used?

The scripted model, then, incorporates the answers to these questions and a switch: if the analyst wants to see the effect of OMGs in a particular game, he can turn the switch on. In some instances he will see a marked (upper-bound) effect; in others, none at all--depending on circumstances such as the availability of operational reserves and NATO close air support sorties. Now, obviously, this form of analysis is limited--and it is not unusual for people to react negatively to the concept of scripted models. However, the rejoinder is also obvious: Is it better to leave out discussion altogether? No, it is not. The next question is whether there is any content to the answer: Is one not seeing only what one puts in? Here, of course, the answer is yes--but with qualifications. After all, *any* deterministic simulation produces only what was put in. The point is that a complex simulation model keeps track of interrelationships and dynamic changes that no individual can consistently keep correctly in mind, even if he made all the initial assumptions. Thus, in practice, good simulations--including those with "scripted models"--often produce results that initially seem surprising, even though in retrospect they appear perfectly intuitive and even trivial.

Another example involves the problem of *early* Pact breakthroughs. Virtually all analytic models preclude seeing such a phenomenon because movements of the FLOT and attrition are driven by force ratios (or by something similar but more sophisticated such as the potential-antipotential calculations). So long as NATO has mobilized to some degree, the force ratios are not generally bad enough to permit--in the analytic models-- an early breakthrough. Hence, the problem goes away. But the problem does not *really* go away because Pact doctrine indicates they will go to extraordinary lengths to achieve such breakthroughs and history indicates that there is enough uncertainty about results of individual battles that we should expect the Soviets to be successful in some. And here is the wrinkle: if we operate usual models with the usual assumptions, the FLOT never breaks until NATO has lost by best-estimate attrition; by contrast, in the real world an early breakthrough *might* result in massive NATO attrition due to breakthrough forces getting into the rear of NATO forces still on the front, with a loss of NATO cohesion and effectiveness. Such effects are simply not captured in axis-of-advance models without special efforts.

If we take the scripted model approach, what do we do? First, we ask some questions:

- Under what circumstances would breakthroughs not predicted by the baseline model be reasonably likely in the real world? (Answer: this is in large part a function of defensive *density* and of competence, surprise, technical uncertainties, and the availability of defensive airpower)

- If a breakthrough occurred, more or less as the Soviets expect, what would be the consequences at our level of resolution? (Here the answer involves greater-than-nominal NATO attrition in the break-through axis, and, perhaps, adjacent axes, and a rapidly moving FLOT)

- Under what circumstances would the breakthrough be likely to bog down for reasons other than those covered automatically by the standard model bringing up operational reserves to confront the breakthrough forces? (Examples of such circumstances might include NATO air superiority and delays in the exploitation phase due to logistics problems.)

Armed with some nominal answers and variable parameters to reflect uncertainties, we could again build a scripted model and perform excursions. One value of this exercise would be to estimate the effects that a breakthrough would have to achieve before it would indeed be a catastrophic event for the defense rather than "business as usual in warfare." We should remember, after all, that the assumptions used in all aggregated models having to do with rate of advance and attrition implicitly average over a range of phenomena that include local breakthroughs and local responses by the defense.

Another virtue of this approach is that it suggests a new measure of effectiveness: performance of the defense given the *assumption* (i.e., prescription) of a breakthrough. How one accomplishes this "prescription" should reflect detailed analyses emerging from war games with human teams and a maneuver-level "board." On the other hand, the results will be predictable and desirable: they will highlight the importance of having early operational reserves that can reliably and efficiently be used on the axes in question (a function of unit locations, experience in rapid maneuver, nationalities, command-control, and experience with cross-national reinforcement operations).

These examples should be sufficient to indicate our general approach. Figure 12 lists some of the model adaptations we have had to make in recent work of this general nature.

Speculation About Possible Results of Multiscenario Balance Assessment   Although it is always dangerous to do so, I would speculate that the results of such a balance assessment would include the following conclusions:

- NATO can defend successfully in many plausible cases--at least for a period of weeks, and *possibly* much longer (a function both of sustainability and of Soviet willingness to commit strategic reserves). In many other plausible cases the Pact could conquer the FRG and, in some cases, most of Western Europe

- Any public image of an *easy or certain* Pact victory is unduly pessimistic, unless one assumes that NATO policymakers will be stupid (e.g., slow to respond), that NATO forces are inferior in quality, or that NATO generals will be incompetent*

- Many measures are available to NATO that would exploit uncertainties and diminish any Soviet confidence in victory

o Sensitivity to different assumptions about readiness and training of lower-quality units

o Scripted models for OMGs and breakthrough operations

o Options to build barriers and prepared defenses over time

o Nation-specific sensitivity to supplies

o Nation-specific mobilization rates and effectivenesses for Pact (and NATO)

o Asymmetric treatment of NATO and Pact attrition, reflecting differences in repair doctrine

o Expert-system reallocation of ground and air forces according to an operational strategy rather than an optimizing algorithm ignoring constraints

Fig. 12. Representative model adaptations

---

*My intention here is not to express optimism--current NATO deficiencies are *very* worrisome--but rather to underline the great uncertainties about outcome suggested by analysis.

- Stalemate leading to a "WWI model" is a distinct possibility--with implications for sustainability

- War outcomes could be quite sensitive to *early* availability of operational reserves and to cross-national command-control (also, of course, to warning time)

On the basis of sensitivity analyses already performed I can also assure you, with no surprise expected, that war outcomes are sensitive to all the issues in Fig. 12. Analyses involving nuclear conflict are even more complex and uncertain.

Coping with the Results of Multiscenario Analysis

In previous times models were sufficiently ponderous that we did not have to worry particularly about multiscenario analysis. That era, however, is behind us. We now have the capability to produce far more simulations than we are prepared to analyze, so new techniques are essential.

So far, we have only begun to cope with this problem. One can talk about postprocessors and the like, but a substantial part of the problem is conceptual: How do you examine many simulations quickly, and how do you portray the results? Eventually, I suspect that we will show results in the form of distributions over ordinally ranked war outcomes, with alternative rankings and alternative measures of outcome. I suspect also that an important measure of effectiveness will be the flexibility--i.e., the options--enjoyed by the NATO commander during the course of the simulated war.

In the meantime, we (and others such as the Blumenthal group at Lawrence Livermore and parts of the Army's Concepts Analysis Agency) have made substantial progress in one area. We have made a significant investment in *graphics-oriented analytic outputs*--partly to make the results more understandable to senior officials and officers unable to spend much time on the issue, but partly because of empirical evidence that man-machine interaction is also greatly enhanced for the *analyst*. Some will always prefer tables, but for pure efficiency and clarity it seems that maps and graphs are inherently superior. Figures 13 and 14 show representative displays, although hundreds of choices are possible. They are available immediately after a simulation on color-graphics monitors (recall that a 30-day European war requires about 10 minutes for an excursion). A hard-copy color print can be produced in about one minute.

There are many options for using such capabilities. For example, one can display graphs of simulation results for excursions overlaid on those for a baseline case; or, one can display results side by side. In any event, it is possible in this way to go through a great many excursions quickly, observe key sensitivities, and determine which runs warrant more careful scrutiny.

Although there is little completed multiscenario analysis as yet, *the era of fast multiscenario analysis of theater conflict is here*. This means, among other things, that *it should be possible efficiently to force convergence on many issues that have traditionally been dealt with in competing essays*. It should now be possible to challenge the advocates of alternative views to become specific enough to allow calculations, to accommodate alternative initial assumptions, and to respond quickly to the predicatable changes of assumption that will emerge after the initial analysis of results. All of this, of course, will come to nought unless

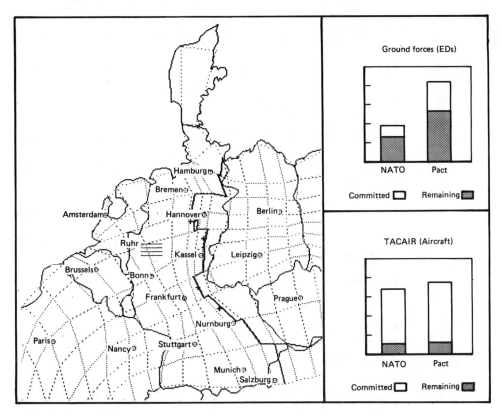

Fig. 13. FLOT locations in Central European theater after a period of strength over time

the models have some credibility and address--albeit imperfectly--the phenomena at issue. Hence the fundamental importance of scripted models and the philosophy of using them regularly (Davis, 1982b).

COMPLEX STRATEGIES AND BASIC MILITARY MISSIONS

Let me now draw on a rather different aspect of our experience so far with game-structured research and analysis. Whereas the previous section dealt largely with combat simulations and multiscenario analysis, here I would like to discuss briefly some of what we have learned in constructing prototype automated agents and the associated analytic war plans.

Effects of the Game Paradigm

Structuring research around the paradigm of a war game has a fundamental effect on people's thinking: it discourages simple-minded focus on optimizing algorithms and mathematically clever but militarily irrelevant models, and encourages a focus on matters global, strategic, and operational.

A second effect is that the game format encourages participants to think about ways to "win"--to frustrate the opponent's strategy and to

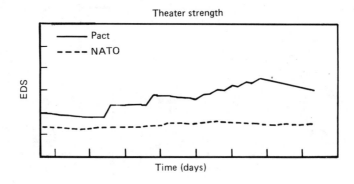

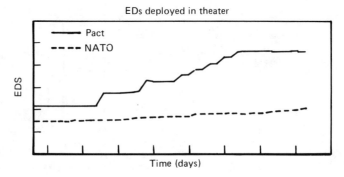

NOTE: ED = Equivalent division.

Fig. 14. Representative simulation outputs showing Pact and NATO strength over time

reach an acceptable outcome. The game paradigm is very different from the more passive paradigm of bean-count comparisons.

Automated Agents

Although work in this area is still relatively primitive, prototype models exist and I am confident that it will be possible to capture in decision models a reasonable fraction of what competent human players have in mind when they participate in political-military war games. That does not mean that the models will be as smart, flexible, or innovative as the best humans--rather, it is a commentary on the limited (albeit rich) scope of political-military war games: the same issues arise over and over again, as do the same decision points.

Another interesting observation from our work in this area is that the process of building automated national-command-level models illuminates issues of deterrence and escalation control (see Davis and Stan, 1984). Unless one undercuts the whole concept by constructing stereotypical decision models rather than more plausible models exhibiting different behavior under different circumstances (what we call "complex" Ivans and Sams), the process of developing decision rules reflecting the various national predispositions is both illuminating and worrisome. Without going into details here, let me merely say that there is a reasonable chance that *if* convergence is ever possible between those who wish to rely primarily upon nuclear deterrence and those who wish to rely primarily upon conventional deterrence (I exclude consideration of nuclear disarmers here), then that convergence might well be achieved by structured gaming with the capability for quick and easy "What if?" queries and the opportunity to test changes in controversial decision rules. Similarly, I believe there is the *potential* for closure on more complex issues of NATO's nuclear-use policy. I do not mean to imply that we now have a panacea for resolving disputes, but to express the view that much is possible because current mechanisms of debate are so crude.

Analytic War Plans

The first thing we learned in attempting to put together analytic war plans is that many people claimed that doing so would be impossible: the building-block approach, it was alleged, does not work. This viewpoint is peculiar to those experienced in conventional military analysis rather than, for example, strategic nuclear analysis. Moreover, it is most assuredly *not* the viewpoint of those most experienced in policy-level work on planning scenarios, regional balances, strategic mobility, and global war games. To the contrary, to those with such experience it seems quite plausible that a moderate number of building-block plans will provide more than enough potential for a wide variety of scenarios. There are, however, serious technical difficulties.

With that background, let me make some more pointed observations from our work so far:

- The requirement to have a war plan for every theater of the world, even if the war plan temporarily consists of nothing more than a one-line operative concept and decisions about force allocations, encourages a strategic view and sensitizes the analyst to problems faced constantly by military planners (especially U.S. planners with their worldwide responsibilities)

- The technical difficulties associated with building adaptive analytic war plans have direct parallels in real-world problems

- Developing analytic war plans is an excellent process for bringing together the cultures of military planner, intelligence specialist, and system analyst

- Allowing someone with a controversial strategy (Soviet or NATO) to have his own plans that can be tested evenhandedly is a good mechanism for encouraging creativity while revealing flaws in argumentation

- The requirement to translate vague operational concepts into formal instructions and plans is an excellent vehicle for improving communications and achieving closure among disparate groups. Often the disagreements originate in implicit assumptions about circumstance: neither group would use their concept under all circumstances, and there can even be some agreement about the circumstances under which the various concepts might be applicable. Disagreements then continue on the likelihood of those circumstances arising, but that is a different issue. In this way, for example, it is possible to turn chaotic feuding into rational discussion about when the Soviets might use airborne forces, operational maneuver groups, naval infantry, etc.

Unfortunately, none of this is yet easy to accomplish technically. It will probably be another six months or a year before the techniques for building analytic war plans efficiently and transparently are well developed.

Complex Strategies

As a by-product of attempts to build plausible analytic war plans and the national command level rules for changing plans, it has become increasingly apparent that many of the nonconverging debates about NATO strategy have their origin in the implicit assumption that strategy is an either-or proposition. In reality, *an enlightened military strategy would have numerous branches*--and room for considerable ad hoc adaptation. In this regard, it seems that an ideal military strategy for NATO might well involve classic forward defense under most circumstances, but other defenses under circumstances such as a surprise attack. Moreover, there is no contradiction between forward defense with heavily mechanized units and the hedge of well-armed and trained territorial reserves suitable for a variety of specialized defense measures in particular sectors.

Moving into more controversial areas, there is nothing contradictory between a principal reliance on conventional defense and having the operationally feasible option for *early* first nuclear use to thwart certain types of surprise attacks (as well as nuclear options to be used later in conflict as necessary). Some would say an analogy exists with the threat of nuclear decapitation of the United States in a surprise Soviet first strike. Under circumstances of such an attack it might not be surprising if the U.S. response were stereotypically massive retaliation (see comments by Harold Brown, in Brown (1983)).

Basic Military Missions

Let me now comment on what I would expect to emerge from more experience with multiscenario analysis, game-structured simulation, and development of automated agents. Basically, I would expect to see far more emphasis on mixed strategies and strategies with explicitly identified multiple components. Analysts (and policymakers) would no longer be able to characterize strategies with "one-liners." Instead, they would have to flesh out their concepts, and in the course of doing so they would identify a longer set of military missions than is usually discussed in analytic papers. These would include, for example (skipping here the usually emphasized military missions of stopping the initial Pact advance and regaining lost territory):

- Worldwide *intelligence* and the ability to integrate it properly (important in monitoring Soviet preparations for war, and, in turn, for judging the feasibility of different Soviet strategies)

- Measures for *early use of strategic warning*--i.e., in a lengthy cold war, but well before mobilization would be seriously contemplated (e.g., well-developed plans for barrier defenses, assuring adequate stocks in all corps sectors, assuring arrangements for timely coverage of forward positions, and heightened security against standing-start attacks)

- Measures for coping immediately in Europe with any *diversion of U.S. and allied forces* to a third area such as Southwest Asia--i.e., without waiting for a European crisis to emerge

- Measures for *adapting military strategy rapidly to surprising results* from early days of battle--e.g., measures exploiting possible Pact coalition problems as well as measures compensating for unanticipated NATO problems

- Measures for *efficient use of existing war reserve stocks* both in Europe and the United States, including measures that would require early preparation of reservists

- Measures for invoking various degrees of *industrial mobilization* rapidly during periods of high tension--before full-scale mobilization of forces if possible, but as soon as feasible in any event, with attention paid to production of high-effectiveness weapons and spare parts

CONCLUSIONS AND RECOMMENDATIONS

The basic thrust of this paper is that concepts and techniques are now emerging that could be a unifying influence for strategic analysis of NATO issues. These will make possible *multiscenario analysis and the development and testing (through simulation) of complex strategies* incorporating a diversity of ideas and capabilities, and reflecting recognition that operational strategy should be adaptive and multifaceted. It is possible that greater consensus will develop within the several analytic and strategic communities, and that this in turn will influence policy.

To achieve such lofty ambitions will be a good trick, but there are ways to start. In my view, such a start would involve a NATO-wide professional association, with NATO sanction, that would seek to bring together the several groups to which I have alluded with the purpose of improving prospects for modeler-analysts (working at varied levels of detail), technologists, and strategists being able to speak in a common language and calibrate their assumptions. Subsequently, it would be useful to compare multiscenario balance assessments--with the objective of seeing whether agreement can be reached on the *complex* strategies and sets of capabilities needed by NATO in the face of continuing threat and uncertainty.

REFERENCES

Betts, R. K., 1982, "Surprise Attack," Brookings Institution, Washington.

Blaker, J., and Hamilton, A., 1977, Assessing Military Balances: The NATO Example, reprinted in: "American Defense Policy," 1982, John Reichart and Steven Sturm (eds.), 5th ed., Johns Hopkins University Press, Baltimore.

Brown, H., 1983, "Thinking About National Security: Defense and Foreign Policy in a Dangerous World," Westview Press, Inc., New York.

Collins, J., 1980, "U.S.-Soviet Military Balance: Concepts and Capabilities, 1960-1980," McGraw Hill, New York.

Congressional Budget Office, 1980, "U.S. Ground Forces: Design and Cost Alternatives for NATO and non-NATO Contingencies" (written by P. Hillier and N. Slatkin), Washington.

Davis, P. K., 1982a, "Observations on the Rapid Deployment Joint Task Force: Origins, Direction, and Mission," The Rand Corporation, P-6751, Santa Monica.

Davis, P. K., 1982b, "Concepts for Improving Military Content of Automated War Games," The Rand Corporation, P-6830, Santa Monica.

Davis, P. K., 1984, "Rand's Experience in Applying Artificial Intelligence Techniques to Strategic-Level Military-Political War Games," The Rand Corporation, P-6977, Santa Monica [also published in: the "Proceedings" of the Summer Computer Simulation Conference of the Society for Computer Simulation, Boston, July 1984].

Davis, P. K., forthcoming, "Concepts and a Prototype System for Game-Structured Strategic Analysis," The Rand Corporation, Santa Monica.

Davis, P. K., and Stan, Peter J.E., 1984, "Concepts and Models of Escalation," The Rand Corporation, R-3235, Santa Monica.

Davis, P. K., and Winnefeld, J. A., 1983, "The Rand Strategy Assessment Center: An Overview and Interim Conclusions about Utility and Development Options," The Rand Corporation, R-2945-DNA, Santa Monica.

Dupuy, T. N., 1979, "Numbers Predictions and War," Bobbs-Merril, Indianapolis.

Enthoven, A. C., and Smith, K. W., 1971, "How Much is Enough? Shaping the Defense Program, 1961-1969," Harper and Row, New York.

ESECs (European Security Council), 1983, "Strengthening Conventional Deterrence in Europe: Proposals for the 1980s," St. Martin's Press, New York.

Graubard, M. L., and Builder, C. C., 1982, New Methods for Strategic Analysis: Automating the War Game, Policy Sciences, Vol. 15, No. 1, Amsterdam.

Karber, P. A., 1984, In Defense of Forward Defense, Armed Forces Journal International, Washington.

Kaufmann, W., 1983, Nonnuclear Deterrence, in: "Alliance Security: NATO and the No-First-Use Question," J. Steinbruner and L. Sigal (eds.), Brookings Institution, Washington.

Levine, R., Connors, T., Weiner, M., and Wise, R., 1982, "Survey of NATO Defense Concepts," The Rand Corporation, N-1871-AF, Santa Monica.

Levine, R., forthcoming, "Flying in the Face of Uncertainty: Alternative Plans and Postures for Interdiction in Southwest Asia," Ph.D. Dissertation, the Rand Graduate Institute, Santa Monica.

Madansky, A., 1968, Uncertainty, in: "Systems Analysis and Policy Planning: Applications in Defense," E. S. Quade and W. I. Boucher (eds.), The Rand Corporation, R-439-PR (Abridged), Santa Monica.

Mako, W., 1983, "U.S. Ground Forces and the Defense of Central Europe" Brookings Institution, Washington.

Marshall, A. W., 1982, A Program to Improve Analytic Methods Related to Strategic Forces, Policy Sciences, Vol. 15, No. 1, Amsterdam.

Mearsheimer, J. J., 1983, "Conventional Deterrence," Cornell University Press, New York.

Posen, B. R., 1984, Competing Views of the Center Region Conventional Balance, in: "Military Strategy in Transition: Defense and Deterrence in the 1980s," K. Dunn and W. O. Standenmaier (eds.), Westview Press, Inc., New York.

Vigor, P. H., 1983, "Soviet Blitzkrieg Theory," St. Martin's Press, New York.

ASSESSING ALTERNATIVE STRATEGIC CONCEPTS

John Elliott

Headquarters, Department of the Army
Office of the Deputy Chief of Staff for Operations and Plans
Washington, D. C.

ASSESSING ALTERNATIVE STRATEGIC CONCEPTS

Beginning any discussion with such an imposing title begs for further introduction. Each word in this title is, in fact, burdened by questions of its own. What is meant by assessment in this context? What kind of analysis? What alternatives to what strategies? What strategies indeed? What is a concept? And what is the time dimension to be considered. Rest assured we may not satifactorily answer any of these rather basic, contentious points using this paper as a "strawman" for discussion of one model to improve military strategy in the long-term. We are especially interested in your views during this initial exchange and plan to develop them in our models as they evolve.

Since I have been posing questions, let me answer at least one by explaining how we came to this subject. This should serve as an introduction and may provide some helpful background on how our Army Staff functions. This past January a group composed of our Deputy Chief of Staff for Operations and Plans (DCSOPS), the Director for Strategy, Plans, and Policy, the DCSOPS Technical Advisor, and myself met briefly to devise a way to engender a thoughtful internal Army debate on future warfighting and deterrence concepts. Out of this session grew first the continuing Colloquium on Alternative Strategic Concepts and later the Army Strategy Processing Model. Both these innovations are active today. I will describe their development and their current status, followed by what we see as the way ahead for their evolution. Description of the Colloquium must be first.

COLLOQUIUM ON ALTERNATIVE STRATEGIC CONCEPTS

Please bear in mind that our Army Staff is a military organization, a very military organization. Most undertakings are very important and quite frequently accomplished under near crisis conditions of time. The sense of urgency is extreme. Usually "now" is the near edge of lateness.

Views presented in this paper are solely those of the author and are not intended to represent any official position of the Department of the Army, Department of Defense, or any other U. S. Government agency.

To introduce an academic instrument as ancient as the Colloquium into these "do it now" pressures of daily stress seemed bent on failure to many. Not so. In fact, the very nature of a colloquium -- its reflective pace and mood --helped ensure its acceptance and utility to the customarily harried participants. Rather than confronting the needs of the Army Staff we genuinely embraced them. This approach is reflected in the Guidelines for the Colloquium:
- Exchanges are limited to one clock hour followed by an informal lunch (to extend discussion)
- Participation is determined by subject matter to ensure the proper participants
- Discussion is off-the-record and not-for-attribution
- There are "no rules" to inhibit discussion
- Colloquia are scheduled by subject and not by calendar
- A one page Gist of the proceedings is circulated after each exchange in order to assign action taskings for accomplishment rather than massive memoranda (this latter product orientation is designed to feed forward into the strategic planning arena)
- Discussion is facilitated by the Director for Strategy, Plans, and Policy and the DCSOPS Technical Advisor with participants seated by discussion expertise rather than protocol.

Participant military rank extends from Lieutenant Colonel to Lieutenant General and civilians include the Under Secretary of the Army. Later we will address the contribution of our most noteworthy presenter todate -- Professor Samuel Huntington of Harvard University. I am sure many of you are familiar with his work.

ARMY STRATEGY PROCESSING MODEL

The basic product of our charter meeting of the Colloquium was another question: What would we do with a good concept if we had one? Some of you have also addressed this challenge. Our answer took the form of the Army Strategy Processing Model. This title was chosen with care because the processing of strategy from ideas to concepts to strategy is precisely what we wanted the model to help us produce. Please recognize that this approach represents "anti-theory" to those who for whatever reasons think military strategy is produced by a Promethean flash of light, a big boom, or similiar crescendo event. Acceptance of this approach required an understanding that strategy could be processed and that consideration of a strategy by the Army Staff did not conflict or compete with production of the national military strategy by the Joint Chiefs of Staff.

The Army Strategy Processing Model takes advantage of innovations provided by the Colloquium and its direct relationship with how the Army processes "raw strategy." Strategy is created in three ways for the Army unilaterally and within the joint arena by DCSOPS. First, self-initiation is triggered when we see a void in national strategy, or previous strategy that has become outmoded. Second, reaction occurs in our coordinated response to documents which establish policy (e.g., National Security Defense Directives (NSDDs)). And, third, revalidation involves making changes on a cyclical basis to policy documents in which strategy is enunciated (e.g., the Joint Strategic Planning Document Supporting Annex (JSPDSA)).

We view the Colloquium as a non-traditional Army Staff mechanism to improve our ability to identify and input future strategy needs into policy formulation and decision making. Our initial emphasis is clearly on self-iniation of strategy and involves the three processes -- Concept Formulation, Planning, and Resourcing. These interdependent processes and their integration with the Colloquium are discussed next.

CONCEPT FORMULATION

We initiate the Concept Formulation phase with recognition and support of the perceived need for change by civil-military leadership. An idea is developed by the Army Staff to resolve that need and introduced into the Colloquium. During the same internal Army debate resulting from these catalysts, Colloquium participants <u>revise</u> the <u>idea</u>, consider consequences of selected alternatives, and <u>achieve consensus on a preferred alternative</u>. These are processed as Action Taskings mentioned earlier. Our goal is to build leverage issues emanating from long-range problem areas (e.g. as identified by the Army Long-Range Appraisal (ALRA)) or current shortfalls and "fight them" through the strategic planning community. This will achieve credibility and legitimacy to ensure adequate resourcing.

PLANNING

Action taskings are refined in the Planning Phase by sequential interaction between Test and Evaluation and Consensus Building in order to validate new concepts well before their entry in the National Command Authority decisionmaking process. <u>Testing and Evaluation</u> is accomplished with assistance of the DCSOPS Technical Advisor and the Army analytical community. Action Taskings are processed concurrently by the Army Staff with the Concepts Analysis Agency, The Army War College, Training and Doctrine Command, Army Materiel Command, and the Chief of Staff's Army Studies Group. As the concept is validated, "soundings" are made to determine its political and bureaucratic feasibility, reaction in the strategic planning and policy community, and assessment of congressional implications. A corporate Army decision facilitates entry into more customary consensus building using established procedures. <u>Consensus Building</u> is accomplished by the Director, Strategy, Plans, and Policy within the joint arena and interagency defense planning activities of the National Security Council, State Department, and Organization of the Joint Chiefs of Staff (OJCS). The resulting OJCS validated and National Command Authority approved strategy is an architecture for organizing a landpower response to accomplish the U.S. goals and objectives for which the strategy was conceived. Implementation of this strategy may require improved joint doctrine and tactics, force design and force structure, sustaining logistics, and deployable hardware. These functional improvements must be legitimized in the Army Plan, the Joint Strategic Planning Document/Joint Strategic Planning Document Supporting Analysis, the Defense Guidance, and National Security Defense Directives in order to compete successfully with the Program Objectives Memorandum (POM) near-term resource competition.

RESOURCING

The Chief of Staff's Army Long-Range Guidance Planning Guidance promulgates results of this planning process and feeds forward into the Army Plan and then on to the POM. Commanders use this guidance to influence the Army Plan, the POM and current budget development. Leverage issues and near-term shortfalls identified by Total Army Analysis (TAA) will be further refined by functional analysis before being input to the Army Plan and POM. We have not yet advanced this model to the resourcing function.

ACTIVATION OF THE ARMY STRATEGIC PROCESSING MODEL

To accomplish our purpose of engendering a thoughtful internal Army debate on future warfighting and deterrence concepts, we chose to activate the model using Professor Huntington's concepts outlined in his article, "Conventional Deterrence and Conventional Retaliation in Europe"

(<u>International Security</u>, Winter 1983/84, Vol 8, No. 3)). Huntington's thesis that: "For a quarter century the slow but continuning trend in NATO strategy -- and in thinking about NATO strategy -- has been from emphasis on nuclear deterrence to emphasis on conventional deterrence... The past several years have seen increasing support for shifting the deterrent emphasis even further in the conventional direction." This trend highlights U.S. joint requirements for forces capable of executing combat operations that are compatible with agreed allied political guidelines, doctrine, procedures, and operations plans.

This conventional forces orientation made Huntington's concept an excellent test vehicle for the Army Strategy Processing Model. This test and evaluation is now being conducted by the Army's Concepts Analysis Agency. We expect a report next summer and are now working on the way ahead for both the Colloquium and the Model.

THE WAY AHEAD

We are exercising the Army Strategy Processing Model to introduce, assess, and validate new strategic concepts generated by the Colloquium. In order for this strategy development process to mature sufficiently to meet our procedural and substantive needs, better linkage with quantitative analysis and simulation models must be achieved. A "best" solution may be direct linkage with a capability such as that provided by the Rand Strategy Assessment Center (RSAC). The RSAC research effort aims to improve methods of strategy analysis using an approach based on automated war gaming and multi-scenario analysis making it possible to combine the best features of war gaming and analytic modeling. <u>We are working on these capabilities now</u>.

Developing alternative strategic concepts yielding strategies has become an important challenge for us all. This challenge is particularily evident in our mutual search for improvements to NATO's conventional strategy in the long-term defense. We hope these deliberations help ensure the success of that search.

SYSTEM DYNAMICS AS A CONCEPTUAL FRAMEWORK FOR LONG-TERM DEFENCE PLANNING INITIATIVES

R.G. Coyle and R. Goad

Shape Technical Centre
The Hague
The Netherlands

ABSTRACT

The paper discusses the problem of evaluating competing or complementary long-term defence planning initiatives. It is agreed that the complex inter-relationships which may exist between them, and between the geographical areas in which they would be deployed, create a need for a framework for conceptual and quantitative analysis. The paper then demonstrates a method for formulating conceptual frameworks which clearly show the issues involved, and which can serve as agenda for discussion or as a basis for a quantitative model. The method is applied in the context of NATO's Northern Region, giving both a diagrammatic and a quantitative simulation model, the latter being based on fictitious data. The paper closes with a brief discussion of the advantages and limitation of the method.

The process of long-term defence planning in NATO is, in principle, very simple; military needs are idenfitied, possible solutions to those needs are proposed and evaluated, and the most promising solutions are implemented, subject to budgetary and political constraints. In practice, matters are more complicated, not least because the evaluation problem is technically very difficult. Different proposals affect NATO's ability to deal with a potential confrontation with the Warsaw Pact in different ways, and a coherent discussion of long-term defence issues requires a common, but tractable, analytical structure which facilitates evaluation and explanation of their relative contributions to NATO security.

This paper outlines such an analytical structure: a System Dynamics formulation of a potential NATO/WP conflict in the context of a developing crisis. The effect of a number of long-term defence initiatives on the ensuing conflict is illustrated by way of an influence diagram of their mutual interactions. The main theme of the paper is to show, by way of the influence diagram, the conceptual relationships between these initiatives, and thus to indicate qualitiatively their potential effect on NATO security. In so doing, a firm analytical basis for quantifying these effects will also be laid, and the paper will give some illustrative examples, using fictitious data.

INTRODUCTION

Ever since the NATO Alliance was formed in 1949, successive Supreme Allied Commanders have put forward priorities for investment and the development of the Alliance's war fighting capabilities. Even before then, there were proposals in the wake of World War II regarding the number of divisions needed for the defence of Western Europe, and over the years there have been countless initiatives extending into missions areas both conventional and nuclear. For example, the Supreme Allied Commander, Europe (SACEUR) has recently established the following key areas of emphasis (listed here in no particular order):

o attack of Warsaw Pact (WP) follow-on forces
o air defence
o reinforcement planning
o mobilizable reserves
o tactical intelligence
o logistics and sustainability of forces
o infrastructure
o nuclear weapons requirements
o command and control.

The last five years have, in addition, seen the well-publicised decision to upgrade theatre nuclear forces in Europe, and in parallel, acceptance by NATO nations that defence spending on conventional capabilities needs to be increased in real terms. These matters are of course largely political, aimed at strengthening deterrence by clear indications to the Soviet Union that NATO possesses the will to take the steps necessary to resist intimidation by the USSR despite by the ever-increasing capabilities of WP forces. Nevertheless proper debate in the nations requires that the contribution to military effectiveness be articulated, and quantified assessment methods have a potentially useful role to play. This is becoming increasingly important, particularly in the context of the current debate on NATO Long Term Planning. (LTP).

For nations to be able to deal coherently with such a list of widely different mission areas, they need (in addition to the political arguments) a clear view of the improvements in military effectiveness that are likely to result from upgrades in one or more mission areas, and they need to know their relative priority. The problem of determining how much of a particular upgrade is desirable, given the competition for available funds and other resources is not trivial. Desirable levels of upgrade across different mission areas are not independent - they are inexorably convoluted in ways which are both complicated and (sometimes) confusing. For example, an upgrade in air defence capabilities that involves the acquisition of, say, more surface-to-air missile systems, will only make sense if, as a minimum:

o the ground on which the missiles are to be deployed is relatively secure (i.e., is not likely to be prematurely overrun by enemy troops);

o adequate Electronic defence capabilities are provided (for survivability);

o adequate Command and Control Systems are available (for operational efficiency);

o adequate logistics/sustainability is provided.

This means that a study of one particular mission area - <u>on its own</u> - will inevitably be of limited usefulness, because it will be unable to take account of complementary and competing upgrades needed in other mission areas - upgrades which would be essential for maximizing the potential military benefits of upgrades in the single mission area studied. What is needed - and this is the methodological challenge - is an analytical framework into which the mission areas and their interactions can be placed in such a way as to allow the evaluation of the relative contribution of each to enhancing NATO security.

This paper is concerned with just such an analytical framework: a System Dynamics formulation of a potential NATO/WP conflict in the context of a developing crisis. The model explicitly represents the LTP missions areas; their impact on the ensuing conflict is illustrated by way of an influence diagram of their mutual interactions. The main theme of the paper is to show, by way of the influence diagram, the structural relationships between the above issues, and thus to indicate qualitatively their potential effect on NATO security.

It is contended that:

o analytical frameworks of this type are relatively easy to construct;

o when constructed they are useful as agenda for discussion and understanding;

o when transformed into quantitative models they can be used to give at least broad indications of the relative benefit of competing system changes.

The proposed method is illustrated in the context of NATO's Northern Region, mainly for the sake of reasonable brevity. An equivalent analysis of the whole of Allied Command Europe (ACE), or even the whole of the NATO military structure, would be feasible, though necessarily a somewhat larger model. The quantitative results too are illustrative, designed to demonstrate how the evolution of a conflict might be charted.

THE METHODOLOGICAL APPROACH

The requirement is for a structured approach that allows mission areas and their interactions to be identified explicitly; and in such a way that the effect of changes in military capabilities in one or more mission areas can be measured in terms of:

o their impact on the overall campaign

o their impact on other (synergistically related) mission areas.

For example, upgrades in NATO's air defence capabilities will almost certainly favourably affect NATO's ground defences, since it should lessen the number of enemy bombers attacking NATO ground forces. This, in turn, should imply that those ground forces will be able to fight for longer, thus increasing logistic support needs ... and so on.

An approach which appears to show much promise in terms of the above is System Dynamics (SD). This is a method of analysing problems in which time is an important factor, and which involves the study of how a system can be defended against, or made to benefit from, the shocks which fall upon it from the outside world. In general, an SD study has a two-fold objective:

o Explaining the system's behaviour in terms of its structure and
    policies (for using resources)

o Investigating changes to structure, policies, or both, which will
    lead to an improvement in the behaviour.

It is not claimed that SD is the only approach that would (or could) "do the job"; merely that it has certain attributes that make it especially suitable for describing and analysing problems of the type discussed in this paper. It should be regarded as a complementary tool to other forms of analysis, certainly not replacing them, but offering opportunities to extend and integrate their results.

SD has traditionally been presented as a method in its own right and has been defined[1] as:

> "a rigorous method of system description, which facilitates feedback analysis, usually via a continuous simulation model, of the effects of alternative system structures and control policies on system behaviour".

An alternative definition is that SD involves bringing the attitude of mind of a control engineer to bear on a managed system, with the objective of increasing the robustness of its reactions to external influences. A system is robust if it always performs as well as the circumstances allow, regardless of what the circumstances are. Of these two definitions, the former describes the procedure of the approach, the latter its essence, and both are necessary for a full understanding. SD has not so far been widely used in the defence community, though SHAPE Technical Centre have incorporated it into several major projects.

The SD approach[2,3] breaks down into an iterative sequence of steps which, in themselves, appear fairly standard, but which differ in many important respects from the corresponding steps in other management science approaches. The steps are:

1. Definition of real-world symptoms to be understood and improved - point A.

2. System description by means of an <u>Influence Diagram</u>.

3. Model formulation.

4. Model verification and validation.

5. Simulation experiments, leading to improved understanding of the problem underlying the symptoms.

6. Redesign of system structures and/or policies in order to improve its dynamic behaviour - point B.

The question then becomes whether the A's from which SD could start are important enough to be interesting, whether the B's to which it is capable of leading are practical enough to be useful, and whether the cost and duration of the journey are low enough to be worthwhile.

Step 2 above is often the most revealing and informative part of the process. The Influence Diagram - simply a diagram showing what influences what - has considerable advantages over flow diagrams and the like from some other methodological approaches. These advantages are:

o   influence diagrams are easy to explain and to be understood by managers

o   they can be drawn quickly and revised easily

o   given a suitable simulation language, large parts of the model can be written down <u>directly from the diagram</u> without a costly and tedious intermediate stage of flow charting.

The bulk of this paper is devoted to the construction and analysis (and contemplation) of an Influence Diagram of a tri-service campaign in the Northern Region of Allied Command Europe.

THE QUALITATIVE MODEL OF NATO'S NORTHERN REGION

The essential object of NATO is to preserve the peace through deterrence, and failing that, in war, to retain or regain control over the territory of its member nations. In some cases, the territories are contiguous, or are geographically related in ways which are militarily significant. In NATO's Northern Region the sea areas are also significant in that it would, for example, be a very difficult and hazardous military operation to send land forces by sea from the UK to Northern Norway if Soviet air and naval forces were able to operate unopposed in the Norwegian Sea. The Northern Region (NR) is therefore particularly interesting from an analytical viewpoint, since all three NATO commands, Europe, Atlantic, and Channel, operate in the geographical vicinity of NR, because NR involves land, air and maritime operations (the Southern and Central Regions do too, but to a lesser extent), and because the NR includes sea areas which are within NATO's area of interest, but which may not be sovereign national territory.

Any conceptual or quantitative analysis directed at the assessment of long-term strategic priorities must therefore include the concept of 'control' of a land or sea area, and it must also address the geographical inter-relationships of these areas. These ideas can be developed in a fairly straightforward way. The starting point is Fig. 1, which indicates that NATO control of North Norway is influenced by the presence of NATO and Warsaw Pact forces there. The arrows indicate that one variable influences another, which is why these diagrams are called Influence Diagrams. The sign on the arrow indicates the general nature of the influence; the plus sign on the link from NATO forces being taken to indicate that an increase in them would lead to an increase in control, and that decreased NATO forces would tend to decrease control. The minus sign on the other link implies that the effect is opposite; an increase in WP forces reducing NATO's control and a decrease in them enhancing it.

Written out at length, that seems to be, and is, stating the obvious. It is one of our central contentions that a structured framework, the individual components of which are obvious and readily acceptable, is more useful for communication with decision-makers, and enables the analyst to capture their expertise more readily, than one which is couched in obscure and opaque mathematical notation.

At this level of simplicity, which is used only for exposition, the links and signs say nothing about the detailed nature of the influences, nor about how rapidly they take effect. It is <u>certainly not</u> implied in Fig. 1 that NATO control of North Norway is a simple matter of force ratio alone, but certainly that it <u>is</u> affected by it. Clearly, Fig. 1 is far too simple, and matters are taken a stage further in Fig. 2, which is arrived at by the very simple process of considering how the forces get to North

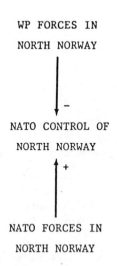

Fig. 1 Simple conceptual diagram for North Norway

Norway. This technique of treating systems in terms of their physical movements and the consequent influences is the key to the SD approach to <u>system description</u>. The power of the method lies in the simplicity of the diagramming technique, and the clear hints each successive diagram gives that it is incomplete. This means that the analyst is led through a series of steps of diagram improvement, and is almost automatically guided to a reasonable first approximation to the degree of detail needed for the problem at hand[6,7]. We suggest that this is a useful attribute for the analysis of difficult problems in complicated systems. This property can be summarized in the phrase 'the model can guide its own evolution'.

In the present case, the diagram suggests that it is incomplete in the sense that reinforcements do not, in the real world, simply appear from nowhere. That idea leads to Fig. 3, in which several factors in Fig. 2 have been dropped from the diagram to reduce overcomplication, though they appear in the simulation model which is discussed below. Since this paper concerns the analytical approach it is important to mention that the diagrams should be used intelligently, so that factors may appear or disappear according to the perspective that the analyst wishes to take. In other words, it is both legitimate and desirable to draw several diagrams for the same underlying model.

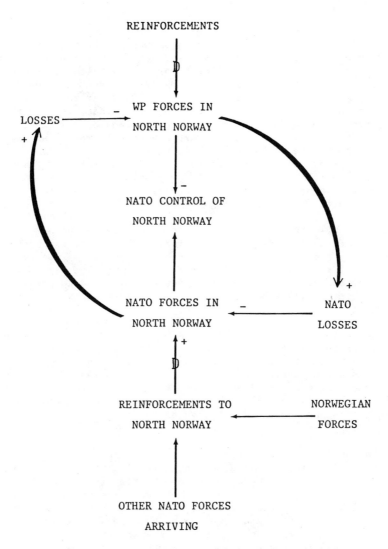

Fig. 2 Extension of North Norway diagram

Figure 3 indicates the influence which "NATO control of the Norwegian Sea" has on reinforcements to North Norway. It also indicates that "NATO control of North Norway" affects the ability to control the Norwegian Sea. Thus, the link marked A implies that the greater the degree of NATO control of North Norway, the more air and naval bases there are from which NATO forces can operate in the Norwegian Sea. Similarly, link B indicates that the greater NATO's control of the Norwegian Sea, the easier it is to protect reinforcements to North Norway, and therefore the easier it is to retain control of North Norway.

Links A and B combine with others to form a very obvious closed chain of influences, a feedback loop, emphasized by the circular arrow marked Loop 1. This is a positive feedback mechanism in which, for example, some loss of control of North Norway might lead to an accelerating collapse of control. The counteracting effects are that the WP losses, which appeared in Fig. 2, may be such that NATO can reinforce rapidly enough to halt, or even reverse, the decline. That, in turn, hinges on the respective WP and NATO reinforcement delays, and that suggests the interesting thought (or irrelevant fantasy) that Norway might make a greater contribution to the Alliance by building roads than by expanding her armed forces. Choices such as that between forces and roads are, however, an aspect of the infrastructure area of emphasis mentioned in the opening section of this paper. Again, we suggest that an analytical approach which stimulates such lateral thinking may be useful.

Figure 3 also includes the reinforcement movement across the Atlantic as influenced by the presence of WP forces there. It is, perhaps, not desirable to expand these diagrams in quite such large stages as we have done in going from Fig. 2 to Fig. 3, but in this paper we do so for reasons of brevity. Figure 3 does, however, lead us to consider how WP forces, particularly submarines, get into the Atlantic and that is the subject of Fig. 4.

Figure 4 includes the idea that NATO control of Iceland's air bases contributes to the effectiveness of the anti-submarine barrier in the Greenland-Iceland-UK (GIUK) gap. That effectiveness, and the ability to inflict losses on Soviet submarines in the Norwegian Sea, in turn affect the Soviet ability to inflict losses on NATO's reinforcements crossing the Atlantic. The diagram also includes the effect that "NATO control of the Norwegian Sea and North Norway" have on reducing the Soviet ability to attack Iceland.

Two points may be made from Fig. 4. The <u>first</u> is the presence of the timing of NATO reinforcements leaving North America vis-a-vis that of Soviet submarines despatched to the North Atlantic from their bases in the Kola Peninsula, as affected by the respective transit delays D_W and D_N. The issues of tactical intelligence and reinforcement planning evidently bear on this, and were two of the areas of emphasis mentioned in Section 1 of this paper, though the diagram clearly shows that these two topics are interrelated both with each other, and with other areas such as command and control and mobilizable reserves. The diagram is thus capable of portraying the interaction of many, if not all, of the areas of concern to SACEUR.

The <u>second</u> point is that the diagram goes beyond being just a rather vivid and clear agenda for debate. It shows the interconnections between the priority areas in terms of the feedback loops on which they operate. It thus allows the analyst to adopt the point of view of the control engineer and attempt to design the interplay between investments made in priority areas and war-fighting strategies, so as to enhance the feedbacks

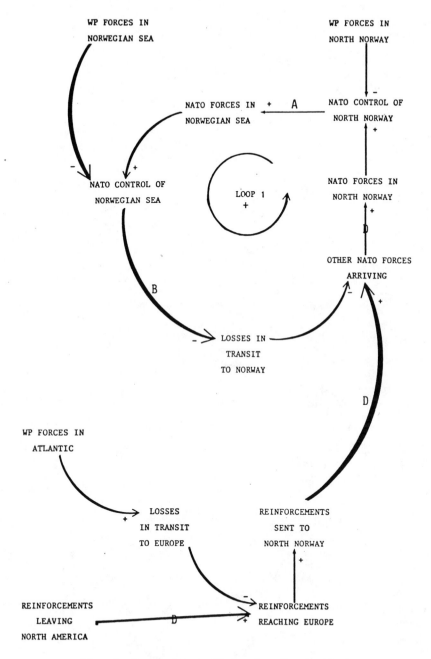

Fig. 3 Extension to Norwegian Sea control

which produce favourable war dynamics for one side, and weaken
those which operate in favour of the other. In other words, it aids the
design of policies for the efficient management of defence assets, aimed at
helping to get the most out of whatever is available. Some examples of how
that might be done are given later in the paper using, of course, fictitious data.

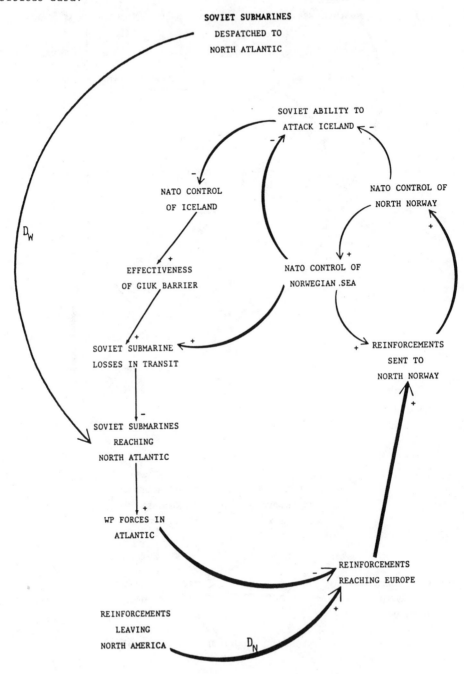

Fig. 4   The inclusion of Iceland

The final stage of the conceptual model is shown in Fig. 5, which incorporates other geographically related areas - the North Sea, Denmark and the UK. For simplicity's sake, some of the factors from Fig. 4 are condensed in Fig. 5, though they remain present in the underlying simulation model. For the same reason, some of the factors in Fig. 5 are not shown in detail. For example, the degree of control of Denmark is represented in the simulation model in the same way as control of North Norway was shown in Fig. 2, but is depicted at an aggregated level in Fig. 5. As can be seen, the degree of control of the North Sea has a positive effect on the ability to reinforce Denmark, just as control of the Norwegian Sea influenced reinforcement of North Norway.

The balance which is, or has to be, struck in the allocation of UK air forces between the competing demands of the Norwegian and North Seas affects the balance between a number of positive feedback mechanisms, and therefore emphasizes the importance of survivable command and control as an area of emphasis. The point is, however, much more profound than the significance of command and control of flexible military assets. The real significance lies in the balance between investment in forces, investment in command and control facilities, and strategic requirements. The two extremes would be absolute priority of resource allocation to the Norwegian Sea or absolute priority to the North Sea. The former would place emphasis on defence of the NR, whilst the latter would emphasize defence of the Central Region.

USES OF THE QUALITATIVE MODEL

In the introduction to this paper, we listed nine areas which SACEUR has nominated as areas of emphasis. Seven of them appear, explicitly or implicitly, in Fig. 5, the exceptions being attack of WP follow-on forces and nuclear weapons requirements. Certainly the former, and probably the latter, could be added to Fig. 5, though at the cost of some complexity. For the purposes of this paper, we will leave Fig. 5 as it is, and indicate how it might be used.

The first level of use is as an agenda for discussion. The nine items on SACEUR's list are, of course, already an agenda, but in the conventional form in which one item follows another, the disadvantage of which is that in discussing any given item it is hard to recall the previous ones, and difficult to project one's thoughts forward to those which are yet to come. The unconventional form in Fig. 5 does, we suggest, allow one to keep an overall view, shared by all participants, while discussing any particular item. We accept that Fig. 5 might need to be redrawn to get the right balance between enough detail and too much complexity, but the principle of the diagrammatic agenda seems to be valuable. Its disadvantage is that the discussion might go round in circles, just as the feedback loops do, and the debate might therefore demand very skilled chairmanship, but, given that, it might be more illuminating than some meetings we have attended.

The second use of the diagram is related to the first, and is its use as a theory tester. That involves taking some theory, or assertion, such as whether the American aircraft carriers should be employed in the Norwegian Sea or in the Atlantic, and attempting to trace out the feedback mechanisms which would be modified in either case. In the first case, the effect would be to strengthen Loop 1, which was shown in Fig. 3, in the second, it

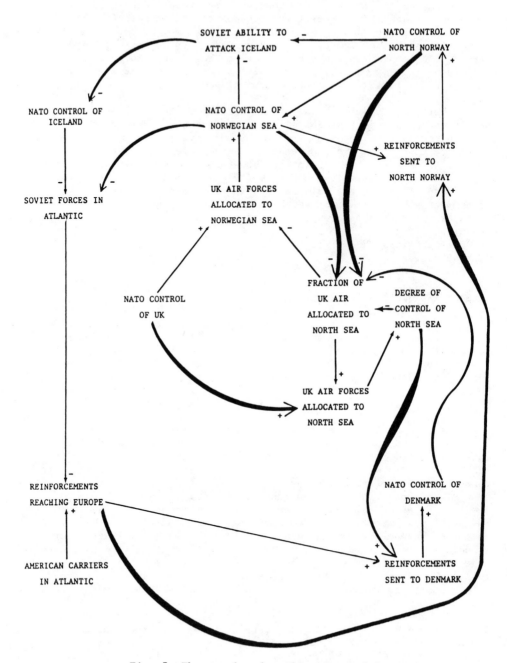

Fig. 5 The completed qualitative model

would be initially to increase the power of the loops, in Fig. 5, which
enhance NATO control over Denmark and the North Sea. This ultimately
affects the control of the more northerly areas and, by arguing about the
time delays, one might get a clearer idea of which is the better use of
these valuable assets. Naturally, such an argument would involve many
judgements about losses and effects, but we suggest that the judgements
would be more transparent than they are in a flat statement about what
carriers should or should not do.

The third use of Fig. 5 is as a basis for a simulation model to
give quantitative indications of the relative merits of different proposals, or to assess the balances between war-fighting intentions and
investment decisions. In particular, one might examine how the intentions
might change as the investments come to fruition. The next sections of
this paper examine this aspect in more detail, using fictitious data.
Naturally in a real analysis, great attention must be paid to data and
validation, issues which we can ignore for the purposes of this paper. It
is, however, worth mentioning that the clarity, transparency and communi-
cability of the influence diagram is an important aspect of securing
acceptance of a quantitative model. Further, it is an attractive aspect of
the method that it provides one with a framework in which the results of
detailed analyses of, say, a carrier battle and the North Norwegian land
battle can be interrelated, even if, as may often be the case, these
detailed analyses are performed by methods different from System Dynamics.

A simulation model based on the detailed version of Fig. 5 could
be written in any one of a number of languages. In practice, it may be
convenient to use a special-purpose language, such as DYSMAP, which is
designed to the structural principles underlying Fig. 5. (For a fuller
discussion of these principles see, for example, refs. 2, 3, 4 and 5.) The
advantage of the special-purpose language is that one can write the model
quite quickly, directly from the diagram without an intermediate stage
of flow-charting. This retains the commonality of viewpoint between
modeller and user, and confers great advantages of modelling speed.
Finally, the DYSMAP format allows the analyst to make use of the companion
DYSMOD optimization package, not for optimization as such[6,7], which would be
naive, but for effective search for robust solutions.

Before turning to the model results, is is worth remarking that
the DYSMAP-type syntax makes it very easy to incorporate non-linear effects, and there are several in the model, for example the effect that
force ratio has on the rate at which control is lost or regained. It is
also very easy to incorporate random variation, though for simplicity we
have not done so in this illustrative model. Finally, although System
Dynamics is traditionally thought of as a continuous simulation approach it
is quite easy to incorporate discrete events. A case in point would be the
carriers; there are few of them, they may have a major effect, and they are
either present or not in any given area. It would clearly be better not to
treat them as continuous variables and it would not be necessary to do so.

SOME INDICATIVE SIMULATION RESULTS

In this section we present some illustrative results from a model based
on a much more detailed version of Fig. 5. The examples are chosen to
indicate the form of the output and a few of the issues which can be
treated. For each experiment five variables are plotted: the degree
of control over five areas, on a scale of 0 to 1 (in which 1 indicates
perfect control). A pattern of line is assigned to each variable by the
package, and that pattern is used to plot the graph for the variable, to

draw its scale and, below the scale in an L shape, to point to the definition of the variable. Naturally, for a real model one might wish to plot more variables (the limit is 124), and one would certainly wish to print numerical tables of any particularly important ones (that limit is 144).

Figure 6 portrays an imaginary base case for the model. The war commences on Day 9, to allow forces to build up (which would allow the analyst to show the effect of alert measures), and continues for 21 days, for illustration. The output indicates that control of North Norway is lost after about 9 days and of Denmark rather later. There is a sharp drop in control of the Norwegian Sea, mainly due to efforts by NATO to attack Soviet submarines on passage, and towards the end of the run, control over the Norwegian Sea is being regained. After about 6 days of combat, NATO's degree of control in North Norway and the Norwegian Sea has fallen to the point that the WP can attack Iceland with acceptable losses, and control there is lost in due course.

Figures 7 and 8 compare cases of increased Norwegian reserves, and the same reserves but a larger rapid reinforcement force (RRF) for Norway. These are the third and fourth items on the list of areas of emphasis given earlier, though we repeat that that list is in no particular order. Figure 7 is quite striking in that there is some loss of control over North Norway, though what is lost is regained later, there is a big improvement in control over the Norwegian Sea, Iceland is not attacked and control over Denmark and the North Sea are hardly affected. Figure 7 does not show the number of Soviet submarines reaching the North Atlantic, but inspection of the detailed output shows that they are hardly affected, relative to the base case. Figure 8 indicates that increasing the RRF by the same amount as the Norwegian reserves were increased in Fig. 7 leads to poorer control of North Norway and of the Norwegian Sea. This confirms the well-known point that reserves and reinforcements have to be considered in relation to the infrastructure by which they deploy and hence the timeliness of their arrival in the combat area. For the purposes of this paper we are, however, addressing two of SACEUR's areas of emphasis simultaneously in the context of geographical relationships.

Figure 9 tests the fairly interesting question of how important it is to be sure about Soviet intentions. The test is done by setting the Norwegian reserves and the RRF back to their base values, and allowing the Soviets to allocate enough forces to attack Iceland immediately, regardless of losses in transit. The effects are the practically immediate fall of Iceland coupled with a better degree of control of North Norway because of the diversion of Soviet forces to Iceland. The loss of the Icelandic air bases is not compensated by the retention of those in North Norway so the degree of control over the Norwegian Sea is worse and, because of the lower attrition of Soviet submarines in the Norwegian Sea and the GIUK gap, there is a reduction in reinforcements reaching Europe. That would have effects in the Central Region which are not shown in this model (though they could be added). The effects further south are improved control over the North Sea, but, because of the inadequacy of the land forces, no improvement in control of Denmark.

Figure 10 tests the effects of improved tactical intelligence for NATO aircraft operating in the North and Norwegian Seas. As might be expected, this leads to better control of those sea areas and, because of greater submarine attrition, improved convoy arrivals in Europe (not shown in the graphs we present, but calculated in the model). There is no noticeable effect on the control of North Norway or Denmark, illustrating that improvements in one asset do not necessarily make up for deficiencies elsewhere (though we reiterate that these are fictitious data).

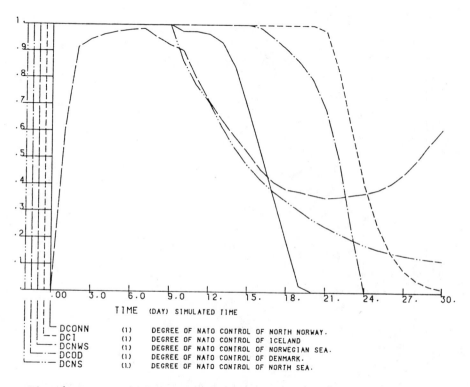

Fig. 6 Base case for model Aggregated model for Northern Region

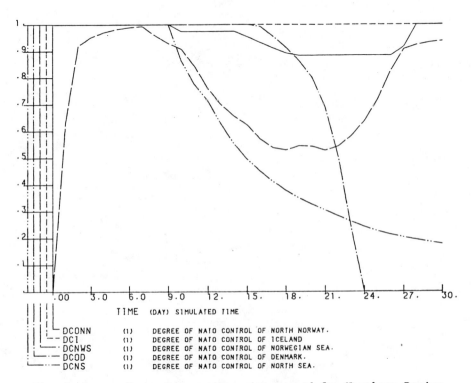

Fig. 7 Larger Norwegian reserves Aggregated for Northern Region

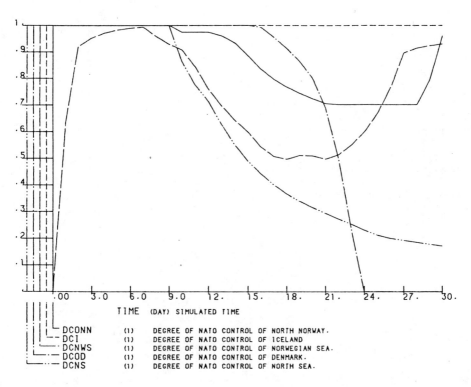

Fig. 8 Larger Marine Amphibious Force (MAF) Aggregated model for Northern Region

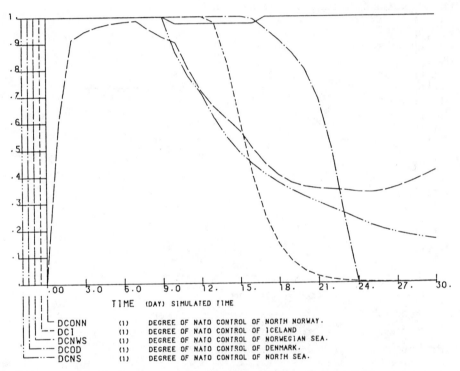

Fig. 9   Immediated Soviet attack on Iceland Aggregated model for Northern Region

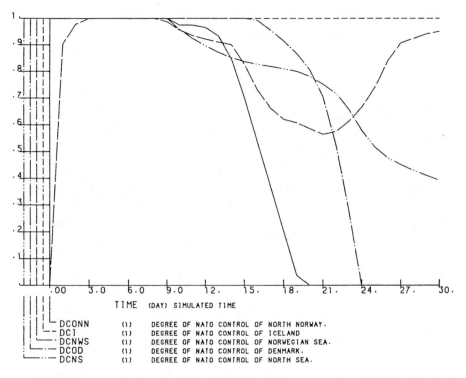

Fig. 10 Better air tactical intelligence Aggregated model for Northern Region

The last experiment in Fig. 11 shows the effects of much larger reinforcements being allocated to Denmark. Not surprisingly, control of Denmark is retained and, interestingly, there is better control of the North Sea and the Norwegian Sea than in the base case. The reason is clearly seen in Fig. 5 that the better control of Denmark means that fewer UK aircraft are needed in the North Sea, and more are therefore available for more northerly duties.

Finally Fig. 12 shows for illustration the wide variation in control of the Norwegian Sea achievable in these different cases. In reading Fig. 12, notice that the pattern for the graph and its scale now point to the run title, with the same variable name in each case. For brevity, we have not provided comparative graphs for the other variables which do not, of course, necessarily show the same sensitivity. Lack of sensitivity may indicate the severity or the irrelevance of a given problem, and care is needed in deciding which is the case. We suspect that an analysis of the true causes of sensitivity or insensitivity in a proper model would be of great value in deciding priorities.

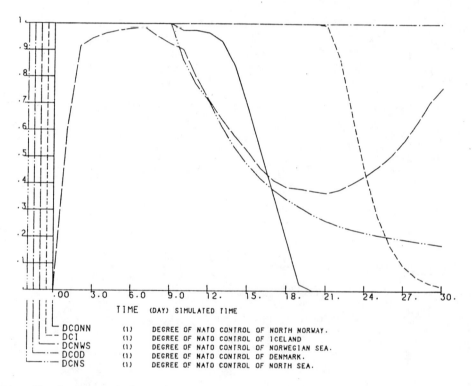

Fig. 11 Larger reinforcements for Denmark Aggregated model for Northern Region

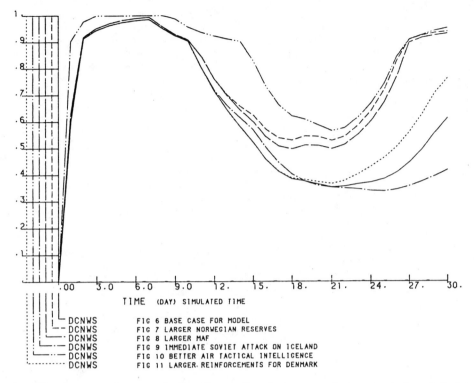

Fig. 12 Comparative graph for Norwegian Sea control Aggregated model for Northern Region

QUANTITATIVE ANALYSIS USING THIS APPROACH

To make full use of quantitative models of this type, we suggest that analysis may evolve through three phases. In Phase I, one does a series of almost random experiments. These usually help to find and eliminate weaknesses in the model. More importantly, though, the analyst gets a better intuitive 'feel' for how the model behaves and, by tracing the results back to feedback loops in the influence diagram, he comes to understand more clearly the importance of the various influences modelled. That leads to Phase II, in which the analyst clarifies and improves his understanding by carefully planned simulation experiments designed to confirm or refute his theories about which loops in the influence diagram are, or are not, important, and how loops can be changed, by adding or reallocating resources, to make the dynamic behaviour more as he wishes it to be. This concept that behaviour can be explained from feedback loops and that loops can be redesigned to produce more favourable behaviour is the cardinal principle of the System Dynamics approach, and is the reason why SD should not be interpreted as a simulation method. Simulation is indeed used, but is merely a guide to analysis.

Phases I and II should lead the analyst <u>and</u> his client to a good understanding of the model and, if it is a good model, of the system, so that sensible objective functions can be formulated to describe the desired system behaviour. At that point, <u>Phase III</u> can be entered in which the very powerful optimization facilities of DYSMOD can be used in the <u>search for robustness</u> of dynamic behaviour.

CONCLUSION

This paper began by arguing the need for analysis methods suitable for exploring some far-reaching system changes, capable of contributing to the debate on prioritization, and even of suggesting other priorities. We have attempted to demonstrate a method which we feel has at least some of the required characteristics. In essence the case rests on four attractive aspects of the method.

1. The Influence Diagram is a vivid and clear conceptual tool, valuable in its own right as an agenda for debate and greatly improving the communication between analyst and client.

2. Once a fairly simple syntax has been mastered, the diagram can be translated quickly and cheaply into a simulation model, providing acceptable data are available. This speed of modelling means that the inevitable false starts are easily rectified, and more is learned than is the case with methods in which an initial model is difficult to revise or abandon.

3. The analytical foundation of feedback loops provides a controllable simulation process, and enables the analyst to give intuitively credible explanations of his results.

4. The ability to link automatically with sophisticated numerical optimization facilities gives a very powerful tool for exploring the model's behaviour and designing more satisfactory dynamics.

It is, of course, very unwise to push any analytical approach too far. For reasons of space, we have said little about the limitations of SD, and this paper should not be taken to imply that we see it as anything more than a useful complement to established and proven methods of military analysis. Certainly, to use SD to do detailed combat simulation would not always be sensible; there may be better methods and simulation languages available. Even within SD, it is necessary to justify very carefully the decision to go beyond the Influence Diagram into a simulation model. That deceptively simple diagram often triggers such insight that quantitative modelling is superfluous.

In summary, we contend that the proper role of SD in military analysis is probably as what we make bold to call an 'architectural model'.
In our view, that means a model which can be used to interrelate results from other analyses, the connections between which might not otherwise be seen. For example, the case we have examined involves, among others, the air/land battle for territory, anti-submarine warfare, air defence of port facilities, sea lines of communication, tactical intelligence gathering, and the operations of carrier battle-groups. For each of these there are already sophisticated and accepted analysis methods and we in no way imply that they should be abandoned. We do, however, suggest that what is lacking is a framework by which their results can be put together, which is why we use the term 'architectural model'. We feel that an SD approach along the lines suggested has much to offer in that role.

REFERENCES

Coyle, R.G., 'The technical elements of the system dynamics approach', European Journal of Operational Research, 14 (1983), 359-370

Coyle, R.G., 'Management system dynamics', John Wiley and Sons, Chichester, 1977

Coyle, R.G., 'System thinking applied to counter-insurgency warfare', Policy Sciences, to appear

Coyle, R.G., 'The use of optimization methods in system dynamics models', Dynamica, to appear

Wolstenholme, E.F., 'System dynamics in perspective', Journal of the Operational Research Society, 33 (1982), 547-556

Wolstenholme, E.F., and Coyle, R.G., 'The development of system dynamics as a methodology for system description and qualitative analysis', Journal of the Operational Research Society, 34 (1983), 569-581

Further information on the software may be obtained from the authors.

Part III

ANALYSIS OF IMPROVEMENT PROPOSALS

ANALYZING ALTERNATIVE CONCEPTS FOR THE DEFENSE OF NATO

Milton G. Weiner

The Rand Corporation

Santa Monica, California

INTRODUCTION

The objective of this paper is to provide a perspective on several aspects of the analysis of alternative defense concepts for NATO. Rather than treating the subject in a broad and general way, the paper uses three specific concepts for the conventional defense of the Central Region as examples. No overall conclusions about their merits are drawn.

The descriptions of the three concepts and some of their military, economic, and political dimensions should raise a host of questions. These can serve to illustrate some of the different factors to be considered in the quantitative analysis of NATO defense concepts.

BACKGROUND

Virtually from its birth over 35 years ago, the North Atlantic Treaty Organization has been faced with crises or controversies. It has had to deal with issues connected with events as diverse as the Berlin Blockade, the invasion of South Korea, the Soviet acquisition of a thermonuclear capability, the formation of the Warsaw Pact, the war(s) in the Middle East, the Hungarian revolution, the proposed creation of a multilateral nuclear force, the French "withdrawal," the invasion of Czechoslovakia, the SALT and MBFR negotiations, the growth of Soviet military strength, the possible deployment of neutron weapons, the invasion of Afghanistan, the deployment of an intermediate range nuclear force (INF), and dozens of other major and minor military, political, and economic issues.

Despite this host of external and internal problems, the Alliance has remained remarkably stable in its membership, basic charter, and cohesiveness. Fundamentally, the military focus of the NATO nations has always been on the deterrence of conflict. That focus will continue to be the major thrust, but there are widespread and growing views that the approaches and mechanisms of the past may not be adequate for the future. To some people the decade ahead will present unprecedented challenges which they perceive as resulting from the growth of military power in both the East and West, the potential for massive defense expenditures, the multi-polarity of international relations, the shrinking pools of military manpower, the impact of anti-nuclear movements, and a variety of other factors.

Although there is concern about NATO's future in the face of these challenges, the remedies suggested for dealing with the future differ considerably. One set of views holds that, despite the history of crises and controversies, NATO survives and adapts because it is a "transatlantic-bargain" and because there is a consensus in the Alliance that there has to be such an Alliance. Thus, even though the members may face difficult individual and collective economic, political, and defense problems, there is no alternative to a commitment to a common defense. Therefore, the remedy for the future is the passage of time and the good offices of the members of the Alliance.

A second set of views considers the current period as propitious for major changes in either the form of the U.S. commitment to European security, i.e., the NATO alliance, or to the commitment itself. For this group, today's conditions are not the same as those that led to the formation of the Alliance in terms of risk, cost, or implications. Therefore, some sweeping changes should be considered. The remedies suggested by proponents of this view include such major changes as unilateral U.S. withdrawal or the establishment of an entirely new Alliance structure. In most cases, the proponents deal with possible directions or alternatives to the North Atlantic Treaty Organization in the long term--ten to 20 years in the future, the emphasis is on the policy aspects of these remedies more than on the military implications.

By contrast to the remedies suggested by these two groups, proponents of other types of remedies concentrate on the "military" nature of the Alliance. They emphasize ways to enhance NATO's defense capabilities. This type can also be divided somewhat arbitrarily into two groups; one includes those with the views that NATO is facing a growing threat in an era in which the United States no longer has the edge in strategic military capabilities. By and large, this group espouses NATO's current strategic concept, but its advocates seek remedies of "more" or "better" capabilities to implement the concept. These include such remedies as a long-term defense program (LTDP), deployment of intermediate-range nuclear forces (INF), enhanced defense capabilities through the use of emergency technologies (ER), etc.

The other group also considers the growth in Soviet power a crucial element in the developing crisis of the 1980s. However, the advocates in this group stress the fact that the desired improvements in NATO's military capabilities require basic changes in NATO's defense concepts and military posture. Although the various proponents of this group endorse MC 14/3 to different degrees, they are uniform in their view that enhancing NATO defense should not be restricted to improvements in current capabilities. They advocate new defense concepts and postures. The changes vary considerably and include such forms as the use of fortified zones or barriers, infantry-heavy area defense units, and various air/land battle concepts.

Even though the four groups espouse different ways of remedying the perceived situation in NATO, they generally agree on several broad issues. These include the desirability, if not the requirement, for improvements in U.S. strategic nuclear capabilities, although there are individual differences as to the type and magnitude of such improvements. And proponents in all groups generally encourage the continual exploration and expansion of arms control measures with the Soviet Union.

In terms of the different groups, the work described in this paper is most relevant to the remedies considered under the fourth group, i.e., alternatives to NATO's current defense concept. An early phase of the work reviewed several classified and unclassified publications that proposed new concepts for the defense of NATO. Summaries of some of the unclassified concepts are published in R. Levine et al, "A Survey of NATO Defense Concepts," The Rand Corporation, N-1871-AF, June 1982. For most of the concepts described in the survey, the individual authors identified the reasons why they believed a change in NATO defense capabilities was required and why the particular change or new concept that was proposed had merit. But few of the authors included or had the resources to undertake even moderately detailed quantitative analyses of their proposals. Without some quantitative analysis, it is difficult to obtain an overall perspective on the proposals in terms of their relative contributions to Alliance defense effectiveness, the magnitude of the investments in resources required, or the variety of military, political, social, or technical issues that they raise.

In undertaking the work described in this paper, we made the conscious decision to favor breadth rather than depth in our approach. Nevertheless, emphasis was on making the work as quantitative as possible commensurate with the level of effort available. The next section describes the methodological approach.

THE METHODOLOGICAL APPROACH

The methodological approach to the study consisted of three parts: the overall research strategy, the techniques or models used for the study, and the development of results and conclusions. For this study, the research strategy was straightforward and comprised:

o developing a general assessment of NATO's current conventional defense capability
o defining three broadly different types of conventional defense alternatives for NATO
o determining the requirements that the defense alternatives would have to meet in order to achieve a stated objective

The stated objective for each of the three alternative concepts was to provide NATO with an effective forward defense. For purposes of this study, an effective forward defense was defined as limiting the Warsaw Pact ground penetration to not more than 50 kilometers into the Federal Republic of Germany. This simple and somewhat arbitrary measure of effectiveness (MOE) was based on the view that NATO endorses a "forward defense" concept and that NATO's wartime posture, although heavily conditioned by terrain and area, in broad terms consists of a covering force area (CFA) extending about 20 to 30 kilometers inside the interzonal border, and a main defense area extending to a depth of about 50 kilometers. Therefore, the halting of Warsaw Pact penetrations within 50 kilometers of the border can be regarded as preventing the Pact from breaking through NATO's main defense area. It should be clearly understood that in using this analytically convenient measure, no implication of the political or operational adequacy of the measure is intended.

The primary tool for analyzing NATO's current conventional defense capability, as well as for analyzing the requirements of the three alternative defense concepts to meet the stated MOE, was a highly aggregated computer model. Since the study was focused on the Central Region and was examining very different defense concepts under a variety of conditions, the theater model was designed to deal with broad concepts like "Mass," i.e., different numbers of NATO and Pact forces with varied capabilities; "Space," i.e., different defense postures and different axes of attack and defense in the different NATO corps areas, as well as different parameters for advancing or withdrawing in FRG territory; and "Time," i.e., different periods of mobilization for the NATO and Pact forces, as well as different periods of combat activity. As a result of this level of aggregation, the model was titled the Mass And Space/Time Evaluation Routine, or MASTER.

MASTER is a theater level, expected value, piston-type, force ratio model. It represents primarily the geographical area of the Federal Republic of Germany divided into 40 regions consisting of eight Corps areas, each of which has five zones. The model incorporates:

o Terrain (four different tupes)
o Forces (brigade/regiment level for NATO; division level for the Pact ground forces. Air forces are represented in terms of 10 to 15 different types of aircraft)
o Timing (six-hour cycles of combat for up to 60 days of war)
o Reinforcements (daily arrivals in the combat area for both NATO and Pact air and ground forces)
o Attrition (modified Lanchester representation)
o Movement (rates of advance for different force ratio, terrain, and posture conditions)
o Posture (different defense postures depending on geographical area, force ratio, etc.)

The model was based on several more detailed theater-level simulations, but it did not incorporate many factors such as weather, logistics, command-control-communications activities, etc. The model outputs included daily and summary information on FEBA/FLOT location, force ratios, sorties, air and ground casualties, etc.

Using MASTER, a series of simulation runs were made to provide a broad assessment of NATO's current capability to conduct a successful "forward defense." As anyone familiar with combat simulations is aware, there are innumerable factors, conditions, and scenarios that can be varied in most theater level models. As a result, any identification of a "base case" is arbitrary and can be considered a device that serves more as an analytic convenience than as a representation of basic capabilities. Thus, while our work did use a base case, it was only as a device for establishing conditions to be used in the assessment of the alternative defense concept. The base case was derived from a series of model runs in which a large number of factors were varied. Among these were different types of ground force ratios, different mobilization periods for both sides, different air and ground force employment strategies, different rules as to when the sides would attack, withdraw, or hold, as well as different values for the attrition and movement variables, etc.

Without going into all the details or trying to identify sets of specific outcomes and the relevant conditions associated with these outcomes, the general results of our assessment of NATO's current defense capability were in line with the results of many theater level studies. In effect, NATO forces under many of the conditions and factors examined were unable to prevent the Pact from penetrations well into and, in many cases, through NATO main defense areas. It was the cases in which the Pact penetrated beyond the (arbitrary) 50 kilometer depth that were used as the standard base for the assessments of the alternative defense concepts.

It is possible to identify at least three very general approaches to the military defense of NATO's Central Region in the event that the Warsaw Pact is not deterred from aggressive action. One approach is literally to prevent the Pact from any significant penetration of the Federal Republic of Germany. A second approach is to allow the initial Pact attack forces to cross the interzonal border but to prevent them from being reinforced by any follow-on forces. A third approach is to allow Pact forces to cross the border, to penetrate in force, but to reduce their capability by maneuver and/or attrition so that they lose the ability to continue their advance before the Federal Republic is overrun.

On the basis of these three broad approaches, we developed a different defense concept for each approach. As an example of the approach that stops Pact forces at the border, we configured a Barrier concept. As an example of preventing the follow-on or second echelon forces from penetrating the Federal Republic, we configured a concept called Forward Response that incorporated an "interdiction belt." As an example of gradually attriting Pact forces as they penetrate, we configured a concept of Distributed Area Defense that utilized small anti-tank units operating throughout the first 50 to 100 kilometers inside the border. The following sections describe each of the concepts briefly and present some comments on various aspects of the assessments carried out in the study. No overall or comparative assessments of the concepts or conclusions about their merit are presented in this paper.

FORTIFIED BARRIER

The use of barriers or fortifications constructed during peacetime for enhancing NATO's defense capability is not new. Over the years, a large number of proposals or studies for various types of barriers have been made in various countries by various people or organizations. In many cases, the work was little more than an appeal for considering the peacetime construction of barriers as an increment to NATO's defense posture. In other cases, the studies were much more detailed. A partial list of some of the studies that have presented design and analytic data includes:

1956	Land Defense of NATO Europe in the Period 1958-1960
1962	Effect of Fortified Barrier Systems on Force Requirements in Central Europe
1963	An Illustrative Area Defense Ground Posture for NATO's Central Front
1964	USAREUR Optimum Barrier Study
1977	Prewar Terrain Sculpturing Concept, Alternative Operations Concepts in Europe (AOCEUR)
1977	Strengthening NATO Capabilities: A Hi-Lo-Ground Force Mix for Area Defense
1979	Heavy/Light Forces Study
1980	Tactical Nuclear Technology in the NATO Context (Project DYNAMIGHT, Phase II)
1982	Peacetime Defense Preparation in Europe
1983	A Fortified Barrier Option for the Defense of NATO

A review of the available studies indicates that virtually without exception they conclude that a barrier would enhance NATO's defense capability. However, there is considerable variation in the studies about the form of the barrier and in its effectiveness. The main elements illuminated by the past studies appear to be:

o Barriers require widths generally measured in tens of kilometers. A single narrow fortified defense line is likely to be inadequate, particularly against modern weapons.
o Barriers generally must be supported by backup forces to counter enemy penetrations. The backup forces (or firepower) require considerable mobility to move to areas where they are needed.

- o Barriers composed of individual positions or strongpoints are likely to be more vulnerable to penetration than those composed of continuous interlocking positions.
- o Barriers tend to limit the contribution of those defense forces at the portions of the barrier that are not under enemy attack. These forces do not contribute directly to attrition of enemy forces nor do they represent an offense threat that requires the enemy to maintain holding forces in areas where he is not attacking.
- o If a barrier of strongpoints, forts, or fortified positions is breached, some of the defense forces in these positions are likely to be bypassed and unable to contribute to subsequent military operations.
- o Improvements in military technology, particularly in sensors, precision weapons, etc., lower manpower requirements.

These conclusions, plus lessons derived from a number of historical examples, led to the outline of the barrier concept. However, to meet the very stringent criterion of stopping Pact penetrations within 50 kilometers of the border, the resultant barrier took on the character of a "modern" Maginot line, i.e., heavy interconnected fortifications in depth with major weapon systems throughout the length of the zone.

The main characteristics of the fortified barrier were:

- o Length
    - Approx. 800 km
- o Width
    - Approx. 20 km
- o Construction
    - Multiple zones of defenses
    - Reinforced concrete/steel
    - Major underground facilities
    - Chemical, fallout safe
    - Interconnected sections
- o Technology
    - Advanced precision fire weapons, rockets
    - Advanced surveillance, sensor, AWX systems
    - Robotic control, computer assessments
    - Remote control
- o Manning
    - Specialized force
    - Reduced troop level for area defended
- o Major support and reserve forces
    - Other NATO forces

Obviously, the characteristics of the barrier could be greatly simplified if the criteria for defense effectiveness were changed. A barrier that simply delays a Pact attack for a short period of time or a barrier that increases the attrition to Pact forces (or decreases attrition to NATO forces) by some small amount, need not have the extensive, massive character of the one configured here.

Using the MASTER model, a variety of delay times and attrition conditions were investigated. Without going into the details, the results were as indicated. In general, they showed that the longer the barrier could hold out, the lower the rate of attrition it had to inflict on the enemy before he was reduced to a point where he could not achieve a deep penetration into NATO territory. However, if the enemy committed a large force to the attack, a barrier that could hold out and also inflict heavy losses on the enemy (with limited losses of the defense force) tended to require the kind of continuous, massive, integrated fortifications and firepower capability of the type configured in the modern Maginot line.

However, it is generally accepted that almost any type of barrier will contribute something to the military effectiveness of NATO. It has generally been non-military considerations, i.e., cost and political issues that have been crucial to the peacetime construction of a barrier. As far as cost is concerned, it depends on the type and extent of the barrier. Limited barriers in selected areas of possible Pact attack could cost in the millions to tens of millions of dollars, while elaborate and extensive fortified barriers of the type described here could run into the tens of billions of dollars. Add to this the potential costs of obtaining land in the border area, as well as some evacuation and relocation of people and business activities from the border to other areas, and the costs could be closer to a hundred billion dollar amount.

The view that not only are such costs unacceptable but that the dislocation of people and businesses in the border area cannot be seriously considered are among the reasons that barriers have never received serious consideration despite their military contribution. In addition, a host of other reasons have been advanced. Although it is outside the scope of this paper to enumerate or examine in detail all the complex political, social, economic, and broad military rationales that have been advanced for not pursuing barrier development, a few of the more common ones can be synopsizes as follows:

o The dangers of defense mindedness. This somewhat vague notion incorporates such diverse views as "only the offense can win wars;" static, linear defenses can be defeated; reliance on fixed defenses can lead to a loss of national willingness to fight. Many of these views grew out of the experience in World Wars I and II, particularly the alleged French dependence on the Maginot line.
o The "legitimization" of a divided Germany. According to this notion, a barrier, particularly one along the border between West and East Germany, would imply NATO acceptance of the permanent division of Germany. Such an acceptance is regarded by some West Germans as disastrous; it is also considered a severe blow to those East Germans who hope that someday the two Germanys will be reunified. To deny this possibility of reunification is assumed to constitute a political concession that no FRG government could make and still remain in power.
o The "reduction" in the commitments of the NATO nations. A barrier that greatly increased the FRG's ability to defend itself could assumably allow other nations, particularly the United States, to reduce forces in the theater. Although ground forces would be the most likely candidates, the reduction could also extend to air forces and eventually to a lessening in the political commitment of the United States and other NATO nations to defend FRG territory.
o The raising of the escalation threshold. This view holds that a greatly increased capability for conventional defense of the FRG would force the Warsaw Pact to emphasize the use of nuclear weapons for offensive operations against NATO. Conversely, if barriers are not effective against a Warsaw Pact attack, NATO would be assumed to have lost flexibility in its current conventional defense and would be forced to escalate.

In summary, this section has tried to illustrate one example of one approach to different defense concepts for NATO and their implications for analytic work. The approach has been to consider ways of preventing Pact forces from penetrating very far into the Federal Republic of Germany in a conventional conflict. The one example discussed has been the use of a barrier, although there are others, including the use of nuclear weapons. The analytic effort indicated that a criterion measure like stopping the Pact in the border area could lead to requirements for a massive and extensive fortified barrier. And, finally, that establishing the military utility of such a barrier was only one aspect of the issues involved in an analysis of alternative NATO defense concepts.

FORWARD RESPONSE

The second broad approach to NATO defense is to consider concepts that would prevent the Pact from following up an initial attack by committing their second echelon or follow-on forces. Most of the concepts for this defense option involve some form of interdiction effort and are proposed in a variety of forms such as "interdiction of the second echelon," "follow-on forces attack," "deep battle," etc. The essence of these concepts is to locate and attack Pact forces before they can enter battle. Although all the concepts involve surveillance, target acquisition, and attack activities, they may differ in when, where, and how these activities may be carried out. In general, emphasis is placed on the value of advanced or emerging technologies for contributing to these interdiction efforts.

Another example of a concept for preventing follow-on Pact forces from entering the battle is a concept that has been called "forward response." The forward response concept envisions a two-phase operation that would be initiated as soon as possible after Pact forces had crossed the interzonal border in force. The concept involves an early, coordinated effort to create an "interdiction belt" on the eastern side of the border.

Phase One would consist of attacks on fixes lines of communication (LOCs) in a pre-designated zone along the border with the immediate objective of disrupting the enemy's scheme of maneuver.

Phase Two would consist of the attack on Pact forces attempting to transit the interdiction belt. The objective of these continuing attacks would be to prevent the Pact from introducing sufficient force into the Federal Republic so that it could continue its advance beyond 50 kilometers.

The interdiction belt is envisioned as a zone 20 to 30 kilometers wide extending approximately 800 kilometers along the eastern side of the interzonal border. One illustrative location of the belt would be about five to 10 kilometers inside the German Democratic Republic and Czechoslovakia.

The concept of an interdiction belt as considered here differs from many of the more traditional views of interdiction operations. In these views, interdiction involves attacks along the enemy's LOCs extending from the combat area back through into the enemy's rear areas, basically in the east-west direction. By contrast, the interdiction belt described here would be across the enemy's LOCs, basically in the north-south direction. In the traditional views, the targets are either "choke points" along the enemy's LOCs to slow movement of forces or enemy units moving along the LOCs. In the interdiction belt, the targets are first the choke points that would impede the movement of enemy forces across the belt, and then the units attempting to go through the area. In the traditional view, interdiction operations may extend hundreds of kilometers behind the combat zone. They may involve going deep into the German Democratic Republic and Czechoslovakia and involve locating and attacking targets somewhere in areas of hundreds of thousands of square kilometers. By contrast, the interdiction belt focuses operations in a narrow geographical area of about 24,000 square kilometers, i.e., 30 by 800 kilometers just east of the FRG border.

The interdiction belt concept raises a large number of questions, only some of which are subject to quantitative analysis. A few of these are illustrated here.

HOW LARGE AN EFFORT IS REQUIRED TO CARRY OUT PHASE ONE OF THE CONCEPT?

Since Phase One emphasizes attacks on fixed LOC targets as a first step in disrupting the enemy's ability to follow up his initial attack, a map analysis of the border area can provide an initial basis for determining likely axes of enemy attack, number of LOCs, available targets on the LOCs, and similar data.

Using as the exemplar a 30 by 800 kilometer belt located about five kilometers inside the border, a map analysis indicated that there are hundreds, but not thousands, of roads (and railroads) that, if cut, would prevent any crossing of the belt on a paved surface. Further analysis indicated that on each of these hundreds of routes, one or more potential targets such as bridges, slide areas, choke points, etc., could be identified. If destroyed, enemy movement across the belt would be impeded while he repaired the damage and/or tried to develop alternate routes.

Thus, even if there were literally no information or intelligence on where the Pact might cross the interzonal border, the destruction of these hundreds of targets would contribute to disrupting the enemy's initial attack plans. To the extent that pre-attack intelligence provided information on the routes that the enemy was using in the border area, this number could be substantially reduced. For example, if the enemy were moving along eight axes and using three or four routes through the belt on each axis of advance, the initial number of targets would not require a major air interdiction effort.

HOW LARGE AN EFFORT IS REQUIRED TO CARRY OUT PHASE TWO OF THE CONCEPT?

To provide some analytic insights into this question, the MASTER model was run under conditions that simulated a number of Pact attacks after different periods of mobilization, with different attack plans involving different numbers of attack axes. Without going into all the details, two of the general conclusions of the simulation should be noted. First, there was no need to try to stop all the enemy forces from successfully crossing the belt. Over a wide range of simulations, the ability to prevent only about one-third of the enemy's fighting vehicles (tanks, armored carriers, artillery, etc.) from crossing the belt was sufficient to reduce the enemy's strength arriving in the FRG to the point where he did not have an adequate force strength to penetrate beyond 50 kilometers of the border against NATO defense forces. In effect, the "leakage" through the belt could be a substantial 60 to 70 percent of the enemy's forces and it would be effective.

The second conclusion, related to the first, was that the effort required by NATO, and particularly by NATO tactical air units, varied enormously depending on the size, timing, and location of the Pact attack. If the Pact initiated the attack with limited forces and the follow-on forces arrived slowly and in small numbers, NATO tactical air could generate sufficient capability to provide the desired attrition level. However, as the size, timing, and location of the Pact attack placed greater demands on NATO tactical air, it reached the point where it was not possible to inflict the necessary loss level on the Pact forces. Under these circumstances, the interdiction belt concept would be ineffective with NATO's current capabilities. However, a series of feasible improvements in NATO capabilities were postulated. These constituted changes in types of weapons systems, weapons effectiveness, all-weather capabilities, aircraft sortie rates, etc., available to NATO. Under these conditions, the interdiction belt concept appeared feasible even against a very heavy Pact attack. But these capabilities could only be introduced into NATO's defense forces over a period of years.

In summary, one concept for limiting the introduction of Pact follow-on forces after the start of conflict is the early establishment of an interdiction belt on the eastern side of the interzonal border. A first phase, considered within hours of the original border crossings, would attack choke points on fixed LOCs through the belt to disrupt the enemy's scheme of maneuver. A second phase would continually attack enemy units piled up behind the choke points and attempting to transit the belt. The concept would permit NATO to concentrate a large portion of its surveillance, target acquisition, and strike assets in a relatively narrow geographical area rather than over a large area extending deep into the German Democratic Republic and Czechoslovakia. By replying to the initial Pact attack in an early, massive, concentrated, and continuing manner, NATO could seize the initiative in defensive operations in a way that is characteristically assumed to be Soviet doctrine for offensive operations. And with a number of improvements in NATO capabilities, it could offer an effective forward defense based on conventional weapons even in the face of a major Pact attack.

As with the barrier, concept, this concept could be militarily feasible, although our analytic efforts have not examined all of the military aspects, including possible Pact countermeasures. But the concept also raises issues of cost and political feasibility. No detailed estimates of the dollar cost associated with developing NATO's capability to implement an interdiction belt were available. In general terms, there are no new surveillance, target acquisition, delivery platforms, or weapon systems required that are not already under consideration. Differences may exist in the extent to which NATO forces are equipped with some of the systems. For example, the Phase Two operations would require a sufficient portion of NATO's aircraft to be equipped with a night and all-weather capability to attack enemy units attempting to transit the belt under those conditions. Therefore, there are likely to be some incremental costs for providing such capability.

On the other hand, because the interdiction belt emphasizes a limited, in-close, geographical area, the numbers of surveillance, target acquisition, and weapons being considered for some types of "deep" interdiction operations may be reduced. In any event, it is highly unlikely that the incremental costs for obtaining the capabilities to implement the interdiction belt concept would involve anything approaching the multi-billion dollar cost of a major fixed fortified barrier.

As to the political issues associated with the interdiction belt, they fall into at least three areas. One area involves political issues associated with implementing a concept that involves all of the NATO countries with forces in the Central Region. Since the belt is likely to be effective only if implemented as a NATO-wide response, it requires agreement on both the specific concept and on the centralization required to do the planning, target selection, allocation of capabilities, etc., so that it can be carried out as a coordinated NATO response to a Pact attack.

A second area involves agreement on the timeliness of carrying out the Phase One operations. The interdiction belt concept calls for virtually immediate implementation following clear evidence that a Pact attack is underway. Implementation, provided that the necessary target selection, weapon tasking, and associated planning has been carried out during peacetime, should take place within a matter of hours after the start of conflict. This will necessitate some pre-delegation of authority for timely implementation of the response and for the attack of LOC targets, as well as military forces in the German Democratic Republic and Czechoslovakia, conditions which have been continuously problematic for NATO.

A third area involves the relative precedence that is given to airpower. Since the concept depends heavily on attacking enemy units before they reach the interzonal border, airpower is the principal capability required. While this emphasis on the use of airpower well forward of NATO's ground forces should result in fewer losses to the ground forces because of the reduced strength of enemy units getting through the interdiction belt, it does not limit the importance of NATO's full ground force capability. The analytic work on the effectiveness of the interdiction belt in stopping Pact forces before they penetrated 50 kilometers was based on the assumption that NATO's current ground strength (and reinforcements) would not be changed. However, political issues could still be raised about over reliance on the use of airpower or on potential reductions in ground forces.

The interdiction belt concept, as is also the case with the fortified barrier case, is only one example of one approach to the topic of alternatives to NATO's current defense capabilities and to the analytic aspects of such concepts. A third approach and one illustrative concept for that approach are presented in the next section.

DISTRIBUTED AREA DEFENSE

A third approach to NATO defense is in some ways similar to NATO's current concept. NATO's current defense concept does not try to stop a Pact attack with heavy fortifications in the border area. It does not involve a massive interdiction effort to prevent those forces that may have already crossed the border from being reinforced by follow-on forces. Rather, it anticipates that, if deterrence fails, NATO will engage in direct defense in the forward area. If the conflict continues at the conventional level, NATO will conduct effective combat operations and stop the Pact. The combination of maneuver and attrition, the nature of the active defense, the form of air/land combat, as well as the possible extent of the Pact advance, the interrelations between conventional and nuclear operations, and the military/political aspects of the conflict and its termination have been subject to continual comment, argument, and discussion. An almost countless number of suggestions and proposals have been made on how to improve NATO's capability to execute its current concept. Among the more innovative of these has been the group that have put heavy emphasis on the use of small, highly equipped, anti-tank units operating over an extended area of the Federal Republic of Germany.

At least two major factors contribute to the interest in this solution. One is the increasing military effectiveness of technologies in precision delivery of munitions, new weapons platforms, command-control-communications, computers, electronic warfare, etc., as well as the promise of new capabilities in the advanced and emerging technology, robotics, and other areas. The second is the changing nature of the potential battleground, i.e., the Federal Republic. The FRG has been undergoing an urbanization, a channeling of traffic, a development of farm and forest areas, etc., that could significantly reduce the capability for the maneuver of large military forces. If they ever existed in this area, the days of continental maneuvering of modern armies are virtually gone.

With this growing recognition that enemy operations are more geographically restricted and the lethality and control of defense forces are increasing, the opportunity exists for defense concepts that put high premiums on small, well equipped, anti-tank units distributed throughout a substantial area of the Federal Republic, particularly the eastern portion.

Although the specific size, organization, equipping, and operational mode of such forces differ in their various proposals, American, British, Canadian, French, and German authors have described somewhat similar concepts using terms like distributed area defense teams, technological guerrillas, techno-commandos, etc.

The version of the approach outlined as the Distributed Area Defense concept in our effort consists of creating a very large force of small area defense units. The units would be of two basic types--direct fire units and indirect fire units. The direct fire units, numbering in the tens of thousands, and the indirect fire units, numbering in the thousands, would be distributed throughout the forward 50 to 100 kilomters of the Federal Republic. These units would be equipped with advanced anti-tank weapons, communications, air defense weapons, etc.

The major objectives of the area defense forces would be to gradually attrite enemy forces as they penetrated FRG territory. The direct fire units operating primarily in wooded areas and in the environs of urban areas would force the enemy to use main routes and roads. The indirect fire units operating from concealed positions would bring large volumes of fire to bear on enemy forces moving through the open areas. In the event of a conflict, all units would operate in pre-assigned areas. However, during peacetime, they would be in garrisons close to their assigned operating areas. Depending on the state of alert, different numbers would deploy from their peacetime locations. In essence, the number of units in the field provide a "variable" response to the level of crisis in NATO.

In the Distributed Area Defense concept, the thousands of small units would be drawn from existing NATO forces and the remainder of the NATO forces available (depending on the mobilization period) would support the area defense units as main defense forces behind the forward area.

The general characteristics of the concepts can be summarized as follows:

AREA DEFENSE UNITS

- o Direct-fire: tens of thousands
    - Equipment
        - o Man-portable anti-tank weapons
        - o Communications
        - o Personal weapons
    - Organization
        - o Assigned sectors for teams
        - o Company areas for support
        - o Battalion areas for administration
- o Indirect-fire: thousands
    - Equipment
        - o Self-contained, precision, indirect fire system
        - o Communications
        - o Air defense weapon

- Organization
    o One for four direct-fire units
    o Operations
        - Peacetime
            o Normal garrison
            o Some alert units
            o Training in assigned areas
        - Transition
            o Variable numbers deployed
        - Combat
            o Deploy to assigned areas (trucks, IFVs, helicopters, etc.)
            o Set up ambush and defense on major attack axes
            o Hit and run attacks
            o Movement to "hides," stay behinds
            o Support, maintenance; local; caches

MAIN DEFENSE FORCES

o 12 to 40 divisions (depending on mobilization time)

The analysis of this concept, like that of the preceding concepts, used the MASTER model. However, because of the importance of terrain, intervisibility, timing of fire and movement, communications, etc., on any assessment of small unit operations, the MASTER model was supplemented by another analytic effort. This effort utilized a three-dimensional terrain board, several computer models, and a manual gaming approach in which a 20 by 30 kilomters area of the interzonal border was represented and combat operations were simulated on a minute by minute basis.

The data and insights drawn from this detailed analysis were extended to the MASTER theater level assessment. Again, without going into all of the variations and details of the assessments, the general results indicated that small direct and indirect fire units, numbering in the tens of thousands and distributed throughout the forward area, could create such heavy casualties on the enemy forces that they would be unable to penetrate beyond 50 to 100 kilometers into the Federal Republic. Even this depth of penetration took place over an extended period of time and with heavy enemy losses.

In terms of the cost and political issues connected with the Distributed Area Defense concept, several points can be noted. If the area defense units are drawn from existing forces, they will require capabilities that are not widespread in current units. For example, very large numbers of direct fire weapons and new, self-contained indirect fire weapons systems. While these items will be additions to the defense budgets, they will reduce the requirement for the larger, more expensive weapon systems when the time comes to replace them in those forces that have been restructured into area defense units. On an extended time basis, it is possible that the concept would involve an actual reduction in defense budgets.

On the political side, the concept raises a number of issues. They range from broader issues of what forces of what nations would be reconfigured to create the area defense forces to such issues as changing garrison locations to conform to the forward disposition of area defense forces and the more rearward disposition of the divisions that constitute the supporting defense force. Related to these are many other issues involving new area command organizations and responsibilities, interrelations with the civilian population and economy, the status of the FRG territorial forces, etc.

SUMMARY

This paper has covered a very broad area at a very general level. It has made a number of assertions and contentions in order to provide a perspective for considering the potential contributions of analysis. The thrust is that:

- o There are a number of different approaches to improving the defense capabilities of NATO.
- o Within these different approaches, there are alternative defense concepts:
    - Several possible concepts have been described.
    - Some analysis of the effectiveness requirements of these concepts has been done.
    - Some of the cost and political implications have been identified.
- o The concepts, the analysis, the issues that have been described should raise a host of questions.

And, finally, the challenge of this presentation is to define concepts and the issues and factors associated with them which the analytic community is capable of addressing in a coherent, credible, constructive, and contributing way.

ON REACTIVE DEFENSE OPTIONS - A COMPARATIVE SYSTEMS ANALYSIS OF
ALTERNATIVES FOR THE INITIAL DEFENSE AGAINST THE FIRST STRATEGIC
ECHELON OF THE WARSAW PACT IN CENTAL EUROPE

Hans W. Hofmann, Reiner K. Huber, and Karl Steiger

Universität der Bundeswehr München
Fachbereich Informatik
Werner-Heisenberg-Weg 39
D-8014 Neubiberg, FRG

I. INTRODUCTION

In the context of this paper, the terms *'reactive defense'* and *'active defense'* are used as defined by Saadia Amiel [1] who considers them as mutually complementary land force elements within the framework of a defensive strategy. In contrast to today's all armour general purpose forces designed to fight in both, the reactive and active mode, Amiel proposes a land force structure *"... of two components: one considering of defensive combined arms teams, committed to reactive defense, where precise and high fire power is at a premium, and the second of offensive combined arms formations, where manoeverability is at a premium"* (S. Amiel [1], p. 62). The reactive defenses would absorb the initial attack, fight an attrition-oriented delaying battle, and provide the time required for the active defenses to deploy at the points of the enemy's main thrust and for counter-attacks into exposed flanks.

Our interest in reactive defenses dates back to the late Seventies when, obviously stimulated by the ideas of Spannocchi [2] and Brossollet [3], Afheldt [4] and Löser [5] forwarded their area defense concepts. However, the arguments in the ensueing debate on the military effectiveness of these concepts forwarded by both, their proponents and opponents, seemed to be based on beliefs more than on analysis. To us, it was obvious that in order to rationalize the debate, tools were required for testing, in a reproducible manner, the basic assumptions underlying these concepts.

Our initial literature search revealed that a great many reactive defense proposals had been published ever since J.F.C. Fuller [6] forwarded his *Archipelago System of Defense* in 1944[*]. Common to all of these proposals is the claim that, compared to active defenses, reactive defenses are much better suited for an efficient exploitation of the inherent advantage a defender has in battle, especially also with a view to the utilization of PGM-type weapon technology (defense efficiency assumption). Our initial investigations by means of a deterministic computer simulation model of the heterogeneous Lanchester-type supported that claim [8,9]. Similar

---

[*] Readers interested in the literature on these proposals are referred to Huber and Hofmann [7], pp. 37-45.

findings were reported by Paxon, Weiner and Wise who used a computer-assisted terrain board game in their studies [10,11]. Thus, all simulation results available at the time suggested that the incorporation of reactive defense elements to fight the initial defense battle promises to reduce, perhaps significantly, the risk of early enemy breakthroughs thereby strengthening NATO's capability for a forward defense.

In addition, an analysis of F.W. Lanchester's mathematical model of modern warfare (i.e., the so-called square law) with a view to stability criteria revealed that, theoretically, the gradual conversion of active land force elements into reactive ones might offer a chance for reducing the imbalance of conventional forces and enhancing crisis stability in Europe, in particular when defense resources are limited [7,12].

Thus, there was sufficient motivation to attempt a new model development that would provide a tool for the validation (or refutation) of our original simulation results[*] and for testing the 'defense efficiency' assumption in a range of scenarios and environmental conditions. To this end, the stochastic battle simulation model BASIS[**] was developed over the past three years. It permits to simulate, in great detail, all essential interactions affecting the dynamics and outcome of ground battles between battalion-size defending forces and a sequence of regimental-size attacking forces. That simulation level appeared to be an expedient compromise with a view to the detail necessary for the simulation of novel structures and tactics on one hand, and the large number of required simulations on the other. It also should provide sufficient a frame for comparisons of reactive defense alternatives to active defense structures with regard to their effectiveness *only* in the initial phase of the battle against the elements of the first strategic echelon of the Warsaw Pact forces.

Before some of the results of the more than 500 battle simulation experiments performed so far will be discussed, a brief summary of the simulation model BASIS is given. It is to provide the reader with information for at least a first order approximation of the model's viability. A detailed description of the model has been published by Hofmann et al. [13].

2. THE BATTLE SIMULATION MODEL BASIS

BASIS is a stochastic Monte Carlo-type battle model that permits the (closed) simulation of battalion-size ground forces defending against a sequence of regimental-size attacker forces accounting, on both sides, for organic as well as higher-echelon fire support. One of the principle design objectives was the development of a flexible and sufficiently detailed tool that would permit, in as realistic a manner as possible, an efficient experimental investigation of ground force structures, equipments and tactics for the initial forward defense battle in NATO's central region. It was to provide a testbed not only for the familiar structures and tactics of present day forces, but in particular also for the many modifications and alternatives that have been proposed or may yet evolve as new technologies emerge. To this end, special emphasis was placed on modelling artillery and infantry as well as on the development of a user-friendly tactical input language.

---

[*] Being of the heterogenous Lanchester-type, the attrition model employed in the original analyses contained a series of assumptions (e.g., on intervisibility, target engagement rules and processes) that by themselves require validation.

[**] <u>B</u>ataillons-<u>G</u>efechts-<u>S</u>imulations-<u>S</u>ystem

2.1 The BASIS Model Structure

BASIS consists of four major program packages comprising a total of about 45.000 lines of code written in PL/1 and implemented on the B7800 mainframe computer of the German Armed Forces University Munich.

Fig. 2.1 shows the basic structure of BASIS. There are two program packages for the generation and testing of input data: (1) The *Tactics Generator* compiles, for each operational plan, the tactics files which define the tactical behaviour of the simulated elements. (2) The *Input Data Processor* tests the input for formal correctness and completeness. A listing of annotated inputs may be printed out for documentation.

The *Evaluation Program* permits to generate, based upon a protocol of the combat history *(Simulation Protocol)*, graphical situation maps, bar charts, diagrams and tables presenting information on, for example, force ratios, movements, fire exchanges, losses and their causes (killer-victim scoreboards), ammunition consumption, costs, etc.

The very *Battle Simulator* consists of a program that simulates, in an event-oriented manner, the battle consistent with the operational plans of the antagonists. Combat units are usually controlled at the level of platoons, the latter consisting of homogeneous groups of infantry, combat vehicles or artillery pieces.

Combat vehicles as well as infantry groups may be equipped with up to three weapon types each. Infantry groups fight either mounted from combat vehicles or dismounted in the open or from cover. Since helicopters are considered as airmobile combat vehicles, the model may also simulate airborne operations. Combat units employ their weapons in the direct-fire mode, fire support is provided by organic or higher-echelon artillery in the indirect-fire mode. Close air support (CAS) is simulated by specifying the CAS-aircraft in terms of (invulnerable) rocket launchers of higher-echelon artillery units with each rocket representing a bomb or missile. Minefields may be deployed either by engineers or rocket launchers. Smoke screens can be placed at selected points in order to provide temporary concealment of friendly units. In addition, the model provides the option to account for visibility deterioration from dirty battlefield effects.

The user is quite free to define, via input data sets, the tactics, weapons and combat vehicles to be employed in the simulation experiments. Thus, a great deal of flexibility exists for the accommodation of novel tactics and new weapon systems. For a given combat experiment, the initial situation and the operational plans of both sides are put into the computer by transferring, by means of a digitizer, the respective information from a map (see, e.g., Fig. 2.2) onto a previously stored digital image of that map.

2.2 Simulation Elements

Except for the infantry, the smallest tactical element explicitly considered in BASIS is the so-called *combat group*. There are four basic types of groups

- infantry (mounted or dismounted)
- combat helicopters (airmobile combat vehicles)
- combat platforms (combat vehicles with elevated weapon platforms)
- combat vehicles with and without gun turrets.

While the combat vehicle groups consist of one vehicle each, the dismounted infantry group may be subdivided into three subgroups of a given number os soldiers each.

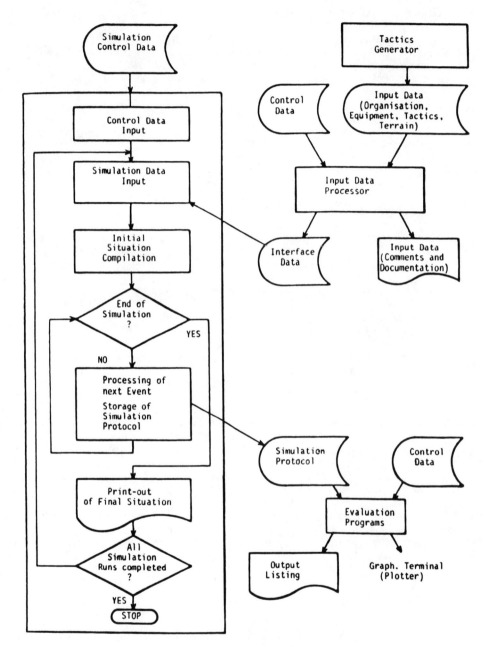

Fig. 2.1 Basic Structure of the Battle Simulation Model BASIS.

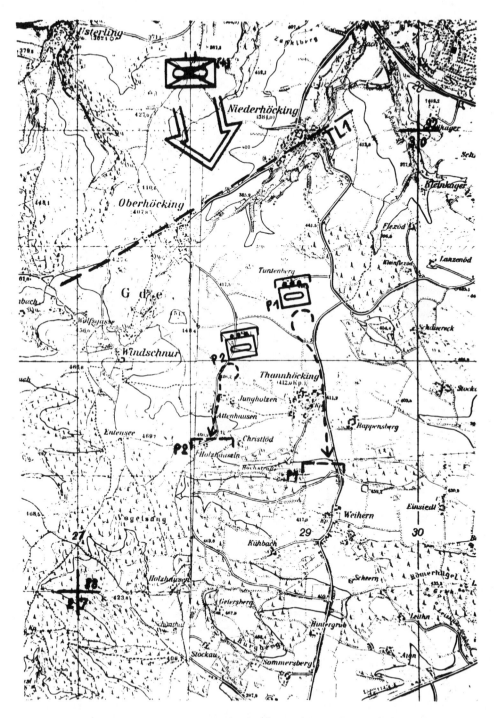

Fig. 2.2 Excerpt from a Tactical Situation and Operations Plan.

All groups may be equipped with up to three out of five (direct-fire) weapon types:

- machine gun
- automatic cannon
- cannon
- guided missiles
- fire and forget missiles.

Combat vehicles employ only one of their weapons at a time. The same is true for infantry when mounted. However, the three weapons of dismounted infantry groups may be employed simultaneously, one by each subgroup. When dismounting, the infantry groups have the option of taking one of the heavy weapons of their combat vehicle, e.g., an ATGW[*], along. When an infantry group suffers casualties, its (in the given tactical situation) least effective weapon is silenced first, the most effective last.

Indirect-fire weapons are of two types:

- artillery guns and mortars
- rocket launchers.

If they are part of the organic fire support units (e.g., the mortars of the defending battalions) they may be subject to attrition from direct-fire weapons. Higher-echelon fire support weapons (e.g., brigade, division or corps artillery) are only subject to attrition from indirect fire or CAS.

With regard to armour protection of combat vehicles or parts thereof[**], the user has the choice from four categories:
- no armour
- light armour
- medium armour
- heavy armour.

Dismounted infantry also exhibits different degrees of protection depending on whether the soldiers are in a crouched posture (when stationary or moving), prone or in foxholes.

For each of these protection states of vehicles and soldiers, the user specifies the protection parameters (probabilities of kill given a hit or lethal radii) versus all weapons that may be employed against them.

Fig. 2.3 shows in a schematic picture of a typical initial situation all the elements that may participate in a BASIS combat simulation. In the center section between attacker and defender units, the figure displays the symbols for designated fire zones of the defender's artillery and for minefields, the broken-lined frame indicating an artillery-delivered minefield, the solidly-lined frame one deployed by engineers.

The user describes such an initial situation by deploying all the elements (platoons and artillery positions) participating in the combat experiment on the respective map through a specification of their location and strength (number of combat groups) and, in case of minefields, their location, size and density. By means of a digitizer, this information is transferred onto the digital image of the map stored in the computer.

---

[*] ATGW = Anti-Tank Guided Weapon

[**] E.g., the turret and the various parts of the hull (top, side, front, rear) of battle tanks usually have different armour protection.

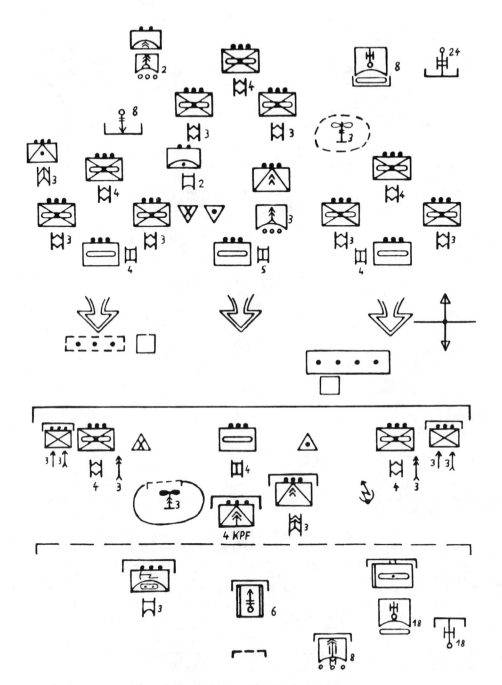

Fig. 2.3 BASIS - Simulation Elements.

The digital maps used in BASIS experiments contain elevation and terrain vegetation and trafficability data for grid sizes of 25, 50 and 100 m. The altitude resolution is 10 cm.

2.3 Simulation Control

In the simulation, combat and fire support elements are controlled by so-called *Tactics Programs*. These programs contain one or more orders to the controlled elements which specify what the elements are to do when certain events occur, i.e., the events trigger the tactics program. In its present version, BASIS incorporates a set of nine orders to combat elements, three orders to fire support elements and, among others, the following trigger events:

Trigger Events

- Occurrence of certain losses or loss thresholds
- Arrival at a specified location
- Crossing of so-called *Tactical Lines* by the attacking party
- Confrontation with a minefield
- Out of Ammunition
- Enemy Contact

Orders to Combat Elements

- Move/March
- Move into a Position and Fire (with optional specification of an open-fire line)
- Move into Disposition Area
- Stop Movement and Fire
- Move and Fire (simultaneously)
- Mount or Dismount (to infantry units)
- Replenish Ammunition
- Dispense Smoke Screen
- Clear Minefield

Orders to Fire Support Elements

- Move and Deploy (to fire position)
- Fire (with fragmentation or smoke warheads) at indicated positions[*]
- Deliver Minefield

In order to illustrate how the simulation control is effected Fig. 2.4 shows how the information displayed in the example of Fig. 2.2 is described in terms of the tactical input language of BASIS. It contains a simple initial situation in which two tank platoons P1 and P2 of four tanks each are mutually engaged with elements of an advancing motorized rifle battalion. The operational plan requires the two tank platoons to retreat, under the cover of a smoke screen and by moving, with a distance of 50 m between individual tanks, to preselected rearward positions when either one of two conditions is met: 1) Enemy tanks or APCs cross the road within a distance of 1000 m to the initial positions; 2) The strength of the two platoons taken together is reduced to 50% of the initial strength. The retreat is to be initiated by platoon P1 on the right, followed by P2 on the left when P1 is ready to fire from its new position. The battle is terminated when the strength is down to 25% of the initial strength, i.e., when merely two tanks survive.

---

[*] Artillery fire (CAS) may be directed by a forward observer (forward air controller) or, if employed against artillery, by anti-artillery radar reconnaissance (leading to reduced ammunition consumption).

The initial situation is defined by two simple data sets: One specifies, for each combat unit (P1 and P2), the type (LEO2) and number (4) of combat vehicles; the other (ANFTP2*)) specifies the order that causes

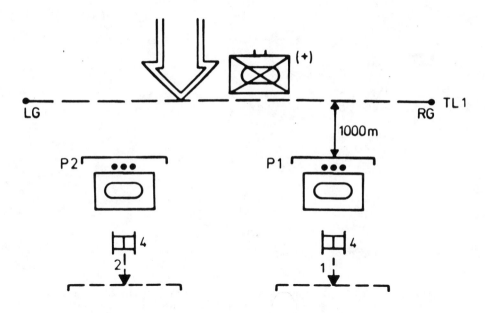

INITIAL SITUATION
      'P1' 'LEO2' 4 'P2' 'LEO2' 4
     'ANFTP 2' 'P1 STG LG RG 2500 NOP'
             'P2 STG LG RG 2500 NOP'

TACTICAL LINE   'TL1 LG RG....AUSW....AUSW....'

COND. LOSS ORDER 'P1' 'P2' 50 'AUSW' 25 'STOP'

TACTICS PROGRAMS

    'AUSW 1' 'P1 NEB AUSP1'
    'AUSP1 1' 'P1 VST POSIT. COORD. 50 0 STGP1'
    'STGP1 2' 'P1 STG LG RG 2000 NOP'
             'P2 NEB AUSP2'
    'AUSP2 1' 'P2 VST POSIT. COORD. 50 0 STGP '
    'STGP2 1' 'P2 STG LG RG 2000 NOP'

Fig. 2.4 Example of Tactics Input.

their initial activity (STG = Move into Firing Position and Fire), the coordinates of the left (LG) and right (RG) boundary of their respective positions, and the distance at which the tanks are to open fire simultaneously.

The conditions for the retreat are specified in terms of a *tactical line* (TL) and in terms of a *conditional loss order* for the combined platoons. The TL-statement indicates the coordinates LG and RG of the endpoints of the tactical line and, in a specified field for the respective combat vehicles, the *tactics program* (AUSW) describing the retreat that is to commence when the enemy combat units (MBT or APC) cross the tactical line. The conditional loss order contains the two combat units (P1 and P2) to which the subsequent loss thresholds (50%) refers and, again, the tactics program (AUSW) being triggered when that threshold is reached. It also contains the order for battle termination (STOP) at 25% of the initial strength.

The tactics program AUSW orders P1 to deploy a smoke screen (NEB) and proceed according to the tactics program AUSP1 which orders P1 to move (VST) to the indicated position coordinates while maintaining a distance of 50 m between tanks. The Zero indicates that the retreat need not be synchronized[**]. When reaching the coordinates, the platoon is to proceed according to the tactics program STGP1 which addresses both platoons (STGP1 2). P1 is ordered to assume firing positions and be ready to fire (STG) between coordinates LG and RG and open fire at enemy elements within a distance of 2000 m. Then, P2 is ordered to deploy a smoke screen (NEB) and proceed according to tactics program AUSP2. Thereby, P2 is ordered to move (VST) to the indicated position coordinates in the same manner as P1 before and, upon arrival proceed according to STGP2. The latter program orders P2 to behave in the same manner as P1 according to STGP1 above.

This example illustrates that the syntax of the tactical order language developed for BASIS permits a fairly simple and quick specification of tactical situations and operational plans. It also shows that, contrary to many other such battle simulation programs, the actual operational plans of the experimenter may be translated in a rather realistic manner not requiring undue simplifications and thus permitting a maximum of flexibility with regard to the testing of tactics.

2.4 Engagement Processes

For given operational plans and forces on both sides, the actual course and outcome of a battle essentially depend on the interactions and outcomes of a large number of basic engagement processes which the combat elements either perform or are subjected to.

The following provides a brief summary description of how some of the principal engagement processes are modelled in BASIS.

2.4.1 Target Search and Detection

In the model, all elements ordered to search for or engage targets (e.g., forward observer or forward air controller, combat vehicles), continuously scan the terrain checking whether there is a line of sight

---

[*]   The '2' indicates that the respective set addresses two combat units.

[**] The digit '1' would indicate that the respective movement is to be pursued in a synchronized manner, i.e., all combat vehicles in the unit move at the velocity of the slowest vehicle.

connection to potential targets. To this end, the altitude at their
instantaneous positions in the digital map is determined by linear inter-
polation between the respective neighbouring grid point altitudes for
both, observer/firer and target. With this information, intervisibility
is tested accounting for such obstacles as houses, woods, dams, seasonal
vegetation and smoke (temporary visibility barrier).

When intervisibility is given, detection is established through Monte
Carlo-sampling for the single scan detection probability determined by the
detection model. This probability is a function of

- firer/observer type and state (e.g., stationary or moving)
- target type and state (e.g., open, covered, moving)
- distance between firer/observer and target
- terrain type
- weather and/or dirty battlefield effects.

Dirty battlefield effects lead to a progressive reduction of the
respective detection probability as the engagement continues. For each
firer/target pair, the extent of the reduction may be defined by the
user consistent with, e.g., the presumed intensity of the engagements
and the type of ammunition employed.

2.4.2 Target Engagement by Direct-Fire Weapons

Since combat vehicles may only employ one of their (up to three)
weapons at a time, the user needs to specify in which sequence these
weapons are to engage given targets. In addition, for each weapon the
priority must be indicated in which the various targets are to be engaged, whether or not it may be employed when the vehicles move, what
its ammunition supply is, etc. Of the detected targets, the target allocation model makes each combat vehicle engage the closest target of the
highest priority employing the weapons according to the specified sequence.
In doing so, on the unit level the model attempts to allocate each vehicle
but one target and to avoid multiple engagements.

As an example, Fig. 2.5 illustrates, in a schematic manner, the
sequence of the target engagement cycle as it is modelled for guns. The
gunner always aims at the center of the visible target silhouette. The
determination of the hit probability accounts for deflection and range
errors as a function of the target distance and whether or not firer and/or
target are moving.

With regard to weapon effects on combat vehicles, the respective
model differentiates between hits of the turret, the hull and the under-
carriage. Depending on the conditional kill probabilities, hits may result in a kill, a loss of mobility or in temporary suppression. When the
target shows no effect, the firer continues firing an a-priori specified
number of rounds.

Against soft targets (e.g., infantry), weapon effects may also be
caused by fragmentation warheads. In this case, the target must be located
within the effective radius around the point of impact.

2.4.3 Target Engagement by Indirect-Fire Weapons

As in the case of direct-fire weapons, BASIS simulates individual
gun rounds. For rocket launchers it establishes the mean point of impact
(MPI) with the individual rockets of the salvo being uniformly distributed
within a circle around the MPI. Thus, for all indirect-fire weapons the
impact points of all of their released warheads are determined. Similar

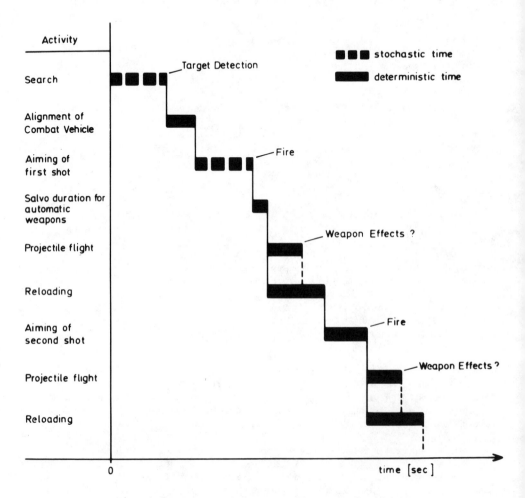

Fig. 2.5 Target Engagement Sequence for Guns.

to fragmentation warheads of direct-fire weapons, the effects suffered by the targets depend upon the location of the latter relative to the respective effective radii around the MPI. The aim point selection for artillery rounds and rocket salvos may account for uncertainties with regard to the available target intelligence.

2.4.4 Minefields

It is assumed that minefields deployed by engineers may only be recognized through the detonation of a mine. Depending upon the size and density of the minefield and the type and formation of the unit entering the field, the model determines the time and the effects of the first detonation. Then the unit has the option to

- change formation and proceed
- clear the minefield before proceeding
- circumvent the minefield.

Artillery-delivered mines may be detected prior to entering and while moving through a minefield. When proceeding through such a field, the speed may be reduced in order to avoid and/or neutralize the mines. In this case, search for and detection of mines is simulated.

2.5 Outlook

The development of BASIS started in early 1982. Essential parts of the model and the computer programs have been contributed by students in form of thesis projects in computer science and systems analysis. So far, the development of the tactics sets involved almost 500 individual combat experiments and many hours of discussion with military experts and analysts. Nevertheless, as the recent series of experiments performed in the course of our studies on reactive defense proposals show, there is still considerable room for extensions and improvements, e.g., with regard to a better accommodation of some of the new weapon developments such as intelligent munitions and mines.

Also a sizeable reduction in the CPU-time requirements for the experiments would be desirable so that the model may be used for large-scale quasi-empirical investigations on the circumstances and dynamics of combat. Presently, one simulation run averages between 0.5 - 1 hr CPU-time when dirty battlefield effects are disregarded. Accounting for those effects tends to double the time requirements. Thus, the current program version limits the number of experiments to about 2-3 per day.

3. THE EXPERIMENTAL FORCES

There are two primary objectives for the first round of experiments discussed in this paper:

1) To test the 'defense efficiency' hypothesis that reactive defense structures exhibit a higher efficiency in the exploitation of the defender advantage than active defenses;

2) To provide some first information if any of the investigated reactive defense options hold the potential for a significant reduction of the risk of early breakthroughs, and which of these appear to be viable candidates for further debate and study.

In order to meet these objectives, a sufficient number of reactive defense options with different structures, equipment, and tactics need to be tested and compared to active defenses in the early forward defense battle.

3.1 The Reactive Defense Options

For the definition of reactive defense options, two existing structures of that type and several proposals on alternative defense concepts published in the open literature were reviewed. From these, we deduced the defense forces (including their organic and higher echelon fire support) and their initial deployment within the 5 km wide sector of an attacking WP regiment.

Thus, the reactive defense options in this paper must not be confused with the defense concepts from which they were taken. They merely represent some of their (forward) elements which seem to be suited, at least in principle, to serve as reactive defenses in a two-tier ground force structure as outlined in the introduction. For this reason, the results of the experiments do not necessarily support or negate any of the alternative defense concepts as a whole. For their assessment, combat simulation experiments on at least the equivalent to a corps level are required in most cases. This is because lower level experiments do not fully capture the operational/strategic implications of such concepts.

The ten reactive defense options of this study may be grouped into one of four basic categories:

- Static Area Defenses (SAD)
- Dynamic Area Defenses (DAD)
- Continuous Fire Barrier Defenses (CFB)
- Selective Fire Barrier Defenses (SFB).

The nomenclature of this classification attempts to capture, in a nutshell, the fundamental operational characteristics of the options subsumed under each category. If they are designed to these characteristics, the cost differences between the options should also follow this classification. Fig. 3.1 illustrates that, by and large, this is indeed the case. It shows the relative investment cost requirements (in multiples of the cost of option E) as they resulted from a first order approximation of the procurement prices for the equipment items in each option including ammunition. A detailed listing of that equipment (except for small arms) is shown in Table 3.1 for each of the reactive defense options.

The rather significant differences between the categories reflect primarily the price to be paid for mobility and armour protection. Major differences within the categories are due to the incorporation of fairly large numbers of modern combat vehicles with elevated ATGW-platforms as in option D, L, M, and of even more expensive dual-purpose platforms capable of launching anti-tank and anti-aircraft missiles (ADATS) as in option N.

The SAD-class options pursue a hedgehog-type defense which is characterized by small combat teams fighting from a network of prepared positions and field fortifications taking advantage of reinforced terrain obstacles and mine barriers[*].

However, within this category, two fairly distinct subcategories must be distinguished: In one, the combat teams have, within their stationary

---

[*] The relative cost figures in Fig. 3.1 do only partially account for the cost associated with the construction of fortifications and terrain reinforcements. However, in no case would their inclusion lead to an increase of the total investment cost by more than about 20%.

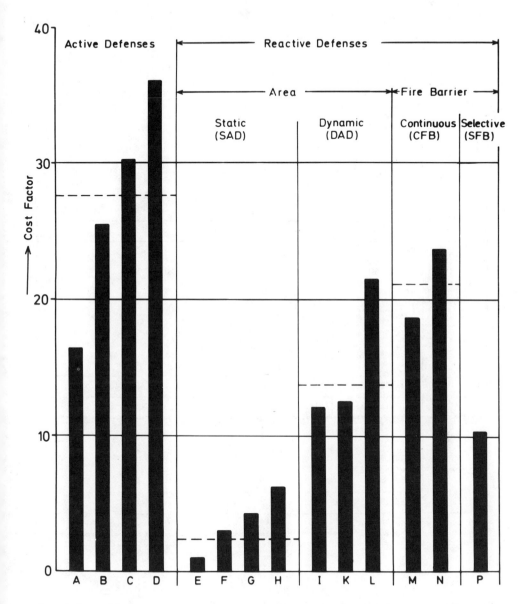

Fig. 3.1 Relative Investment Cost Requirements for Basic Forward Defense Options.

area of operations, about two alternate positions to which they evade whenever they are threatened to be overrun or their losses approach 35-40%. The options E ('Technokommandos') of Afheldt's *Area Defense Concept* [14] and G (the infantry forces in the SAS[*]) proposal [15]) belong to this category[**]. In the other, the combat teams remain stationary in their positions and continue fighting until they are virtually wiped out. This is the case in options F (the infantry forces of the *Swiss Territorial Defense System* [16,17,18,19]) and H (the infantry forces of the *Austrian Area Defense* [20,21,22]).

The options of the DAD-class are distinguished by their tactical mobility and the utilization of space in order to maintain a favourable loss exchange ratio. Fighting a mobile attrition-oriented delaying battle

Table 3.1 Equipments of Reactive Options in a Sector of 5 km Width.

Weapon Class	Item[**] / Depth(km) OPTION	E	F	G	H	I	K	L	M	N	P
		10	5	8	5	7	5	8	8	8	5
Direct Fire Weapons	HMG SP					13	20*				
	ATK gun stat.				6						
	ATK gun SP					15*	10*				13*
	LRCL	4				10		8	28	18	54
	HRCL		56	16	36		20		32	18	
	ATGW	10	24	9		10					27
	ATGW SP					3*	10*		60*	36	6*
	ATGW SPEP			2		6	4	40			6
	ADATS SPEP							2		18	
	AARCL	(3)		(6)		(6)	(16)				(6)
	AA gun/AAM SP				(5)		(3)	(2)			
	MBT					8					
	Total DFW	14	80	27	57	50	64	50	134	90	106
	Avg.Total per km²	0.3	3.2	0.7	2.3	1.4	2.6	1.3	3.4	2.3	4.2
Indirect Fire Weapons	mor 81mm	2	12	3	6						
	mor 120mm					3	9	3	15	18	6
	mor 120mm SP				18						
	Lhow 105mm		18					18			18
	Mhow 155mm SP								15		
	LRLS	5		4		3	8	8		18	8
	Total IFW	7	30	7	24	6	17	29	30	36	32
Helicopters	AT hel			4		6	7	7	6	8	

*Fighting vehicle or APC   **For abbreviations see IISS: Military Balance
                              (EP = Elevated Platform)

---

*) Studiengruppe für Alternative Sicherheitspolitik

**) When they run out of alternate positions, Afheldt's combat teams move into prestocked hideouts from which they attempt to harass the enemy forces in their rear. According to the SAS proposal, they are supposed to withdraw from their area of operations to reinforce identical forces further back. However, the proposal's transportation capability of two half-ton commercial vehicles per platoon of 28 men hardly seems sufficient for such an operational movement.

by falling back, through a series of prepared and partially reinforced positions, the options I (the so-called shield forces in Löser's *Area Defense Concept* [23,24]), K (the batallion-size cavalry regiment of the SAS proposal [15]) and L (the anti-tank teams of Füreder's *Cellular Defense Concept* [25]) adhere to a tactical philosophy that may be described as *dynamic density defense**).

The CFB-category includes concepts that foresee a continuous fire belt along the demarcation line acting as a barrier that the attacker has to penetrate. In option M (Gerber's *ATK-Sam Belt* [26,27]), the forward edge of the belt (16 km) is reinforced by minefields and obstacles and defended by highly mobile anti-tank battalions equipped with light fighting vehicles capable of quickly digging themselves in and having elevated ATGW-platforms. A substantial number of LARS and heavy mortars are available to these battalions for fire support. Option N (Hannig's *Fire Barriers* [28,29]) is characterized by a 4 km deep belt in which attacking formations are showered by artillery-delivered anti-tank mines and, when thus halted or slowed down, hit by long-range anti-tank weapons delivered by anti-tank defense battalions deployed behind the fire belt. These battalions also target and control a very substantial higher-echelon fire support by LARS and heavy mortars. When incapacitated or having spent their ammunition, the battalions withdraw and the fire barrier is taken over and maintained by the battalions of a second wave in standby behind those of the first. Upon having been resupplied, the former first wave battalions will eventually replace, as a third wave, the second wave battalions, etc. (ladder tactics).

In contrast to the latter two options designed as continuous fire barriers, the authors of this paper composed option P being a light infantry battalion which, as part of a '*barrier brigade*' counting four of these battalions and one engineer battalion, would be employed to provide a selective fire barrier (SFB). These barrier brigades are to be considered as additional forces assigned to the (possibly somewhat reduced) divisions of the active defenses. They would be deployed by the division commander or the commander of the superordinate corps consistent with the tactical situation. Except for some senior officers and cadre NCOs and enlisted men, their personnel would consist primarily of reservists residing in the vicinity of the respective battalion area of operation. Their equipment would be maintained by active cadre personnel and held ready for periodic reserve exercises. In suitable terrain, these brigades would be assigned to fight the initial forward defense battle largely from field fortifications assembled prior to combat from prefabricated (commercially available) structures stored in the vicinity of their usage. Thus, the armoured battalions of the active defense could assume the role of tactical and operational reserves for reinforcing the barrier brigades and for counterattacks.

---

*) This concept was theoretically substantiated in a joint working paper by Vector Research and BDM (May 1976). Accordingly, it takes advantage of the observation that the instantaneous offense/defense-exchange ratio as defined by the quotient of the fractional loss rates of defender versus attacker increases as a function of elapsed battle time since the concealment advantage accrued the defender wears off. For the same reason, the instantaneous exchange ratio is less dependent on the force ratio early in the battle. In fact, due to additional advantages to the defender (e.g., first shot and delayed reaction of the attacker), it must be assumed as being initially almost independent of the force ratio and very low. Therefore, an outnumbered defense should be deployed over some depth and fight a series of short battles as its units evade, thus continually increasing its density and improving the force ratio for a decisive battle.

3.2 The Active Defense Options

In order to provide a reference basis for a comparative assessment of the reactive defense options, three active defense alternatives were defined that resemble structural variants implemented within today's German Army Structure 4 (Heeresstruktur 4) [28,29,30,31]. Of these, case A corresponds to the (normal) reinforced armoured infantry battalion (verst. PzGrenBtl) and case B to the mixed reinforced armoured infantry battalion (verst. gem. PzGrenBtl) of the armoured infantry brigade (PzGrenBrig). They differ primarily in that the latter battalion contains a mix of armoured personnel carriers (APC) and main battle tanks (MBT), while the former has no MBTs and a somewhat higher share of anti-tank guided weapons (ATGW) and recoilless rifles (RCL). Case C is identical to the mixed reinforced tank battalion (verst. gem. PzBtl) of the tank brigade (PzBrig). An equipment list for these battalions (including the higher-echelon fire support systems available in our experiments) is compiled in Table 3.2. All of their weapons are either mounted or armoured fighting vehicles or transported, together with their crews, in armoured personnel carriers. Their high mobility reflects the German Army's preference for a mobile defense requiring that all of its combat units must be employable in each of the three basic phases of a defense battle: 1) the initial *delaying phase*; 2) the *defense phase*; 3) the *counterattack phase*[*)].

Table 3.2 Equipment of Active Defense Options (Maneuver Btls and Fire Support)

Weapon Class	Item**	A	B	C	D
Direct-Fire Weapons	HMG SP	22	22	11	21
	ATK gun stat.				
	ATK gun SP				
	LRCL	18*	12*	6*	
	HRCL	9*	6*	3*	18*
	ATGW	27*	18*	9*	
	ATGW SP	6	6	6	
	ATGW SPEP				6
	ADATS SPEP				
	AARCL				
	AA gun/AAM SP	(3)	(6)	(6)	(3)
	MBT		13	26	13
	Total DFW	85	77	61	70
	Avg.Total per km²	3.4	3.1	2.4	2.8
Indirect-Fire Weapons	mor 81mm				
	mor 120mm				
	mor 120mm SP	6	6		6
	Lhow 105mm				
	Mhow 155mm SP	18	18	18	18
	LRLS	8	8	8	8
	Total IFW	32	32	26	32
Helicopters	AT hel	7	7	7	7

* dismountable   ** For abbreviations see IISS: Military Balance (EP = Elevated Platform)

---

*) For a comprehensive discussion of defense tactics in general and the active defense in particular the reader is referred to P.A. Karber [34].

In addition to these current structural variants, a further hypothetical active defense option has been defined based upon the proposals by Koch [32,33]. This option D, the so-called reinforced armoured infantry battalion 90 (verst. PzGrenBtl 90), may be considered as a modernized version of option B. The latter's APCs and self-propelled mortars are replaced by new combat vehicles equipped with 25 mm automatic cannons, 120 mm anti-tank guns and improved 120 mm mortars. In addition, there are 12 120 mm self-propelled anti-tank guns. The ATGWs available from higher-echelon fire support are launched from elevated platforms. The operational employment and tactics are essentially identical to those practiced by today's German Army.

3.3 The Threat Forces

The threat forces considered in the combat simulation experiments consist either of motor rifle regiments (BMP) of the Soviet motor rifle division or of tank regiments of a Soviet tank division. Their organization, equipment and tactics were specified from Wiener [35], Hartung [36], Kreker [37], Baginski [38] and Karber [39]. Table 3.3 presents a listing of their equipment and the higher-echelon fire support systems available to them.

Table 3.3 Equipment of the Threat Options

Weapon Class	Item*	Threat	MR Regt (BMP)	TK Regt
Direct Fire Weapons	MBT	T-72/T-80	39	90
	AFV	BMP-2	126	42
	AFV	BRDM-2	9	
	AGS	2/BMP-2	18	6
	AARCL	3/BMP-2	(27)	(9)
	AA gun	ZSU-23-4	(4)	(4)
	AAM	SA-13	(4)	(4)
	Total DFW		192	138
Organic Indirect-Fire Weapons	mor	82mm	4	
	mor	120mm	24	8
	Mhow	122mm SP	24	24
Higher-Ech. Indirect-Fire Weapons	Hhow	152mm SP	48	96
	can	130mm	24	
	Hhow	152mm	24	
	MRL	BM-21	24	24
	Total IFW		172	152
Helicopters	AT hel	HIND D	6	6

* For abbreviations see IISS; Military Balance

In the simulation experiments, the typical regimental attack has two reinforced battalions*) attacking abreast as first echelon forces over a sector of ca. 5 km width (see Fig. 3.2). The third battalion follows as a second echelon force attacking in either one of the sectors of the two forward battalions. The attack is supported by organic and higher-echelon artillery forces and by attack helicopters.

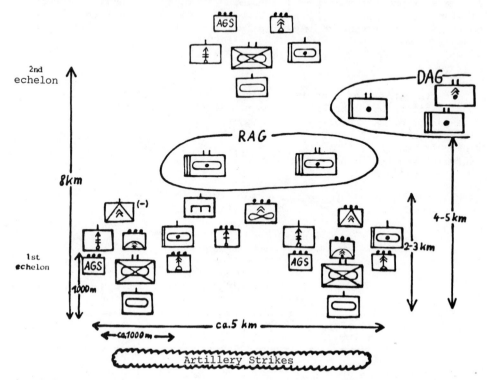

Fig. 3.2 Organization of a typical Attack of a Soviet Motor Rifle Regiment (BMP).

The attack of the reinforced motor rifle battalion is spearheaded by the tank company followed closely by two motor rifle companies as first-echelon elements and by the third motor rifle company as a second echelon element (see Fig. 3.3).

The reinforced tank battalion's attack is spearheaded by two tank companies operating abreast, one being closely followed by the reinforcing motor rifle company. The third tank company follows as second echelon force (see Fig. 3.4).

In addition to these typical attack plans, several variations were investigated in order to test the defenses' sensitivity toward adaptions in enemy behaviour.

---

*) In the motor rifle regiment, the three companies of its tank battalion reinforce its three motor rifle battalions spearheading their attacks. In the tank regiment, the three companies of its motor rifle battalion reinforce its three tank battalions.

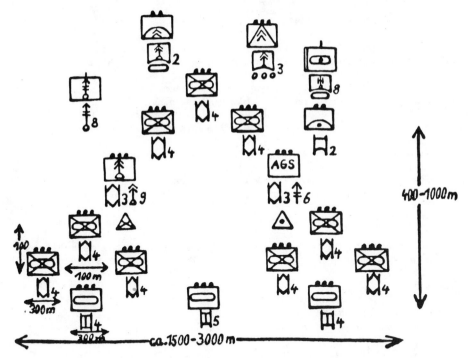

Fig. 3.3 Organization of a Typical Attack of a Soviet Reinforced Motor Rifle Battalion (BMP).

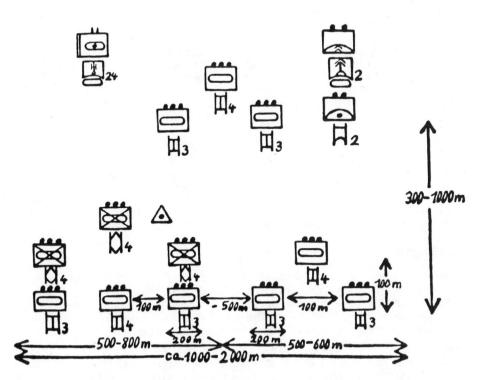

Fig. 3.4 Organization of a Typical Attack of a Soviet Reinforced Tank Battalion.

4. THE SIMULATION EXPERIMENTS

Considering the very objectives of our experiments, it is not sufficient to test a number of different defense options in a few 'typical' situations. In order to gain insights into the sensitivity or robustness of the options, the scenarios underlying the experiments need to encompass a reasonable spectrum of the possible operational and environmental variations that must be expected to affect the performance of the candidate options[*]. Thus, as the number of experiments one may perform within a given time is limited, the design of relevant scenarios is not a trivial task, especially when the model employed for the experiments is fairly rich. Also, in that case it is often rather difficult to arrive at meaningful criteria for measuring, based upon the analysis of the simulated combat histories, the comparative performance or utility of options.

4.1 The Scenarios

In addition to the threat forces and their operations as outlined in the previous section, the main parameters describing a BASIS scenario are related to
- terrain
- visibility conditions
- artillery environment
- the tactical organization of operations.

Presently, digital maps of four 6x10 km pieces of real estate in West Germany are available for simulation experiments. They resemble the following terrain types:
- mountaineous/wooded (Furth i. Wald)
- rolling hills/partly covered (Bubach)
- flat/partly covered (Donnersdorf)
- flat/open (Grettstadt).

Except for a few excursions involving attacks by tank regiments in the Grettstadt terrain, to date most experiments were performed in the Bubach area under three visibility conditions in each case, namely
- good visibility ($\geq$ 5.000 m)
- dirty battlefield (initial visibility of 1.000 m deteriorates down to 350 m at a rate of 10% per minute)
- poor visibility (350 m).

In the standard experiment, the maneuver units of both sides are supported by artillery fire controlled by forward observers. In order to test their artillery sensitivity, the respective defense options were subjected to additional experiments involving artillery barrages preceding the attack. Tactical variations mainly involved local counterattacks by the defenders and different defense organizations.

4.2 The Measures of Effectiveness

Recalling our original motivation of wishing to test the 'defense efficiency' hypothesis, criteria must be defined that facilitate the comparison of reactive defense options to active defense structures with regard to their effectiveness in the initial forward defense battle against the elements of the Soviet/WP first strategic echelon.

---

[*]   Recent research by Farrell [40] has shown that variations caused by terrain/tactics parameters frequently exceed those caused by weapon system parameters and, in Monte Carlo-simulations, by the random nature of combat processes.

Of the many indicators one may deduce from the rather detailed battle accounts provided by the simulation model BASIS, we decided to base the comparisons on *relative force value ratio* (RFVR) measures because they tend to capture the direction in which the battle is developing. In this paper, the RFVR are defined as the quotient of the relative value (with respect to the initial value) of the respective defense option and the relative value of the threat formation surviving at the end of the battle. Thus, at the beginning of a combat simulation experiment the RFVR = 1. Generally, for RFVR > 1 the situation can be considered to develop in favour of the NATO defenders as compared to the initial situation, regardless of how good or bad the initial situation may have been. For RFVR < 1 the opposite is the case. Therefore, it is obvious that a value RFVR > 1 must not be interpreted to mean that a successful defense is necessarily possible. It only implies that the *probability* of a successful defense increases as RFVR increases. For the same reason, in a given scenario defense options become more preferable as the values of RFVR increase.

However, even though we do not have to worry about absolute values, using the relative force value ratios for measuring force effectiveness does not eliminate the often controversial issue of what the term 'force value' actually implies. If at all, the relative value in terms of the fraction of surviving major weapon systems makes sense only when the rather homogeneous forces of the active defense options are compared to each other. Otherwise, a weighting scheme is necessary that permits to account for the sometimes very different elements in the reactive defense options.

Of course, one might consider to derive the weights from the killer-victim scoreboards, thus expressing the relative contributions of the various items to whatever course the battle may have taken. However, in addition to not being independent of the particular circumstances of the respective battle, the thus established weights reflect upon the past contribution of the particular items and not necessarily upon their remaining relative capability. For this reason, it was decided to simply let its investment cost determine an individual item's weight.

4.3 Selected Results

When considering the results presented in the following sections, two aspects should be kept in mind:

(1) The results are valid only for the very initial phase of an offensive against NATO when the forward divisions of the WP's first strategic echelon attack NATO's forward defense elements. They reflect upon the latters' comparative capability in standing their ground under certain (variable) conditions and the assumption that there is sufficient warning for them to fully deploy prior to the enemy's onslaught.

(2) The time available for this series of experiments limited both, the number of scenarios in which the options could be tested and the number of replications that could be performed for each scenario-option combination. While the small number of replications need not concern us too much[*], the limitation with regard to scenarios is a more serious problem, in particular with respect to the organization

---

[*] In a large number of previous test runs, the final states of the involved forces resulting from different replications of the same experiment differed at most by 2-3% when the number of involved direct-fire elements was sufficiently large on both sides. This appears to be the case in all of the experiments reported here since the above margin was not exceeded in any of the performed replications.

of the defense in options which exhibit a great deal of tactical mobility. However, based on the findings reported by Farrell [40] and the few results available from our experiments, it is estimated that a deviation in the relative force value ratio of 20% of the mean ratio should encompass about 80% of all tactics/terrain-induced variations in the organization of the mobile defense battles of the active defenses. Owing to their comparatively little mobility, this margin of uncertainty should be fairly small for the reactive defenses.

4.3.1 Active Defenses

Table 4.1 presents, in terms of three measures of effectiveness (MOE), average results of experiments involving the four active defense options A, B, C, and D defending against the first attacking Soviet motor rifle regiment (1st division echelon) under three different visibility conditions. In addition, for option B a local counterattack into an exposed enemy flank was tested and for options C and D the attack of a second motor rifle regiment (2nd division echelon). In each of these excursions good visibility conditions were assumed to prevail.

The MOEs differ in that the RFR-CV considers the relative force values on both sides to be presented by the fraction of their surviving combat vehicles (tanks and APCs), while both RFVR imply a force value definition in terms of the monetary value of the surviving direct-fire weapons (D) or all surviving weapons employed in the battle (T).

Since combat vehicles are by far the most expensive items, the high degree of armour on both sides generally results in the RFR-CV and the RFVR-D to assume rather similar values. However, the RFVR-D usually exceeds the RFVR-T by a significant margin in all scenarios exhibiting good visibility.

This difference is caused by the fact that under good visibility conditions the indirect-fire weapons have a comparatively higher survival chance in our simulations than the direct-fire weapons, an effect that is even more pronounced on the Soviet side due to its numerical artillery superiority. For one thing, the artillery systems are mostly out of range of the enemy's direct-fire weapons. Further, when visibility is sufficient a large share of the fire support is directed by forward observers against direct-fire systems. That artillery support is allocated to enemy artillery positions whenever visibility conditions deteriorate below the range between observers and direct-fire system targets.

For each of the three MOEs we notice an improvement under all visibility conditions as we move from the (least expensive) active defense option A to the (most expensive) option D. However, the improvement is generally less marked for the poorer visibility, a fact which attests to the rather significant impact visibility conditions on the battlefield have on all of these defense options.

The reinforcement by anti-tank helicopters notwithstanding, in all experiments on option A the defense forces turned out to be too weak to prevent the break-through of the attacking Soviet regiment's second echelon battalion.

Option B provides the defender with sufficient forces to hold off the attack under good visibility conditions. How well that is done appears to depend largely on the useage of the tanks (which are not available in option A). Three alternative tank employments were tested which resulted in deviations of 15-25% from the mean MOE-values shown in Table 4.1. They

Table 4.1 Final Defense/Offense Relative Force (Value) Ratios (Terrain: Bubach)

SCENARIO	Threat / Ops / Artillery / Visib'ty [m] / Option	1st Motor Rifle Regiment Defense FO > 5.000	1st Motor Rifle Regiment Defense FO ≤ 1.000 / > 350	1st Motor Rifle Regiment Defense FO 350	1st Motor Rifle Regiment Def. + Counter-attack FO > 5.000	2nd MR Rgt Defense FO > 5.000
MOE						
RFR-CV	A	0.55 b	0.44 b	0.52 b		
	B	1.40 dh	1.08 i	0.68 b	0.97 bd	
	C	2.19 h	1.63 i	1.29 i		2.37 h
	D	2.18 h	1.82 i	1.30 i		2.61 h
RFVR-D	A	0.56	0.52	0.52		
	B	1.57	1.30	0.87	1.17	
	C	2.08	1.38	1.13		1.88
	D	2.42	1.48	1.13		2.60
RFVR-T	A	0.85	0.67	0.67		
	B	1.16	1.20	1.19	1.05	
	C	1.56	1.27	1.08		1.51
	D	1.87	1.36	1.19		1.97

b = break-through   h = attack thwarted
i = penetration   d = attack narrowly stalled

differed primarily with regard to the number of tanks that were rapidly
redeployed to intercept, from cover, the second echelon battalion of the
motor rifle regiment on the move to resume the attack of its stalled pre-
decessor.

Under dirty battlefield conditions, the attacker always accomplishes
break-throughs against option B defense forces without the defender being
necessarily attrited down to his break-point (penetration). Employing all
tanks available in option B in a company-size counterattack (into the
flank of the Soviet motor rifle regiment's second echelon battalion) did
not help the defender's situation. On the contrary, in three out of four
experiments the increased loss of tanks in the counterattack weakened the
defense to a degree that made it impossible to subsequently prevent the
Soviet break-through.

Both, options D and C can be expected to contribute significantly
to a stabilization of the early forward defense, option C by virtue of
its relatively large number of tanks and option D through its effective
combination of tanks and modern combat vehicles. In our experiments, the
sequential attacks by two motor rifle regiments were beaten back in
option C and by three in option D when good visibility prevailed. The MOEs
of this narrowly stalled third regimental attack (not shown in Table 4.1)
resulted as 1.03, 1.27, and 1.28. However, under dirty battlefield conditions, more than half of the elements of the first attacking regiment
were able to penetrate the battalion defense area more or less unseen in
both cases.

With regard to their vulnerability from artillery, the results of
the experiments involving a preparatory barrage of 30.000 rounds*) produced
very similar results for all four active defense options. On the average,
it neutralized about 40% of the (lightly armoured) APCs and combat vehicles,
25% of the tanks, and (a surprisingly low) 10% of the dismounted infantry
in field fortifications**). Only in options C and D would these losses
leave the defenders with a capability to hold their ground against the
subsequent assault by one motor rifle regiment, provided the visibility
is not impaired by the preparatory fire.

Summarizing these results, it appears that the implementation of the
recent long-term proposal [32,33] for equipping the armoured infantry in
the German Army along the lines of option D would undoubtedly lead to a
sizeable improvement in the early forward defense capabilities, provided
that there is sufficient warning for a full deployment and the preparation of defense positions. However, a considerable risk still remains
as all active defenses seem to be rather sensitive to dirty battlefield
effects***) and exhibit a high degree of vulnerability from concentrated
artillery barrages.

As far as the cost-effectiveness of option D is concerned, one can
be reasonably certain that it will not be any worse than the cost-effectiveness of the other active defense options. This is shown by Fig. 4.1 in
which the range of RFVR-D values observed for the various options is

---

*) This corresponds to the total rounds available to a Soviet Army for
preparatory fire in sectors earmarked for break-throughs. Of these, 15%
or 4300 are assumed to be 'aimed' at defense positions.

**) The lethal area of an artillery round against a tank or an APC is be-
tween 2.5 - 4 times the lethal radius against soldiers in small field
fortifications.

***) Considering the dramatic force effectiveness degradation resulting
from a visibility deterioration, field tests of the dirty battlefield
hypotheses underlying our experiments are strongly recommended.

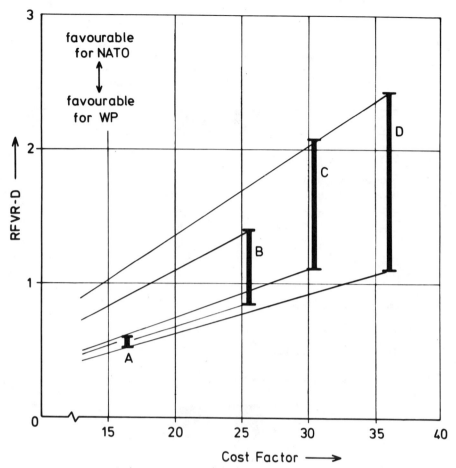

Fig. 4.1 Relative Defense/Offense Force Value Ratio for NATO Active Defense Options at the end of the first attack by a SOviet Motor Rifle Regiment (BMP).

plotted over the relative investment cost requirements for these options. The diagonal lines connect to the (not depicted) origin of the diagram. Thus, their inclination represents the relative effectiveness/cost ratio of the respective option, indicating that it is almost identical for all options at their lower end. Only under optimistic assumptions (good visibility, enemy pre-attack artillery strikes can be neutralized or evaded) would this ratio be approximately doubled when comparing concepts C and D to A. However, as the share of the operational and support cost tends to increase as the degree of mechanization and the technological level of the equipment rises, one must expect that the cost factors of C and D would increase more than those of A and B if they were based upon life-cycle cost rather than the investment cost only. Therefore, including the operational support cost would shift the options further apart, thus very likely eliminating the gains in cost-effectiveness to be expected under optimistic operational assumptions.

4.3.2 Reactive Defenses

The basic principles underlying the reactive defense options investigated in this study are illustrated in Fig. 4.2. They are distinguished by stationary or mobile *modules* which comprise the experimental forces

Static Area Defense (SAD)
- Stationary Modules
- Weapon Density
  - Evasive Tactics : 0.3 - 0.7 per km^2
  - Hedgehog Defense : 2.3 - 3.2 per km^2

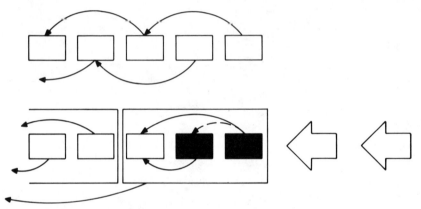

Dynamic Area Defense (DAD)
- Mobile Modules
- Weapon Density : 1.3 - 2.6 per km^2

(Fire) Barriers

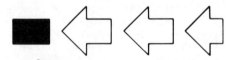

- Stationary Modules
- Weapon Density : 2.3 - 4.2 per km^2

Fig. 4.2 Reactive Defense Concepts.

described in Table 3.1 and their area of operation. Within each module, the forces may defend either in a stationary manner from strong points or evasively from a sequence of a priori-prepared positions.

The static area defense (SAD) modules are stationary. Within these modules, the forces of option E and G pursue evasive delay/screening tactics, those of options F and H defend from strong points (hedgehog defense). Typical for the modules practicing evasion is their rather low weapon density. When one module is overrun or penetrated, the attacker is faced by a new one. Thus, the defender attempts to gradually attrite and slow down the enemy forces as they have to move through a network of modules. In contrast, the strong point options are characterized by a rather high weapon density. Their modules may be either arranged in a fortified belt or interspersed among 'evasive' modules (such as in the concept from which option H was deduced).

The dynamic area defense (DAD) modules are mobile in that they are to withdraw before being overrun and resume the battle in a module further back, either by themselves after having been replenished or as reinforcements of the respective module's forces. A string of modules may be combined into a superordinate module which, when considered as a unit, acts more or less as the regular modules do. Within the modules, the forces usually practice a delay/screening defense. Contrary to the SAD forces, the DAD modules are highly mobile and usually have some armour at their disposal.

The (fire) barrier options may be considered as consisting of one module only within which the forces basically pursue a positional defense. However, the modules of options M and N each are neighbouring modules of a continuous belt extending along the demarcation line while the module of option P is deployed selectively in appropriate terrain, complementing active defenses acting as operational reserves. In option P, the infantry forces fighting from strongholds are supported by light tanks and mobile ATGW-platforms.

Most of our experiments, in particular those testing sensitivities, involved the forward modules only. A few experiments with the second modules were to provide data for an estimation of the operational depth required by area defense forces. In the standard scenario, a Soviet motor rifle regiment (BMP) attacked, without a preparatory artillery barrage, in the Bubach terrain under good visibility conditions. Being of the partly covered/rolling hill type, the Bubach area is considered to be rather favourable for an infantry defense as practiced by most of the investigated options.

All reactive defense options were equipped with weapons of contemporary technology (i.e., no smart ammunitions except directional mines). Thus, it is not surprising that the experiments involving one module in the standard scenario support the old military truism that the effectiveness of a defense increases monotonically as the number of weapons available to the defender grows. This result is shown in Fig. 4.3 where the effectiveness is measured in terms of the force value ratio RFVR-T, i.e., the (monetary) force value accounts for all surviving weapons employed in the experiments[*]. For weapon

---

[*] For good reasons, option H falls outside the general pattern. Resembling the infantry of the Austrian defense forces, its equipment does not include any ATGWs which represent, more or less, the backbone of the defense in all other options. For this reason, H is a comparatively weak and expensive option.

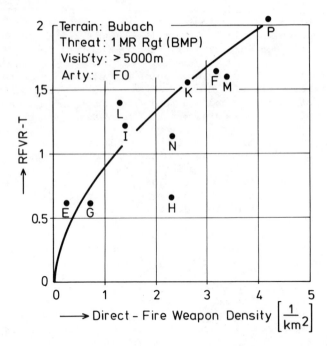

Fig. 4.3 Relative Defense/Offense Force Value Ratio as a Function of the Direct-Fire Weapon Density in the Reactive Defense Options.

densities ≥ 1 we notice that the relationship between effectiveness and weapon density is linear, an indication that none of the investigated reactive defense options are 'over-equipped' in the sense of diminishing (effectiveness) returns on weapon density. However, considering each of them as a candidate source of a blueprint for the development of reactive defense elements aimed at improving the stability of NATO's forward defense, one needs to know more about their critical sensitivities and the implications of their effectiveness differences with regard to defense resource requirements such as cost and operational depth.

To this end, one may first take a look at the losses the reactive defense modules can be expected to inflict upon an attacker. Averaged over all experiments, Table 4.2 presents the fractional losses suffered by the attacking Soviet motor rifle regiments. They refer to the regiment's major equipment items (tanks and APCs). In addition to the initial attack under varying visibility conditions, the robust defense options capable of thwarting the initial attack were subjected to a second and, if still viable, to a third regimental attack.

When attacked by but one regiment, all options designed to hold their ground (i.e., F, H, M, N, P) are able to do so except for H, provided visibility is good and the assault not prepared by an intensive artillery

Table 4.2 Fractional Losses of Soviet Motor Rifle Regiments attacking Reactive Defense Options (Terrain:Bubach)

SCENARIO / CATEGORY	Threat / Ops / Artillery / Visib'ty [m] / Option	1st Motor Rifle Regiment — Defense — FO			2nd MR Rgt — Defense — FO	3rd MR Rgt — Defense — FO
		> 5.000	≤ 1.000 > 350	350	> 5.000	> 5.000
SAD	E	0.21 $_i$	0.16 $_i$	0.10 $_i$	0.03 $_i$	
SAD	F	0.66 $_h$	0.69 $_h$	0.62 $_h$	0.62 $_{db}$	
SAD	G	0.23 $_i$	0.14 $_i$	0.14 $_i$		
SAD	H	0.46 $_b$	0.45 $_b$	0.42 $_b$		
DAD	I	0.26 $_i$	0.30 $_i$	0.32 $_i$		
DAD	K	0.52 $_i$	0.36 $_i$	0.24 $_i$		
DAD	L	0.65 $_h$	0.25 $_i$	0.12 $_i$		
CFB	M	0.65 $_h$	0.55 $_i$	0.50 $_i$	0.62 $_h$	
CFB	N	0.64 $_h$	0.35 $_i$	0.24 $_i$		
SFB	P	0.70 $_h$	0.65 $_h$	0.71 $_h$	0.70 $_h$	0.70 $_{db}$

b = break-through   h = attack thwarted
i = penetration   d = attack narrowly stalled

barrage. However, due to their rather one-sided equipment structures, the options L and N are extremely sensitive toward a degradation in visibility. This is because the share of ATGWs in the direct fire weapon inventory is close to 90% in option L and 60% in option N. In contrast, owing to their relatively large number of heavy recoilless rifles and/or anti-tank guns, options F, H, and P are hardly affected by poor visibility[*]. On the contrary, as the results in terms of the relative force value option RFVR-T shown in Table 4.3 indicate, reduced visibility may even be a condition favouring a defense of sufficient density, especially if it is equipped with a fairly large number of anti-tank guns such as in option H. Low visibility greatly reduces the effectiveness of tanks covering the advance by aimed suppressive fire on the defender's anti-tank strongholds. As a consequence, the loss exchange ratio improves in favour of the defender.

As done in case of the active defense options, the artillery sensitivity of the medium and high density reactive defense options was tested by means of experiments involving a preparatory artillery barrage of 30.000 rounds immediately preceding the attack. With regard to lightly armoured vehicles, tanks and infantry in field fortifications, the results were almost identical to those experienced with the active defense (i.e., ca. 40, 25, and 10% losses). However, contrary to the active defense options, many of the reactive options (i.e., I, K, L, M, N) are equipped mostly with light, and thus soft and cheap combat vehicles of which nearly 60% did not survive the artillery barrage.

Trying to evade the artillery through a retrograde movement directly in front of the barrage appears even more of a problem for reactive defenses than for active ones. This is because, when the barrage stops, the time available for the force elements to move into the prepared positions is rather short as the attacking enemy elements advance closely behind the barrage. However, having to fight in the open means yielding the defense advantage. Thus, evading preparatory artillery barrages while simultaneously trying to maintain the defense advantage could well mean an additional abandonment of terrain.

In addition to being fairly robust vis-à-vis a visibility deterioration and, to a lesser extent, artillery preparatory fire, options F and P both appeared to have sufficient strength left to take on another regiment. The respective experiments revealed that there should be a one in three chance for the forces of option F to (narrowly) stall the attack of a second motor rifle regiment[**]. Whenever they succeeded in breaking through, the attackers did so just before they reached their break-point. In case of option P, the second Soviet regiment suffered the same losses as the first while enough defense forces survived to even stand the ground against a third motor rifle regiment's attack in two out of three experiments. When being reinforced by a flight of seven anti-tank helicopters, the defender were able to thwart the third regiment in all cases.

These results suggest that, among the 'stationary' options, only F and P may be regarded as viable candidates for further consideration. This is the more true as the continuous fire barrier (CFB) options M and N are among the most expensive reactive defense options in terms of their investment cost requirements (see also Fig. 3.1).

---

[*] The small (< 7%) variations in the average values shown in Table 4.2 are most likely of random nature and caused by the yet limited number of replications of each experiment.

[**] Provided visibility is good, the forces of option M are judged to have approximately the same capability as those of F.

Table 4.3 Final Defense/Offense Force Value Ratio RFVR-T (Terrain:Bubach)

SCENARIO	Threat / Ops / Artillery / Visib'ty [m] CATEGORY \ Option	1st Motor Rifle Regiment — Defense — FO			2nd MR Rgt Defense FO	3rd MR Rgt Defense FO
		> 5.000	≤ 1.000 > 350	350	> 5.000	> 5.000
SAD	E	0.62 i	0.70 i	0.69 i	0.30 i	
SAD	F	1.65 h	1.72 h	1.67 h	1.56 db	
SAD	G	0.62 i	0.93 i	0.96 i		
SAD	H	0.65 b	1.11 b	1.09 b		
DAD	I	1.22 i	1.03 i	0.96 i		
DAD	K	1.57 i	1.27 i	0.96 i		
DAD	L	1.40 h	1.04 i	0.91 i		
CFB	M	1.60 h	1.21 i	1.09 i	1.18 h	
CFB	N	1.13 h	1.09 i	0.88 i		
SFB	P	2.06 h	1.55 h	1.75 h	1.26 h	1.01 db

b = break-through   h = attack thwarted
i = penetration   d = attack narrowly stalled

Concerning the area defense options which attempt to trade space for losses, the results in Tables 4.2 and 4.3 indicate that, good visibility prevailing, the performance of the two SAD alternatives E and G is almost identical. Within the operational depth of 10 respectively 8 km, their forward modules should kill about 20% of the enemy's tanks and APCs[*]. In doing this, the experiments on option E show that they must be expected to lose between 50-80% of the personnel manning the ATGWs and about 25-30% of those manning recoilless rifles and machine guns. Therefore, it is not surprising that in subsequent experiments involving the attack of a second regiment they were only able to kill a mere 3-4% of the Soviet combat vehicles[**].

Under deteriorating visibility conditions, the survivability of the option E and G combat teams increases relatively more than the survivability of the attackers. This is obvious from the slight improvement in the RFVR-T values in Table 4.3 and the simultaneous decrease of Soviet losses as shown in Table 4.2. In both cases, at about 60-80% the surviving strength would be sufficient in order to inflict some damage (below 10-14%) on the following second motor rifle regiment, provided it is at all possible to operate in the enemy's rear.

There were several experiments in which, after having penetrated the first module at a loss of 21 respectively 23%, the first motor rifle regiment attacked the second module under good visibility conditions. In all of these experiments, the Soviet losses were nearly identical (deviation < 10%) to those suffered in the regiment's battle with the first module. This was to be expected in a battle environment characterized by an abundance of threat targets confronting a low density defense. In such a situation, the threat losses depend almost exclusively on the defense's targeting capability which is the same for all consecutive modules, provided the terrain characteristics do not change significantly. Thus, in order to attrite three Soviet motor rifle regiments as in options P and D, depending upon the attacker's behaviour about 9-12 consecutive modules are required for option E and 8-10 for option G. At an average operational depth of 10 km for the E-modules and 8 km for the G-modules, this translates into required operational depths of between 90-120 km for option E and 65-80 km for option G[***]. Since it is unlikely that the favourable (to an infantry defense) terrain of Bubach underlying these figures would persist throughout such long distances, these figures must be considered to represent lower bounds.

Contrary to options E and G in which the modules are stationary, the operational depth required by DAD options for the neutralization of three motor rifle regiments cannot immediately be determined from the simulation

---

[*] This kill rate was reduced to 15% in experiments in which the attacker adapted his behaviour so that the width of the regimental attack was lowered and the battalions proceeded in file rather than two abreast and one following.

[**] For these experiments it was assumed that the individual performance of the survivors would not be impaired by the high casualty levels they had witnessed before. Thus, Afheldt's assumption that, after having been by-passed, the combat teams would be able to effectively harass the follow-on enemy forces is very likely at fault.

[***] A depth of ca. 90 km respectively 80 km is postulated by Afheldt[14] and the SAS[15] in the proposals from which the options E and G were derived. However, contrary to Afheldt, the SAS concept does not propose a homogeneous infantry force within this area of operation. Additional modules such as the one of option K are available to support the infantry.

results. However, with two simplifying assumptions one may provide an upper bound estimate for the operational depth and a lower bound estimate for the required number of modules. For one thing, it is assumed that the defending modules always kill the same number of enemy targets[*] and, for the other, that, each time they break off the battle (I and K at 35% losses, L at 50%), the modules withdraw and resume the battle in the second module to their rear as soon as the attackers have penetrated the module in front of them. With these assumptions, the (maximum) operational depth d and the (minimum) number n of modules required results as

- d = 50 km ; n = 4 for option I
- d = 20 km; n = 2 for option K
- d = 24 km; n = 2 for option L.

Due to the tacit assumption of a favourable terrain persisting through the entire operational depth, these estimates may, at least for the options I and L, turn out to be much less than an average obtained from larger scale experiments covering the entire depth.

Summarizing these observations, we arrive at Fig. 4.4 which shows the operational depth and the relative investment cost (in multiples of the cost

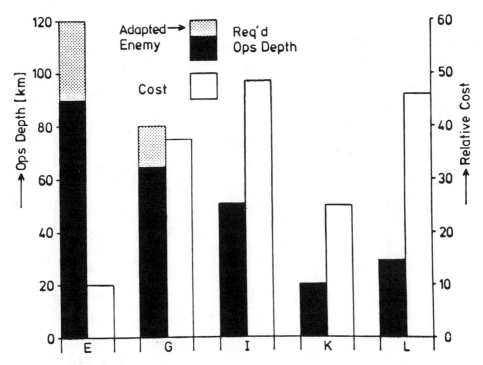

Fig. 4.4 Operational Depth and Investment Cost Requirements of Reactive Defense Options for the Attrition of three consecutive Soviet Motor Rifle Regiments (BMP).

---

[*] Within a range of less than 5% around the average values, this assumption is supported by the experiments involving the attack of the first motor rifle regiment against the second module in option I.

of one E-type module) required by the 'mobile' area defense options for the attrition of three consecutively attacking motor rifle regiments, good visibility conditions and Bubach-type terrain prevailing throughout the entire operational area. From these results we conclude that, except perhaps for option K, none of the area defense modules tested can be seriously considered as a viable candidate for a reactive defense design aimed at improving the *forward* defense capabilities of NATO. With the investment cost of one module of option P being approximately the same as of 10 of modules of option E, the one tenth-figure of the relative cost depicted in Fig. 4.4 represents the factor by which the investment cost of the area defense options would have to exceed those of option P in order to only meet the latter's attrition capability.

The results of our experiments on the reactive defense options also permit to specify the relationship between the two mutually substitutable operational resource parameters of *fire power* and *operational depth*. This is examplified by Fig. 4.5 in which the operational depth required for the attrition of three consecutively attacking Soviet motor rifle regiments is plotted over the direct-fire weapon density of several reactive defense options. In case the *availability* of these operational resources were not limited, all points on the dashed curve would represent pairs of equal effectiveness or of indifference with regard to the *requirement of being able to defeat* three attacking regiments. Increasing this requirement would shift the indifference curve to the right, relaxing it to the left.

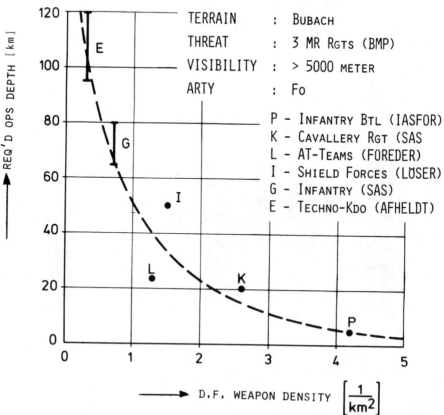

Fig. 4.5 Operational Depth required for the Attrition of three consecutively attacking Soviet Motor Rifle Rgts as a function of the average Direct-Fire Weapon Density of various Reactive Defense Options.

Thus, taken together, the evidence obtained from our combat simulation experiments performed so far permits to conclude that, among the reactive defense options tested, options F and P both represent the foremost candidates for a reactive defense that would contribute toward a significant improvement of the *initial forward defense* capabilities of NATO in partly covered rolling hill-type terrain. It is therefore recommended that both of these options be studied further, not the least with regard to their personnel requirements and losses. A preliminary estimate revealed that, notwithstanding the very similar performance in the standard scenario, both in terms of losses inflicted upon the attacker and in terms of the relative force value ratio (based on investment cost), the personnel losses of F might be rather high compared to those of P. This is apparently due to the fact that F's forces fight primarily from stationary strongholds at a rather close range (70% of their direct-fire weapons are HRCLs of 500 m range) so that they become easy targets for the highly accurate tank guns after they revealed their positions. In contrast, P's infantry forces, in addition to having longer range ATGWs at their disposal, are supported by light tanks and ATGWs on elevated platforms so that the enemy may be engaged at much longer ranges. The personnel losses of option P are presumably on the same order as those of D.

5. PRELIMINARY CONCLUSIONS AND RECOMMENDATIONS

When comparing the reactive to the active defense options, it is interesting to note that, with regard to the return-on-investment characteristics, the active defense options A and B obviously do not belong to the set of options of 'contemporary' technology and/or efficient tactics. As Fig. 4.6 shows, option A should be of the same set as option H which, being deprived of modern ATGWs, had turned out to be among the least (cost-)effective of the reactive defense options under standard scenario conditions. Option B might be attributable to an intermediate set that might also include the reactive fire barrier option N, the latter not for reasons of inferior technology but because of its very one-sided structure and inflexible tactics. Therefore, the proposed evolution of the active defense forces toward option D can be interpreted as what it is meant to be: the attempt to incorporate modern contemporary weapons technology into the existing force structure.

It is for these reasons that comparisons to the reactive defenses should be based on the active defense options C and D. In this context, it should be pointed out that in our previous studies [8,9] the reactive options E and I were compared to the active option B. In fact, the results then computed with the initially mentioned deterministic heterogeneous Lanchester model are almost identical to the average results now obtained from the detailed simulations of options B and E in the standard scenario. The new results on option I are somewhat better, mainly because Löser has increased the strength of his modules by replacing APCs by main battle tanks and adding ATGWs with elevated platforms. Thus, subject to further analysis of the large amount of data generated in the battle simulation experiments, we may consider the aggregated battle model as validated on a preliminary basis and under the environmental conditions that characterized the previous analytical experiments.

When translating the weapon densities shown in Fig. 4.6 into investment cost (including the cost for the (mostly indirect) fire support weapons), one notes that the 'modernized' active defense options C and D rank at the low end on a cost-effective scale (see Fig. 4.7). In fact, the cost-effectiveness of option P is about three to four times higher than that of options C and D in the standard scenario. As a corollary to this,

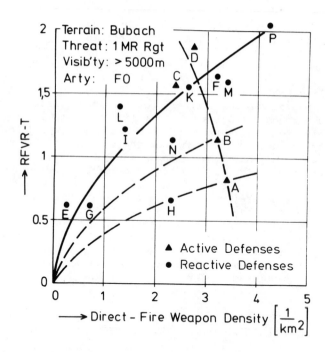

Fig. 4.6 Relative Defense/Offense Force Value Ratio as a Function of the Direct-Fire Weapon Density in the Reactive Defense Options

the investment cost requirements for obtaining the same effectiveness (of being able to repulse the consecutive attack of three Soviet motor rifle regiments) are about three to four times higher for option D than for option P (see also Fig. 3.1).

Of course, their high armoured mobility provides options C and D with capabilities that options P and F do not possess. However, in the scenarios underlying our tests these capabilities were of little value. It is true that we did not, in this series of experiments, look deeply into this matter. Yet, in none of the few tests on option B that involved tactical counter-attacks by various numbers of tanks did the overall situation of the defense improve. On the contrary, the additional loss of tanks in these attacks tended to weaken the defense posture so that a subsequent break-through by the enemy could not be prevented in most cases. However, due to the

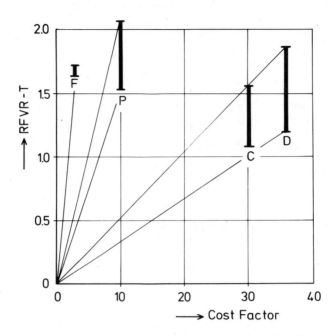

Fig. 4.7 Relative Defense/Offense Force Value Ratio of Defense Options at the end of the first attack by a Soviet Motor Rifle Regiment versus Option Cost (Terrain:Bubach)

limited number of respective experiments performed, this conclusion must be considered as preliminary, at best. We hope to find the support to, among others, incorporate a sufficient number of counterattack plans into our experiments. In addition, systematic research on the basis of higher level (at least division and corps) models is strongly recommended. This is because the operational utility and (cost-)effectiveness of being able, by virtue of a high mobility to quickly redeploy forces in order to meet unforeseen threats and changing enemy efforts may adequately only be tested at higher levels. This is also true for operational level counter-attacks into exposed enemy flanks that would possibly become fairly standard operations for active defenses being primarily the operational reserves for the forward deployed reactive defenses within a two-tier defense structure.

Concerning option F, it is certainly true that its implementation would result in some kind of a barrier along the demarcation line the appearance of which could, however, be quite different in different sectors depending upon the prevalent terrain*). Well aware of the fundamental aversion one tends to have toward such barriers for military (Maginot line syndrome) or political reasons (visibility), one cannot escape to observe their potentially high cost-effectiveness. In the standard scenario, the cost-effectiveness of option F was about three times that of option P and twelve times that of the active defense options C and D. It is for this reason, that their potential should be studied further. Also with due regard to the terrain differences in the Central Front defense sectors, it appears quite plausible that a reactive defense could well be a combination of options F and P.

Finally, a few observations shall be added concerning the *'defense efficiency'* hypothesis which implies that reactive defenses are better suited than active defenses for an efficient exploitation of the inherent advantage a defender has in battle. To this end, the reader is referred to Fig. 4.8 which shows the relative (to option D) offense/defense loss

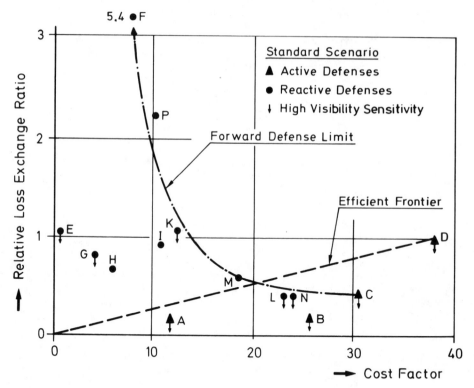

Fig. 4.8 Offense/Defense Loss Exchange Ratio Versus Relative Investment Cost

---

*) For example, in the North German plain it might well be organized along the lines of the British village or framework concept. In the covered hilly and mountaineous Central and Southern parts it might require the storage of prefabricated parts for the quick assembly of strong points and field fortifications.

exchange ratio (RLER) of the investigated active and reactive defense options in the standard scenario over their relative (to option E) investment cost. In this ratio, the losses represent the capital investment values lost by both sides in the battle including the ammunition spent and destroyed by the enemy.

Since it dominates all other active defense options in terms of the RLER to be obtained for the (monetary) investment, option D may be considered to represent a point on their so-called *'efficient frontier'*. Being the set of options that are not dominated, the efficient frontier is also known as the 'Pareto optimal set'. There exists no reactive defense option which would, for a given amount of capital investment, yield a higher RLER than the (hypothetical) option on the efficient frontier. However, we notice that this efficient frontier is dominated by all but two of the reactive defense options. Due to their rather one-sided equipment structure, these two options had already been diagnosed as being extremely sensitive toward visibility degradation and of little flexibility.

Thus, subject to the results of further experiments designated to test the threat and terrain sensitivity of the options, one may consider the defense efficiency hypothesis as not having been falsified, if not validated, at least in the economic terms of capital investment. However, based upon some preliminary estimates of the personnel losses to be expected for the various options, it seems very likely that the active defenses would dominate several reactive options, in particular those of the SAD category. For this reason, it is strongly recommended that empirical models be developed for the estimation of permanent and temporary personnel losses.

Strictly on the basis of economic considerations, the results also support the old military wisdom that a defense may be practiced the more efficiently, the more operational depth a defender has available. This is evident when one compares, for the reactive options E, G, I, and K, the ratio of the RLER to the investment cost obtained from Fig. 4.8 to the required operational depth depicted in Fig. 4.5. We note that for both of these parameters the value sequence results as $E > G > I \geq K^{*)}$, and as a corollary, that there is a limit to the pursuit of efficiency, depending upon the available operational depth.

For example, let us assume that a fair chance for a successful forward defense were given if the modules can be expected to repulse the initial assault of two consecutively attacking Soviet motor rifle regiments at essentially no loss of terrain (i.e., less than 5 km). In that case, the options F, M, and C could be considered to be members of the set defining the *forward defense limit* (see Fig. 4.8). If the forward defense criteria would be relaxed (e.g., by reducing the number of regimental attackers to be repulsed), this limit would shift to the left. In any case, only reactive defense options located in the sector 'north' of the efficient frontier and 'east' of the forward defense limit (including these bounds) could be considered as militarily and economically viable candidates for the design of a reactive defense component that is to supplement and, in the long term, even partially replace the traditional active defenses of NATO (see Huber and Hofmann[7], p. 19).

---

*) However, if in addition to the military capital investments, the defender losses would also include the damage to the civilian infrastructure, the value sequence of RLER would presumably be reversed. Since approximately 25-30% of West Germany's economic infrastructure is located within a belt of 100 km west of the demarcation line [41], option E's thus extended RLER might indeed not be far from Zero.

Overall, the results of our experiments suggest that the incorporation of properly designed reactive defenses into NATO's existing force structure could indeed contribute to a significant improvement of NATO's forward defense at acceptable cost and without having to rely on 'emerging technologies', the operational performance of which tends to be overestimated, especially with regard to enemy adaptability and the demands of a battlefield environment.

ACKNOWLEDGEMENTS

The authors express their deep appreciation to Christa Beckh and Klaus Bielesch for their invaluable work in the testing, maintenance, and documentation of the BASIS computer program, and to Carin Flitsch-Streibl for the dedicated and faultless technical production of this report.

REFERENCES

1. Amiel, S.: Deterrence by Conventional Forces. Survival March/April 1978, pp. 58-62
2. Spannocchi, E.: Verteidigung ohne Selbstzerstörung. In: Verteidigung ohne Schlacht. München-Wien 1976, pp. 15-91
3. Brossollet, G.: Das Ende der Schlacht - Versuch über die "Nicht-Schlacht". In: Verteidigung ohne Schlacht. München-Wien 1976, pp. 93-211
4. Afheldt, H.: Verteidigung und Frieden - Politik mit militärischen Mitteln. München-Wien 1976
5. Löser, H.J.: "Raumdeckende Verteidigung" gegen "Raumgreifende Operationen". Europäische Wehrkunde 9/1977, pp. 444-453
6. Fuller, J.F.C.: Armor and Counter Armor, Part 3: Defense Against Armored Attack. Infantry Journal, May 1944, pp. 39-43
7. Huber, R.K., Hofmann, H.W.: Some thoughts on Unilaterally Reducing the Conventional Imbalance in Central Europe - Gradual Defensivity as a Force Design Principle. Bericht 8402, Institut für Angewandte Systemforschung und Operations Research, Fachbereich Informatik, Hochschule der Bundeswehr München, Feb 1984
8. Huber, R.K., Steiger, K., Wobith, B.-E.: Über ein analytisches Modell zur Untersuchung der Gefechtswirksamkeit von Heeresstrukturen. Wehrwissenschaftliche Rundschau 1/1981, pp. 1-10
9. Huber, R.K., Steiger, K., Wobith, B.-E.: On an Analytical Quick Game to Investigate the Battle Effectiveness of Forward Defense Concepts. Journal of the Korean OR Society, Vol. 6, No. 1, Apr 1981, pp. 33-55
10. Paxon, E.W., Weiner, M.G.: A Method for Evaluating Advanced Systems and Concepts for Ground Combat. Rand Report R-2365-ARPA, Nov 1978
11. Paxon, E.W., Weiner, M.G., Wise, R.A.: Interactions between Tactics and Technology in Ground Warfare, Rand Report R-2377-ARPA, Jan 1979
12. Avenhaus, R., Fichtner, J., Huber, R.K. (1983): Conventional Force Equilibria and Crisis Stability - Some Arms Control Implications of Analytical Combat Models, Workshop on Supplemental Ways for Improving International Stability. IFAC-IIASA. Laxenburg, Sep 1983
13. Hofmann, H.W. et al.: BASIS - Ein Gefechtssimulation system auf Btl/Rgt-Ebene, Band 1: Beschreibung des Gefechtsmofells. Bericht 8401, Institut für Angewandte Systemforschung und Operations Research, Fachbereich Informatik, Hochschule der Bundeswehr München, Jan 1984
14. Afheldt, H.: Defensive Verteidigung in Europa. Hamburg 1983
15. Studiengruppe Alternative Sicherheitspolitik (Hrsg.): Strukturwandel der Verteidigung - Entwürfe für eine konsequente Defensive. Opladen 1984, pp. 156-173

16. Marti, P.: Schweizer Armee 80. Frauenfeld 1979
17. Senn, H.: Kann die Armee ihren Auftrag erfüllen?, in: Beilage zur Allgemeinen Schweizerischen Militärzeitschrift Nr. 3/1979, pp. 1-14
18. Schauer, H.: Die Schweiz - Neutraler Kleinstaat mit optimaler Verteidigung. Truppenpraxis 9/1978, pp. 693-699
19. Schauer, H.: Die Landesverteidigung der Schweiz (I). Wehrausbildung in Wort und Bild Nr. 10/1982, pp. 426-430
20. Marolz, J.: Raumverteidigung und Mechanisierung. Österreichische Militärische Zeitschrift, Heft 5/1978, pp. 374-379
21. Hochauer, G.: Raumverteidigung und Landwehrkonzept. Österreichische Militärische Zeitschrift, Heft 1/1979, pp. 11-19
22. Pleiner, H.: Herbstübung 77. Österreichische Militärische Zeitschrift, Heft 1/1978, pp. 7-15
23. Löser, J.: Vorneverteidigung der Bundesrepublik Deutschland. Österreichische Militärische Zeitschrift, Heft 2/1980, pp. 116-123
24. Löser, J.: Weder Rot noch Tot - Eine sicherheitspolitische Alternative. München 1982
25. Füreder, G.: Non-Nuclear Defense of Europe: Example Germany, Part I and II. Working Paper, 1983
26. Gerber, J.: Fordert die Wirtschaftlichkeit eine neue Struktur des Heeres? Heere International, Band 3, Herford 1984, pp. 39-52
27. Gerber, J.: Bundeswehr im Atlantischen Bündnis, Abschnitt 10: Analytischer Rückblick und prognostischer Ausblick. Regensburg 1984
28. Hannig, N.: Die Verteidigung Westeuropas mit konventionellen Feuersperren. Internationale Wehrrevue 11/1981, pp. 1439-1443
29. Hannig, N.: Abschreckung durch konventionelle Waffen: Das David-Goliath Prinzip, Berlin 1984
30. Greiner, D. et al.: Die gepanzerten Kampftruppen und Kampfunterstützungstruppen im Heeresmodell 4. Kampftruppen/Kampfunterstützungstruppen 1/1978, pp. 8-27
31. Bahr, J.: Gedanken zur Verteidigung der gepanzerten Kampftruppen. Kampftruppen/Kampfunterstutzungstruppen 3/1981, pp. 10-110
32. Koch, G.: Panzergrenadiere 90. Truppenpraxis 12/83, pp. 880-885
33. Koch, G.: Konzeptionelle Vorstellungen für die gepanzerten Kampftruppen der 90er Jahre. Europäische Wehrkunde/WWR 2/84, pp. 90-94
34. Karber, P.A.: In Defense of Forward Defense. Armed Forces International, May 1984, pp. 27-50
35. Wiener, F.: Das sowjetische MotSchützenregiment BMP. Truppendienst 5/1977, pp. 339-341
36. Hartung, H.-J.: Sowjetische Grundsätze für die Gefechtsgliederung von Panzern im Angriff. Kampftruppen/Kampfunterstützungstruppen 4/1978, pp. 174-177 and 5/1978, pp. 217-220
37. Kreker, H.-J.: Hinter den Panzern steht die Artillerie. Kampftruppen/Kampfunterstützungstruppen 1/1983, pp. 29-31
38. Baginski, E.: Die Panzerabwehr der Kampftruppen. Wehrtechnik 8/1983, pp. 18-25
39. Karber, P.A.: To Lose an Arms Race: The Competition in Conventional Forces Deployed in Central Europe 1965-1980. In: The Soviet Asset-Military Power in the Competition over Europe (Nerlich, U.(Ed.)). Cambridge, Mass. 1983, pp. 31-87
40. Farrell, R.L.: How Non-Weapon-System Parameters Affect Combat Results. In: Systems Analysis and Modeling in Defense (Huber, R.K.(Ed.)), New York 1984, pp. 615-626
41. The Federal Minister of Defense: White Paper 1983 - The Security of the Federal Republic of Germany, Bonn 1983, p. 144

SOME LONG-TERM TRENDS IN FORCE STRUCTURING

Walter Schmitz, Otto Reidelhuber, and Klaus Niemeyer

Industrieanlagen-Betriebsgesellschaft mbH
D-8012 Ottobrunn, Federal Republic of Germany

1. FUNDAMENTAL PROCEDURE

1.1 Problem

In the 1979 Defense White Paper, the task of the Federal Armed Forces is described as follows: /1/

"Article 87a of the Basic Law stipulates that armed forces shall be built up for defence purposes. This constitutional rule is the yard-stick for the Federal Armed Forces' operational concept, training, and equipment. In peacetime, Bundeswehr *planning and activities are aimed toward achieving an effective defence posture. The purpose of the armed forces' operational readiness is to safeguard peace through deterrence. Moreover, ready forces are an instrument of crisis management. In times of crisis they ensure freedom of political action of the Federal Government. The Alliance concept provides that in a state of defence our armed forces, together with the allied forces, operate on the ground, in the air, and on the seas, in an integrated forward defense effort. This includes the mission of restoring the integrity of the territory of the Federal Republic of Germany, if need be".*

This statement reflects the three fundamental objectives which, from the German viewpoint, NATO's military forces are to meet: They must be capable of

- maintaining a high degree of operational readiness in peacetime;
- holding up an attack as far forward as possible (forward defense);
- regaining lost territory by counter-attack.

Thus, with a view to these objectives several facts and premises need to be considered which tend to a-priori eliminate certain structural alternatives for the defense system of the Federal Republic of Germany:
- Alternatives to forward defense which imply the surrender of territory are in fact feasible but cannot be seriously considered, as the essential prerequisite, namely territory, is not available.

- As from the middle of the 1980's a steep decline in the available numbers of those liable to conscription is forecast. Thus, manpower-intensive structures are then disadvantageous and could pose serious problems.

- It has to be assumed that, under normal circumstances, the defense budget will be limited. The consequence is a limit to the procurement of defense materiel from both the quantitative and qualitative viewpoints.

- An increase in the quality of weapon systems leads, in many instances, to a disproportionate cost increase. Thus, the budgetary limits result in the acquisition of fewer weapon systems as their quality improves. However, quantity frequently dominates quality in the contribution to the total effectiveness of the defense structures. Therefore, given improved quality and no increase in the budget, total effectiveness may, under certain circumstances, suffer a dramatic decrease.

- The rapid technological development leads to new possibilities for ordnance design. In particular, micro-electronics and sensor technology promise revolutionary innovations which will have a decisive influence on the battlefield of the future.

- Availability of infrastructure is an important constraint for the design of force structures. It may only be relaxed rather slowly in the course of time. Similarly, it must be borne in mind that the capacity of the existing infrastructure for military operations may be limited as it is predominantly designed for peacetime use.

- The threat analyses show that an enormous quantitative and qualitative increase of the offensive potential has been achieved by the Warsaw Pact countries. A continuation of this trend is expected in the future.

- Alliance-related constraints have to be taken into account which cover a wide area, such as, for example, the assignment of defense sectors to national formations, the joint development and procurement of defense materiel or the coordination of combat principles and doctrines.

- The defense system like any other complex living system or organism requires steady adaptation. To this end, potential improvement options need to be continuously tested and compared with a view to their feasibility, effectiveness, and robustness in a wide range of possible scenarios and taking into account all of the above indicated factors and their interdependence. However, as the human brain may only consider a limited number of system entities and interrelations simultaneously, new tools and methods become necessary to support the planning and structuring of forces.

Since they permit to account for the complex interactions of modern day combined arms combat and its synergistic weapon effects, *Systems Analysis* approaches do provide the requisite basic instruments. Yet it must be kept in mind that any analysis does have its limitations due to very practical reasons such as, for example, the availability of data, time, and personnel. Consequently, the work presented in this paper is necessarily incomplete and must be considered merely as an illustration of the approach in support of force structure planning as it has evolved at IABG over the years recognizing that the traditional cost-effectiveness analysis at the weapon system and small unit levels is insufficient for the assessment of force structure improvements (see also Schlesinger /2/ and Huber /3/). To this end, the defense systems must be analyzed, not only at intermediate levels such as those of brigades and corps, but also at high levels accounting for land/air/sea interactions, likely enemy reactions, and the range of possible scenarios.

This paper presents some analyses at the intermediate level aimed at the "optimization" of bridgade structures from the results of which certain trends can be observed. In the calculations, the above mentioned constraints, in particular the manpower and budget limits as well as the synergetic effects have been considered in a quantitative manner. Other constraints have been introduced implicitly at the initial definition of the basic brigade structures.

1.2 Methods

1.2.1 Methodical Principles

Large and complex systems such as the Federal Armed Forces are always hierarchically organized /4/. Basically, three hierarchical levels, using the land forces as an example, might be differentiated (Fig. 1):

Hierarchic Level	Components	Frame	Time Resolution	Geographic Characteristic	Command Process
High	Major Units	Land Forces	Days	Topography	Operational Level
Intermediate	Formations	Major Units (e.g. Div., Corps)	Hours	Terrain Feature	Tactical Level
Low	Weapons	Formations (e.g. Btl., Comp.)	Minutes	Local Conditions (e.g. line of sight)	Duel Level

Fig. 1 Hierarchic Levels.

- <u>Low Level</u>   On this level, the system is physically identifiable in its components such as men, weapons, equipments, vehicles, etc. These components are combined into formations which have a particular but restricted task to fulfill: restricted in terms of location, time, and aimed at a specific opponent. The time resolution is on the order of minutes since the duels between modern weapon systems are generally decided in a relatively short time. The influence of the surrounds have a direct bearing, i.e., the outcome of a duel is dependent on the presence of a direct line of sight to the opponent.

- **Intermediate Level** On this level, the system elements resemble the formations of the low level. These may be joined into major units such as brigades, divisions or corps and undertake particular yet wider ranging targets and tasks. The time resolution at this level is usually in the order of hours, as, in addition to the duels, some time is required to carry out reconnaissance, to take the appropriate command measures and to position the formations in the desired places. The results of the battle are determined by a large number of duels whereby it is sufficient to consider the terrain in its general features using appropriate maps.

- **High Level** At this operational level, the system is made up of the intermediate level units. The time resolution is in terms of days since in addition to the combat operations on a tactical level a wide variety of logistical, reconnaissance, command and control, preparation, support, and movement processes, all of which require time, are taking place. The command may satisfactorily be based on rather large scale maps.

It is important to define the level in the discussion of structures in the defense system since, at every level, there are specific problems. It is not possible, for instance, to arrive at a new structure at the highest level on the basis of the consideration of duels at the lowest level only. Thus, from the systems analysis viewpoint, preference is given to the analytical procedure, i.e., to the decomposition of the whole system into its individual parts rather than the synthetic procedure, i.e., the putting together of the whole from its constituent parts since the overall interactions and objectives do not get lost. This top-down approach may be followed by a bottom-up approach in a sort of feedback with possible further iteration steps.

The highest level should be the starting point for assessment of structural alternatives both from the point of view of expenditure as well as effectiveness. This is because only at this point may the missions of the armed forces be defined as part and in terms of the overall defense task and substructures be seen as part of the entire system.

On the other hand, an assessment at this level is only possible if it is based on the effectiveness data of the intermediate level. It is, however, possible in such an examination to assume the results of the intermediate level (or, in analogy, those of the lowest level) in form of hypotheses that may subsequently be validated at the lower level. In this way, inefficient structural alternatives can be eliminated early so that only the promising ones are subjected to the more detailed analyses at the intermediate and lower hierarchic levels.

Closely linked to the hierarchic structure of the land forces, the development and application of simulation models and war game procedures have proved to be advantageous. The advantages are:

- Investigations and studies can be adjusted to the particular problems at the respective levels. In the pragmatic point of view, the input and output data have to be manageable for the user, the model-process has to be clear, at least in general terms, and the data volume has to remain within the work limits of the computer.

- The model can be constructed more efficiently with modular software technology. Thus it is possible to exchange simple, less detailed modules with more complex ones and vice versa. Given the availability of standard data structures and interfaces, comprehensive modular systems can be developed in this way.

A considerable disadvantage is that it is necessary to develop procedures for the aggregation of data such as, for instance, Lanchester coefficients or terrain typification from the detailed models of the respective lower hierarchical levels. This process demands the user to have a relatively high abstraction capability and is often not understood. However, as there are generally some overlaps between the hierarchical levels, it is possible to reciprocally check the model functions in an iterative manner.

A further dimension is the type of model. In addition to war games or simulation models there are the analytical models with the degree of abstraction increasing in this order. The higher the degree of abstraction, the more variations may be performed on the parameters under examination and there is the possibility of determining new solutions using mathematical optimization techniques. However, simultaneously with the increased degree of abstraction, the number of explicitly considered entities in the model diminishes. Therefore it is necessary to develop appropriate aggregation procedures similar to the aggregation procedures for the hierarchical levels. But as the possiblity exists of checking the results of the models iteratively, the disadvantages of the abstraction can be compensated. This iterative model application is a qualitative improvement in systems analysis /5/.

In the following chapters the iterative model application is described as it was employed in the compilation of the results presented in this paper. The detailed simulation in the lower hierarchical level was carried out to generate a data base for the loss calculations at the medium level in a war game /6/. This process can be understood as a *hierarchical aggregation*. The war games were then used in interplay with a planning model. The planning model, in turn, requires aggregated characteristic data from the war games. This process can be understood as a *methodological aggregation*. In the feedback process, the structures determined from the planning model were tested in the war game, whereby new aggregated characteristic data were produced /7/.

In this way, it was possible to arrive at new "optimal" structures that were validated by means of interactive simulation. However, as the optimization algorithms in the planning model are based on linear approaches, which are only approximately valid within certain limits determined by the respective war game results, the planning model may only find its optimum within these limits. Hence, the established solutions may represent relative optima which depend on the initial structure as the so-called zero-approximation structure for the war game. Thus, in order to be able to start from a fairly good initial structure, a series of very different alternative structures was investigated in a preceding analysis, whereby the war game was again used as the evaluative instrument. The optimization model represented the search algorithm in the overall heuristic process which was comprised of the following:

- Detailed simulations in order to establish the data base for the hierarchical aggregation;

- Assessment of alternative structures on brigade level for the identification of the initial structure in the iterative model application;

- Iterative search for the optimum.

1.2.2 Simulations and Hierarchical Aggregation

Fig. 2 outlines, in a schematic manner, how detailed simulations support the wargaming experiments on the next higher level. These company/battalion level high resolution simulations permit to determine the operational pros and cons of future weapon systems in different types of terrain and changing tactical situations. Characteristic values or coefficients for parameters such as

- average active combat ratio,
- tactical firing rate and
- kill probability per salvo and distance category

can be derived from the simulations within the hierarchical aggregation process.

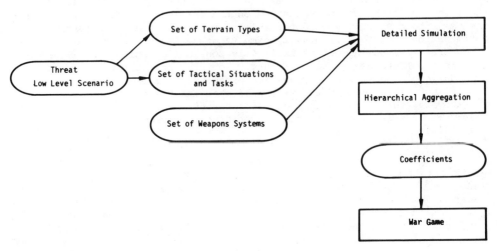

Fig. 2   Detailed Simulation.

These characteristic values are determined for all duel pairings as a function of terrain, distance category and combat mode. They form the data basis for the war game model as described by Niemeyer, Reidelhuber /6/ and Schmitz /7/. The war game model simulates the combined arms combat on the next higher level (Fig. 3). From the war games, the values for the same parameters are established which now account for all the influences of the support systems of the Air Force and the Army. Thus, they take into account the particular circumstances of the combined arms combat.

With due consideration of the cost and performance trends for modern weapon systems, the analyses of the simulation results suggest that there are certain principles that should be observed when defining a basic force structure as a departure point for the subsequent "optimization". Among others, it appears that, in the context of land warfare, weapon systems designed for specific tasks should be preferred over multiple-capability systems. This is not only because their design is simpler, their maneuverability better and the availability for their specific tasks greater. Also it permits to avoid, to a large extent, the exposure to enemy action of several components when only one need be deployed. Thus, armoured combat troops might consist of a mix of some or all of the following main weapon systems /8/:

- Main Battle Tank (MBT) with a high performance cannon capable of neutralizing all tanks up to a certain distance;

- Armoured Personnel Carrier (APC) with an automatic cannon capable of neutralizing modern APCs on a distance of about 1500 m;

- Anti-Tank Vehicle (ATV) equipped with an anti-tank missile effective up to medium distances;

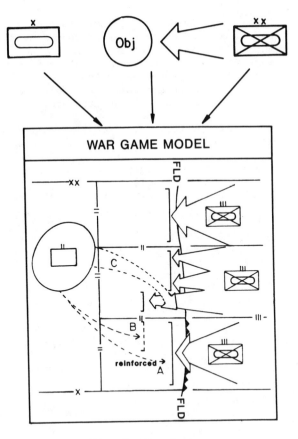

Fig. 3   War Game.

- Anti-Helicopter Vehicle (AHV) with a cannon or guided missile for ranges of 4000 meters or more;
- Mortar Vehicle (MV) with a range of about 8000 meters;
- Tank Destroyer (TD) with anti-tank missiles effective up to a distance of 4000 meters. An elevated platform would increase its effectiveness considerably;
- Anti-Tank Weapon System (ATWS) for medium distances;
- Bazooka (BAZ).

1.2.3 Assessment of Alternative Structures on Brigade Level

Despite the stringency of defense budgets of most nations, NATO needs to increase its conventional combat strength in order to satisfy the forward defense requirements of its strategy. Basically, an increase in conventional defense strength may be obtained from the implementation of improvements in either one or any combination of three fundamental areas:

1) Improvements of the effectiveness of existing weapon systems and/or introduction of newly developed systems; 2) procedural and doctrinal adaptions; 3) organizational and structural changes. In reference to both German and American sources, Huber /3/ points out that there might be room for procedural and structural measures which would permit to increase force effectiveness at considerably lower cost than those required by the procurement of additional and/or new hardware.

Moreover, authors such as Löser /9/, Afheldt /10/, Uhle-Wettler /11/, and Hannig /12/, amongst others, have put forward ideas and alternatives which imply non-traditional operational outlines and weapon system mixes to repel a conventional attacker. And last, but not least, planning is also affected by the demographic developments: A manpower shortage is expected for the 1990's in most of NATO's armed forces practicing conscription.

With due consideration of these facts and aspects, five alternative force structures were subjected to war gaming experiments. These structures resemble brigade-sized combat units which differ primarily with regard to their weapon systems mix and the requisite adapted tactics and operational employments. Table 1 provides an overview of the relative composition of the alternative structures in terms of the weapon systems introduced in section 1.2.2 above.

Combat support is nearly identical for all structures and comprises
- artillery,
- anti-tank helicopters,
- light fighter bombers,
- air defense,
- engineers.

TABLE 1: WEAPON SYSTEM DISTRIBUTION [PER CENT] IN THE ALTERNATIVE STRUCTURES

Alt. Structure \ Weapon System	MBT	APC	ATV	AHV	MV	TD	ATWS	BAZ
A	24	26	15	3	4	3	-	25
B	-	-	21	-	-	43	11	25
C	-	-	-	-	-	8	55	37
D	-	-	-	-	5	21	37	37
E	-	18	37	5	7	12	-	21

In the war games, each of these structures was analyzed and tested in the same terrain sector and in the defense combat mode. Additionally, the initial structure A for the optimization was tested in the other modes as well. The threat consisted of a reinforced motorized rifle division of the 1st Army echelon and a back-up tank division of the 2nd Army echelon.

The analysis was performed in the way that is illustrated in Fig. 4: The five structures were investigated in a given scenario, taking into account their operational objectives and specific weapon systems and structural tactics, in which the combined arms combat and also elements of raid type actions and operations from field fortifications were considered. The effectiveness of the structures was determined with the help of the war game. The cost defined here as life cycle cost, made up of the procurement cost plus operational cost, and the manpower requirements were estimated by a suitable model. Effectiveness, life cycle cost and manpower requirements were - in accordance with the questions raised - the predominant criteria for the comparative assessment of the structural types.

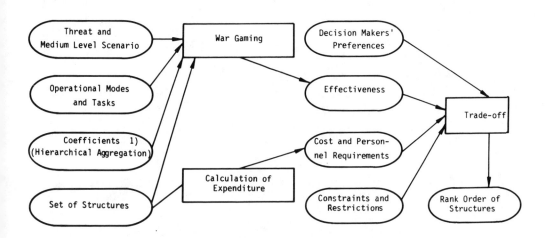

1) Detailed Simulation

Fig. 4 Assessment of the Basic Structure.

1.2.4 The Optimization

Fig. 5 shows an overview of the entire methodological process for the determination of optimal force structures:

- The data basis for the war game is generated with the help of the detailed company/battalion-level simulations (see section 1.2.2);
- The war game investigation starts with the initial structure as zero-approximation structure which is deployed both for defense and delaying action and counter-attack against a defined opponent;
- The analysis of the war game results yields the basis for the calculation of an improved weapon mix (methodological aggregation);
- The suggestions obtained from the planning model's optimization are incorporated into the structure and examined again in the war game;

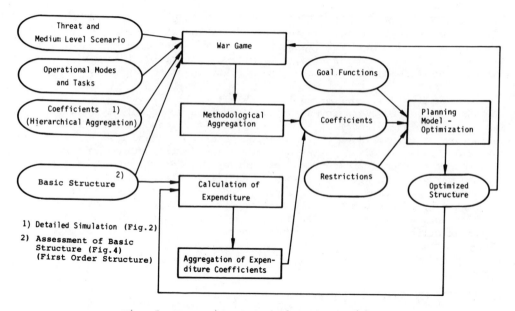

Fig. 5   Iterative Search for the Optimum.

- The process of gaming and optimization is continued iteratively until such time as no improvement in the mix is ascertainable. Only then one can speak of an optimal mix.

Thus, the "optimization" in the planning model links effectiveness, cost, and personnel requirements respectively to constraints in order to determine improved weapon system mixes. In doing so, the demand placed on the improved mixes is that they destroy at least as many enemy weapon systems as did the initial structure, given the cost and personnel restrictions.

With regard to cost, the model may differentiate between procurement, ammunition and life cycle cost which include the procurement, ammunition and operational cost. The improved mixes must not be more expensive than the initial structure in any of the three categories.

The structural specifications for the optimization include
- the maximum manpower requirements
- the minimum and maximum dismounted strengths
- the desired weapon systems mix of an armoured infantry company
- the desired number of combat vehicles the companies or platoons should have.

These structural data represent desired values that may be varied within certain limits.

2. RESULTS OF THE INVESTIGATION OF THE ALTERNATIVE STRUCTURES

Among others, the evidence obtained on the structures A to E (Table 1) from the analysis of the war game results relates to

- the characteristics and capabilities of the structures in comparison to one another;
- the role of the most important weapon types in the individual structures;
- the combat support for the structures.

2.1 Characteristics and Capabilities of the Structures

A comparative assessment of the structural types in terms of the criteria effectiveness, life cycle cost, and manpower requirements is shown in Fig. 6. Accordingly, E dominates A, followed by D, C and B.

This rank order is valid, as has been emphasized, only for brigade-size structures in the defense combat mode. In the context of a corps battle, these standards could vary considerably, particularly when delaying action and counter-attack operations are taken into account. Despite these limitations, however, various interesting conclusions can be drawn.

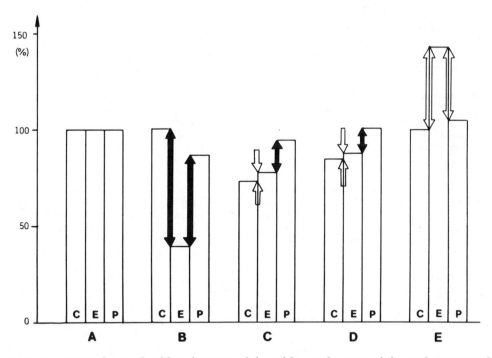

Fig. 6 Comparison of Effectiveness (E), Life Cycle Cost (C), and Personnel Requirements (P) for the Structures A to E.

It is quite obvious that the appropriate weapon systems mix has a special significance. This becomes clear both from the tactical assessment of the war game and from the resulting quantitative assessment of the war game runs.

The suitability of the mix is, of course, governed by the mission, in this case, to carry out a defense operation, and by the nature of the threat, i.e., the mix and the assumed deployment modes and sequences of the attacker. Given this framework, the suitability is determined above all by the criteria firepower, vulnerability cover, and mobility. The firepower must fulfill a target spectrum oriented echelonment in depth of its ranges, and must similarily guarantee a cost-effective target destruction by means of the deployment possibility of varying types of ammunition.

In this sense, structures A and E appear to be rather balanced considering their weapon mix composition as presented in Table 1 and the firing ranges of the weapons. Structure E has a clearly higher proportion of missile systems. The high proportion of armoured vehicles ensures a good chance of survival and increases the mobility of the infantry forces, whereby terrain and artificial obstacles can be used more profitably, permitting among others, a quick concentration of firepower. Given its large number of battle tanks, structure A may be also employed for counter-attacks, a capability that is not accounted for in the effectiveness of a strictly defensive battle. Being tailored to such a battle, it is not surprising that A's effectiveness is lower than E's, because E without battle tanks is more a structure specialized on defense.

Taking as a prerequisite that the cost effectiveness of a formation should remain unaltered, the results also show that the criteria echeloned firepower, armoured protection, and mobility can only be substituted for one another to a limited extent.

Structure B's effectiveness depends on the firepower of the tank destroyer over longer distances and on the capacity of the anti-tank vehicle for the medium range combat distances. When the tank destroyer vehicles are forced to take evasive action and give up terrain, the link to the static infantry forces, operating basically from field fortifications, frequently breaks down and the elements of the structure have to fight isolated rearguards actions. A mobile attacker with a strong force of infantry and the ability to concentrate his firepower exploits this situation.

Thus, structure B must be considered as insufficiently equipped in respect of survivability and mobility of its infantry forces; the firepower of its tank destroyer vehicles cannot compensate for these inadequancies, particularly in the face of strong infantry forces. Its procurement cost are comparatively high, as can be seen from Fig. 7.

Structure C has only few combat vehicles and is composed mainly of infantry forces equipped with medium range guided missiles which are deployed over the area to be defended by the brigade. The lack of mobility and survivability of these forces when changing position reduces their effectiveness to a degree that they cannot prevent the attacker's advance, and their action results to be more a delaying than a defensive one.

As in B, firepower is the dominant component in structure D. However, the comparatively large number of tank destroyers with their long weapon range warrants an enemy attrition that permits the infantry forces to successfully cope with the enemy armour penetrating within their effective weapon range. The results for structure D suggest that, as long as mobility and armoured protection can be done without for a change of position, the specialization on target destruction at long range is effective. If these prerequisites are not valid any longer, the area to be defended is very quickly lost.

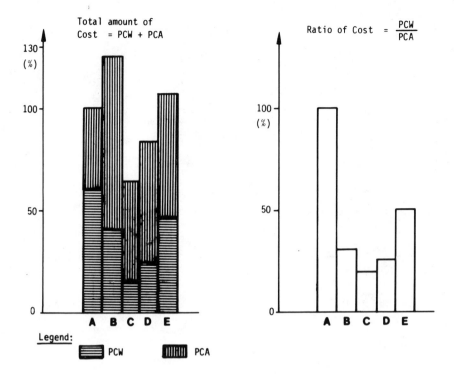

Fig. 7 Comparison of the Procurement cost of Weapon Systems (PCW) and Ammunition (PCA) for the structures A to E.

2.2 Selected Results on Weapon Systems Effectiveness

With regard to insights on the cost effectiveness of the individual weapon systems in the structures, the reader is referred to Fig. 8 presenting the relative cost of the weapon systems in the five structures and the relative effectiveness contribution of the direct-fire weapons. It shows what the individual weapon systems are capable of, given the premises underlying each structural type at the time of its drafting. There seem to be no complete "failures" amongst the weapon systems, even if the relative cost effectiveness varies from structure to structure. This is probably only a small reflection of a quality difference. Much more important is the influence of the differing roles to be played in the respective structure by the weapon types. If, for example, infantry forces prevent penetration by the attacker, then they may improve the cost effectiveness factor of the anti-tank forces equipped with guided missiles. Thus, it follows that it is not primarily the cost effectiveness factor of the weapon types which must be considered but rather their efficiency in the structure, i.e., their role in the combined arms combat situation.

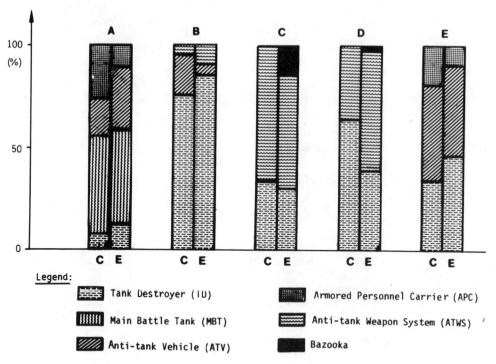

Fig. 8 Comparison of life cycle cost (C) and effectiveness (E) for important weapon systems of structure A to E.

2.3 Some Comments on the Effectiveness of Combat Support Means

The combat support means were available to the differing structures in almost equal measure. They had considerable influence on the attrition of the attacker.

Of particular interest is the direct mines had on the attacker's combat vehicles: in all wargaming experiments, mines were the cause of significant losses. A prerequisite, however, is a sufficient capacity for mine-laying and for installing horizontal mines. Furthermore, sufficient preparation time and local knowledge are similarily important. Difficult to gauge are the indirect effects of mines. However, it appears that the more balanced structures, in the sense described earlier, could derive greater indirect use from mines than could the specialized structures: the tank destroyer at long range and the anti-tank vehicle at medium range could gain advantages in respect of target detection and target destruction. At the same time, the armour offers protection against increased artillery fire from the attacker during the crossing of a minefield. In addition, the enemy attack helicopters can be restricted in their effectiveness by anti-helicopter combat vehicles and other air defense systems.

The rapid availability of anti-tank helicopters significantly supports the concentration of fire power for the defending side. The exchange ratio, which the anti-tank helicopter achieves in combat with armoured vehicles, makes it a cost-effective weapon system. The problematic aspect for this system is, however, the high density of air defense systems which the attacker has at his disposal near the FEBA.

Special consideration is earned by those artillery weapons which fire target-seeking ammunition. This target-seeking ammunition has proved itself to be effective, also indirectly, i.e., when it succeeds in destructing enemy systems which, in turn, fire target-seeking ammunition. However, it should be emphasized that a number of prerequisites for these successes are assumed, for example, with regard to detection, target area reachability or target selectivity, the technical and tactical realization of which cannot yet be reliably gauged.

3. SOME RESULTS OF THE SEARCH FOR THE OPTIMUM

The example that illustrates the process of optimization is based on structure A as the initial structure.

3.1 Weapon Systems Effectiveness

Hardware-related planning data are available from the war games in form of the losses caused to either side's combat troops by the weapon systems in opposing force structures. This shall be discussed using artillery as an example.

The *analysis* of the war gaming results indicates that some future rocket launcher artillery systems can be expected to destroy a-times as many targets as today's systems which are equipped with guns. This effectiveness increase is primarily a result of the rocket systems' superior range, high firing rate and extremely effective ammunition. However, these advantages must be paid for by a b-fold higher life cycle cost for these systems. If, for simplicity's sake, it is assumed that the existing cannons cause no further expenditures, then the future artillery mix, made up of x launchers and, in total y cannon systems, whereby y_1 cannons have already been purchased and y_2 are still to be purchased, will result in the following cost C and effectiveness E (a > b):

$$C = b \cdot x + 0 \cdot y_1 + 1 \cdot y_2 \quad / \text{ monetary units } / \qquad (1)$$

$$E = a \cdot x + 1 \cdot y_1 + 1 \cdot y_2 \quad / \text{ destroyed targets } / \qquad (2)$$

In answer to the question how large x and $y=y_2$ should be, there are two possible objectives one may pursue:

- maximize effectiveness at fixed cost C_{fix} ;
- minimize cost at a given effectiveness E_{fix} .

Maximization of the Effectiveness at Fixed Cost

If an upper cost C_{fix} is specified for the mix, then only such mixes are permissible, the cost of which, C, are the same or lower than C_{fix}.

Therefore, given the cost function above, we obtain

$$b \cdot x + 1 \cdot y_2 \leq C_{fix} \quad \text{or}$$

$$y_2 \leq C_{fix} - b \cdot x .$$

It is then only possible to purchase at most only so many guns and launchers so that the equation

$$y_2 = C_{fix} - b \cdot x \qquad (3)$$

is correct.

On the other hand, the number of cannon systems to be acquired can be calculated as a function of the effectiveness.

$$y_2 = E - y_1 - a \cdot x . \qquad (4)$$

Fig. 9 shows a graphic representation of the relations (3) and (4) which illustrates how the optimal solution is optained. All (x_o, y_o) points to the left of the cost line C_{fix} represent permissible mixes, the effectiveness of which, however, is smaller than that of the mix $(x_{max}, y_{max}) = (x_{max}, y_1)$, as the intersection points of the effectiveness lines show on the y-axis. This solution indicates that no further cannon system should be purchased. The existing guns are to be incorporated into the mix and the remaining money should be spent entirely on launchers.

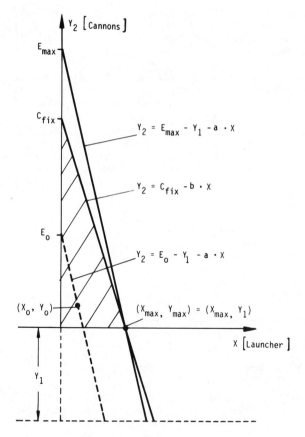

Legend: X = Number of launchers to be acquired
Y_1 = Number of cannons already acquired
Y_2 = Number of cannons still to be acquired

Fig. 9 Optimal solution-mix with fixed cost and maximum effectiveness.

Minimization of Cost for a Given Effectiveness

If the minimum effectiveness E_{fix} is specified then only those mixes are permissible, the effectiveness of which is greater or equal to E_{fix}.

Equation (2) which describes the effectiveness of any artillery mix, then modifies to

$$a \cdot x + y_1 + y_2 \geq E_{fix} \quad \text{or}$$

$$y_2 \geq E_{fix} - y_1 - a \cdot x \ . \tag{5}$$

Therefore, at least as many cannons and launchers have to be acquired that the equation

$$y_2 = E_{fix} - y_1 - a \cdot x$$

is fulfilled. The cost of this mix is obtained from equation (3).

In analogy to Fig. 9, the relationships (3) and (5) are presented graphically in Fig. 10. All (x_o, y_o)-points to the right of the effectiveness line E_{fix} represent permissible mixes, the cost of which, however,

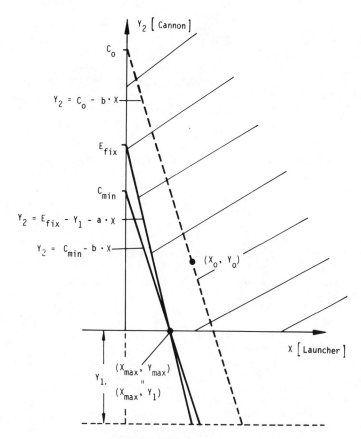

Legend : X = Number of launchers to be acquired
Y_1 = Number of cannons already acquired
Y_2 = Number of cannons still to be acquired

Fig. 10 Optimal solution-mix with specified effectiveness and minimum cost.

are higher than of the mix $(x_{max}, y_{max}) = (x_{max}, y_1)$, as the intersection points of the cost line on the y-axis show. The optimal solution obtained when minimizing cost is identical to the one maximizing effectiveness. Thus, even when making extremely favourable assumptions for the cannons, the same result is achieved from both directions so that an increase in launcher strength can be deduced from this result, as the best procurement policy.

3.2 Combat Modes

Usually, the proponents of alternative force structures aim at the removal of weaknesses from the existing force structure as they are perceived with regard to the possible courses of a war in which the forces might become involved. However, the derivation of improved structures by simply removing, one by one, the perceived weaknesses while retaining the strengths may lead to proposals that are in conflict with important restrictions such as, for example, minimum requirements for the fulfillment of all sub-tasks or upper limits for cost or manpower. But even when all the conditions are fulfilled, it is not possible to exclude the existence of still better and/or cheaper structures.

It is for this reason, that the approach discussed in this paper explicitly considers restrictions in this search for improved structures thus permitting to observe the influence of restrictions on the design of force structures. This type of sensitivity analysis is particularly important when restrictions or requirements are considered which are based solely on value judgements rather than being the result of a reproduceable analysis. In order to illustrate how such value judgements affect the design of force structures, a few planning model calculations results shall be discussed in which the force structure effectiveness in the three main combat modes (defense, delaying action, and attack) was alternatively maximized subject to given cost and personnel constraints and certain minimum requirements as to the capacity in the other two combat modes.

Fig. 11 shows the results of these calculations in terms of the relative contribution of the main weapon systems in the "optimal" brigade mixes to the brigade's effectiveness when the latter is maximized in the indicated combat modes. In each case, the brigades are required to hold a certain line.

<u>Defense</u> The main battle tanks, tank destroyers and armoured personnel carriers are the mainstay of the defensive operation. They are supported by the mortar vehicles and anti-helicopter vehicles. This mix covers the range of defensive operations so well that the anti-tank vehicles are not required. Thus, when the anti-tank vehicle is provided as a means of anti-tank defense in the mechanized infantry company, it has to be clarified, how the battle tanks and the tank destroyers are to be organized so that they can effectively make up the then deficient anti-tank capacity of the mechanized infantry. The problems raised by a lack of anti-tank capacity of the mechanized infantry are discussed further in section 3.4.

<u>Delaying Action</u> As the delaying action is mainly carried out over long distances, the planning model requires longer-range weapon systems. The number of battle tanks is raised considerably. The number of tank destroyers remains unaltered. The number of mortar vehicles is raised as well. The number of anti-helicopter vehicles remains the same and the armoured personnel carriers are taken out of the mix completely.

<u>Attack</u> The highly mobile attack operation is essentially sustained by battle tanks. As in the delaying action, many battle tanks are incorporated into the structure. As, however, in the attack situation the tank destroyer must transport its fire to the enemy, it cannot always make full use of its

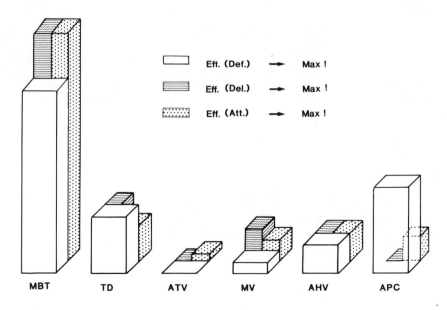

Fig. 11 Combat Mode Influence.

maximum range. It is also thereby more vulnerable which makes it sensible that the tank destroyers are partly replaced by anti-tank vehicles. The mortar vehicles might also be reduced while the anti-helicopter vehicles remain unaltered. Because of the shorter combat distances in the counter-attack situation, some APCs are included in the mix.

However, all three of these structures exhibit an insufficient dismounted strength. Because of this, the manpower level always remains below the upper limit. Given the fact that in all the structures there is a large number of battle tanks, the specified cost framework is, to a large extent, drained of resources. This raises the interesting question as to which weapon system will deleted first, if the cost have to be reduced.

3.3 Influence of Cost

In order to illustrate the influence of cost on the structures presented above, we look at a case in which the life cycle cost were minimized subject to certain minimum requirements being met in all the combat modes. The result is depicted in Fig. 12 which shows that the most expensive system - the main battle tank - is greatly reduced in numbers compared to the case when the defense effectiveness was maximized. Similarily, the number of tank destroyers should be reduced in favour of anti-tank vehicles such that the total number of anti-tank missiles remains unaltered. The number of mortar vehicles and the anti-helicopter vehicles remain unaltered while personnel carriers should be reduced to a similar extent as the tanks.

3.4 The Anti-Tank Capability of Mechanized Infantry

Armoured personnel carriers and anti-tank vehicles are the main weapon systems for the mechanized infantry. The APC is to be deployed against enemy armoured personnel carriers and the anti-tank vehicles against enemy battle tanks. Given the large number of main battle tanks and tank destroyers, the anti-tank vehicle disappears almost entirely in the above discussed structures. The mechanized infantry is hence deprived of its anti-tank capacity which should lead to considerably difficulties in the deployment of its companies. In order to avoid this, one may require that each mechanized

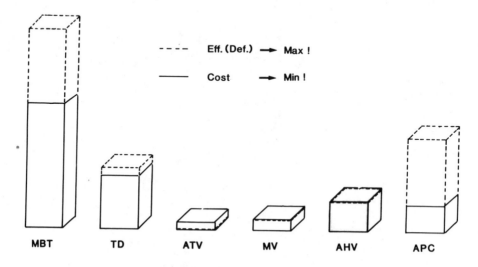

Fig. 12   Influence of Cost.

infantry company is equipped with m APC and n anti-tank vehicles. Fig. 13 illustrates how such a requirement would effect a structure that is otherwise optimized in the defense role. It shows the original structure on the left, and the structure with the n:m requirement to the right.

This comparison indicates quite clearly that an anti-tank capacity of the mechanized infantry may only be attained at the expense of battle tank numbers. The battle tank numbers would be reduced and additional anti-tank vehicles would be included in the mix. All other numbers remain the same. However, the life cycle cost increase slightly at approximately the same extent as the effectiveness decreases.

3.5   The Influence of Dismounted Strength

With a view to situations in which visibility is reduced (e.g. covered terrain or dirty battlefield), one might assume that the dismounted strength of the above structures is insufficient. As the dismounted strength is directly linked to the number of armoured personnel carriers, this means that an increase in dismounted strength automatically implies an increase in the number of armoured personnel carriers. Thus, one needs to know what structural changes would result if the dismounted strength is increased.

Fig. 14 shows the influence of an increase in dismounted strength (DS) in comparison to the previously calculated structure with the n:m mix requirements (see also Fig. 13). Here too, the trend of reducing the number

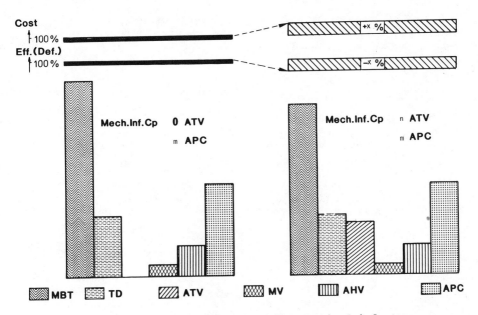

Fig. 13 Anti-tank capability of mechanized infantry.

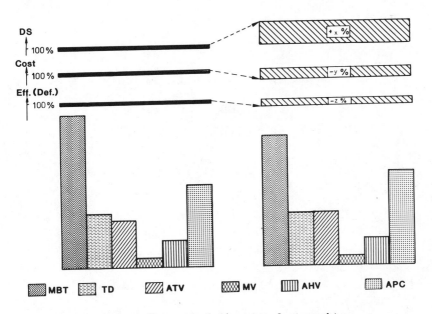

Fig. 14 Influence of dismounted strenght.

of battle tanks is continued. The new structure deletes a tank company and includes an additional mechanized infantry company. Thereby, the dismounted strength is actually increased but, at the same time, the cost and effectiveness decrease marginally.

3.6 Simultaneous Influence of the Restrictions

From the above discussion it is obvious that, when considering manpower and cost restrictions only, the force structures are rather sensitive as to which combat mode represents the primary design requirement (see section 3.2 and Fig. 11). Similarily, the analysis showed that entering, one by one, additional (structural) requirements or restrictions caused the force structure to change in the case of the defense combat mode, usually at some decline in effectiveness. This is, of course, no surprise as the available space for force structure decisions is narrowed by a-priori requirements.

That additional restrictions lead to similar consequences when either one of the other two main combat modes becomes the primary design criteria is obvious from Fig. 15. It shows that, when all the above discussed restrictions are entered simultaneously, the "optimal" structures are practically identical in all three combat modes. Only in the counter-attack situation is the number of mortar vehicles increased at the expense of tank destroyers. As mentioned before, this latter effect is caused by the higher vulnerability of the tank destroyers over the shorter operational distances when employed in an attack mode.

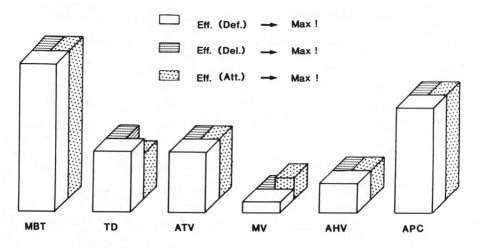

Fig. 15 Combat mode influence given extended restrictions.

As was the case when considering an effectiveness requirement only, Fig. 16 shows that the minimization of life cycle cost leads to a reduction of main battle tanks and tank destroyers when all requirements are considered simultaneously.

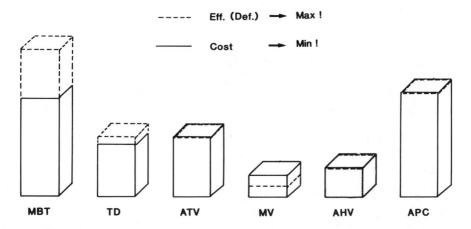

Fig. 16   Influence of cost extended restrictions.

Now one could assume that the robustness of the new structure is predetermined by the extended restrictions. To refute this suspicion, the influence of cost is examined. As Fig. 16 shows, an increasing fluctuation is ascertainable if the life cycle cost are to be minimized within this extended framework. The number of main battle tanks is reduced considerably and the number of tank destroyers decreases slightly. Only the mortar vehicles might increase. All other systems remain unaffected. It is worthwhile to mention that this structure fulfills all minimum requirements for the three combat modes. At the same time life cycle cost are lower.

3.7   Specialized Structures Versus Balanced Structures

In order to arrive at what might be called a "balanced structure", a procedure was developed that applies Fuzzy Set Theory to determine a compromise solution from the "optimal" solutions obtained with different objective functions. A detailed description of this procedure is provided in the appendix to /7/. It basically attempts to satisfy all objective functions to the greatest possible extent. The fuzzy term "to the greatest possible extent" implies that the values for the objective functions must not fall below a-priori specified lower bounds.

Fig. 17 shows the thus derived compromise solution in comparison to the above discussed solutions obtained for the four different objective functions under extended restrictions as presented in Figs. 15 and 16. Accordingly, the compromise solution differs from the "defense" respectively "delay" solutions only in the number of battle tanks. The number of all other weapon systems remains the same.

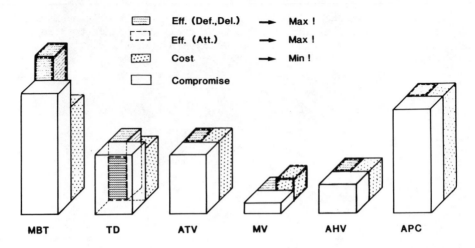

Fig. 17 Compromise Solution.

On the other hand, the differences between the "compromise solution" and the "minimum cost solution" are slightly higher. The "compromise" demands more battle tanks and tank destroyers but fewer mortar vehicles. That is the reason why the compromise solution's life cycle cost are higher than those of the minimum cost solution.

In comparison to the three structures presented at first (see section 3.2), the relatively small number of tanks in the compromise solution is striking. This shows that the objectives and restrictions have to be selected very carefully, in order to make sure that certain structural solutions are not a-priori eliminated.

3.8 Summarized Trends from the Optimization Process

From the results discussed above, the following trends may be deduced:

(1) Main battle tanks have a high tactical value in all combat modes, but particularly in highly mobile conflict situations.

(2) The lower the cost limits are set the fewer is the number of main battle tanks in an "optimized" structure.

(3) The demand for increased dismounted strength is made at the expense of main battle tanks.

(4) In the future, tank destroyers will have to be provided in greater numbers than today.

(5) Given the expected helicopter threat, an adequate number of anti-helicopter vehicles is absolutely necessary.

(6) Reductions in resources have a decisive influence on the force structure.

Having recognized these trends, the fact is stressed that restrictions and objectives must be examined very carefully so that structures can be found which are both realistic and feasible.

4. CONCLUSIONS

(1) Using systems analysis methods, valuable information can be acquired with respect to the suitability of weapon systems, the organization of force structures and their possible improvement. Although the methods used till now have been appropriate to solve the problems posed, it is important that a continuous methodological development and adaptation to an ever-changing military environment takes place.

(2) The group of combat vehicles which were taken into consideration permits the development of effective and robust structures with regard to changing requirements. The specialization of individual weapon systems for a particular task is preferable to a multi-purpose role. The key question is the proper weapon system mix within the structures.

(3) Given the prerequisite and considering the criteria

- echeloned firepower ranges, with an adequate mix of cannons and missile systems,
- survival protection and
- mobility,

it must be concluded that balanced structures are preferable to specialized structures where firepower is over-emphasized. The latter are less robust to equipment changes and to tactical variation on the part of the attacker.

(4) A considerable part of the total effectiveness is provided by combat support systems. Their size, equipment, and structuring, together with varying forms of interactions with the combat units, must similarily be examined in more detail.

(5) The structure investigations presented here are merely partial and illustrative contributions to long-term structural planning, the objectives of which are derived from the role of the Federal Armed Forces as part of the Alliance. It is the task of the planner to decompose the overall structural planning problem, in a top-down process, into appropriate individual problems which may then be examined by means of systems analysis methodologies. The results provide the planner with essential information on the synthesis process of organizing suitable force structures.

REFERENCE

/1/ Bundesminister der Verteidigung: Weißbuch 1979, Bonn 1979

/2/ Schlesinger, J.R.: The Changing Environment for Systems Analysis. In: Systems Analysis and Policy Planning - Applications in Defence (Quade, Boucher Eds.), New York 1975, pp. 364-387

/3/ Huber, R.K.: Die Systemanalyse in der Verteidigungsplanung - Eine Kritik und ein Vorschlag aus systemanalytischer Sicht. Wehrwissenschaftl. Rundschau 5/1981, pp. 133-143

/4/ Niemeyer, Klaus: Zur Struktur einer Hierarchie von Planspielmodellen. In: Operationsanalytische Spiele für die Verteidigung. (Huber, Niemeyer, Hofmann Eds.), München-Wien 1979

/5/ Niemeyer, Klaus: Systemanalyse, Management-Enzyklopädie. Verlag Moderne Industrie, München 1971

/6/ Niemeyer, Klaus, Reidelhuber, Otto: Das Planspiel als Methode der Verteidigungsplanung. In: Operationsanalytische Spiele für die Verteidigung. (Huber, Niemeyer, Hofmann Eds.), München-Wien 1979

/7/ Schmitz, Walter: Application of a War Game and an Analytical Decision Model to Planning of Military Structures. In: Systems Analysis and Modeling in Defense. (Huber Ed.), London 1984

/8/ Koch, Gero: Gedanken über die gepanzerten Kampftruppen der Zukunft. Truppenpraxis 3/1982, pp. 177-186

/9/ Löser, Jochen: Weder rot noch tot. München 1981

/10/ Afheldt, Horst: Verteidigung und Frieden, Politik mit militärischen Mitteln. München-Wien 1976

/11/ Uhle-Wettler, Franz: Gefechtsfeld Mitteleuropa - Gefahr der Übertechnisierung von Streitkräften. München 1980

/12/ Hannig, N.: Die Verteidigung Westeuropas mit konventionellen Feuersperren. Intern. Wehrrevue 11/1981, pp. 1439-1443

Part IV

ASSESSMENT GROUP SUMMARIES

MILITARY RATIONALE AND OPERATIONAL ROBUSTNESS: The Impact of Emerging Technology and Experimental Tactics on the Future of Infantry

Phillip A. Karber
Vice President, BDM Corporation

MILITARY RATIONALE

Since the adoption of Forward Defense as an operational doctrine, the overall structure of NATO's armies on the Central Front has remained remarkably stable. However, while the number of divisions deployed in Central Europe in peacetime has remained virtually unchanged, and the growth in the quantity of subordinate brigades marginal, there has been significant change in the armament and structure of the maneuver battalions, with particular focus on the introduction of "new" technology. Over the last two decades, every Western army has experimented with and introduced a major reorganization, equipping the vast majority of battalions with a new generation of weapons technology. This includes both the introduction of entire new classes of combatant systems (ATGM, attack helicopter, battlefield mobile SAM, infantry fighting vehicle, etc.), and radical changes in components (hypervelocity guns, robotic loading, automated fire control, laser range finders, thermal imaging, special armor, digital communications, smart bombs and missiles, scatterable and self-disarming mines, improved lethality submunitions, etc.). Given the scope and magnitude of this modernization, and the fact that so little of this technology has been tested in battle, the sheer energy of all this change is more than sufficient justification to improve our understanding and analysis of the potential impact of advanced technology on the nature of modern combat. To the extent that operations research and simulation of combat via mathematical modeling can assist professional military judgement in cutting through the fog of increasingly complex battlefield interactions, not to mention informing a growing public and political concern over the effectiveness of conventional forces, they provide a major contribution to European defense.

The papers and analysis presented at the symposium represent the "cutting edge" of military operations research in the FRG, US and Britain, and show not only professional analytical rigor, but a serious attempt to explore both new tactics and new force structures to take advantage of emerging technology. This workshop was unique in that it provided a rare opportunity for a comparison of research findings oriented to a common theme. This comparison was valuable in several ways: first, the highlighting of differing national concerns and simulation approaches; second, the contrasting of results and insights from different models, each with its own strengths, that covered a range of analytical levels of combat -- from battalion and brigade (where individual weapons duels can be examined on real terrain and with realistic tactics) through corps and theater wide aggregations addressing broader political and economic issues; third, the research was not limited to a search for a single "solution", but rather examined a wide variety of proposed mixes of weapons technology and alternative tactics in order to compare the strengths and weaknesses of each to current force structures.

The common theme, cutting across virtually all of the "new" options and contrasting simulations presented at the symposium, is how to optimize (via equipment procurement, tactics, and unit organizational design) the contribution of NATO infantry to the alliance objective of Forward Defense. This preoccupation with infantry is not only evident in the growing number of reform proposals by non-governmental experts, [1] but is increasingly a subject of concern within the professional military establishment. [2] There are several reasons for this:

- o As illustrated in Figure 1, infantry make up the largest component of NATO's maneuver battalions -- if one is searching for structural innovation with proportionally the most impact, this is where to start.

- o Upon mobilization of reserves and arrival of reinforcements the role of infantry increases, yet historically the European reserve contingent has been the least capitalized (in terms of modern equipment) and much of the manpower potential is not organized into combatant units but diffused in holding pools for individual replacement of battle casualties.

- o Warsaw Pact forces are organized and offensively designed for mechanized combat in hopes of achieving an early and decisive penetration of the defense with rapid and deep exploitation. Given the nature of the opposing offensive operational concept and Warsaw Pact emphasis on tanks and infantry combat vehicles, NATO infantry must be able to defend against armor to remain viable.

- o In sharp contrast to the tank (which has experienced evolutionary technical development and whose tactical employment is well established) the role of infantry on the modern battlefield has

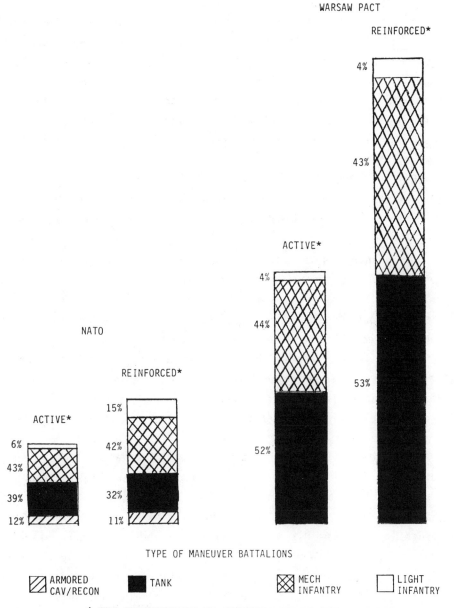

Fig. 1. Current structure of opposing maneuver forces in Central Europe[3]

gone through a radical change in perceptions and the current debate is far from settled.

o While individual armies are evaluating the merits and proper mix of heavy vs light infantry, NATO countries demonstrate a wide and growing divergence of needs.

In the 1950s, dismounted infantry was perceived to be doomed by the order of magnitude increase in fluidity and dispersion presumed on the nuclear battlefield. With the massive mechanization of 1960s, an inherent contradiction arose as to whether the infantry should fight mounted (with marginal firepower but escorting and securing the main battle tank) or continue the fight on foot and use their APCs as taxis (a transport vehicle offering a modicum of protection between dismounted force deployments).[4]

In the 1970s, this dilemma was exacerbated by two developments: creation of the infantry fighting vehicle (IFV); and the mounting of heavier armament (which provided a mobile platform to engage enemy APCs and tanks and the simultaneous proliferation of the medium-range man-portable ATGM. Today the infantry is so saturated with antitank systems that they have become static (tied to dispersed entrenched positions to simultaneously reduce their vulnerability and maximize the density of ATGM fire), divorced from their tracked carrier, and weighed down so they cannot use their inherent human mobility in closed and built-up terrain.[5]

These dilemmas are reflected in the internal agony which individual NATO armies are currently going through. The Bundeswehr is concerned about overloading mechanized infantry with too many diverse weapons on a multi-mission platform. The individual vehicles possess ATGM systems for long-range fire, rapid firing APC cannon at mid-range, and small arms for close range combat. Other countries, unable to afford the luxury of outfitting all of their infantry with IFVs, are searching for new tactics as a means to keep their dismounted troops from becoming irrelevant. The US, having made an enormous investment in the multi-mission IFV as a complement to its' new M-1 tanks, and basing the cornerstone of its' new maneuver oriented "Airland Battle" doctrine on the synergy of the two vehicles, now faces a disconnect due to the wide asymmetry in their relative survivability.[6] As the Soviets recognized (but did not solve) a decade ago, the lightly armored ICV is vulnerable to many more weapons than the tank. A hit tends to be much more catastrophic, and when fighting mounted, produces double jeopardy -- the loss of both crew and rifle squad.[7]

A successful defense against armor has traditionally been structured around two key parameters: <u>depth</u>, the ability of the defense to engage the exposed attacking vehicles before they can close with and penetrate the defenders tactical integrity -- thus, providing a favorable loss exchange ratio for the defense; and <u>density</u>, a sufficient quantity of surviving systems to simultaneously engage the majority of exposed vehicles and occupy key terrain to prevent a rapid overrun. Both of these approaches, taken to extreme, have severe limitations. While the defender is most efficient in keeping the attacks at arms distance, in essence using terrain features to create an ambush then withdrawing to repeat the process several kilometers to the rear, the price that must be paid is the loss of his own territory. If the terrain permits the rapid movement and concentration of enemy armor, the pace of the attack can move too deep too quickly and the cumulative effect of abandoning positions (with less time and fewer assets to organize at each successive site) will soon break the defenders' cohesion. On the other hand, positional defenses in which a large quantity of weapons are dug in over a limited space rather than preserving their mobility, can inflict a much higher loss rate against the attacker. Nevertheless, positional defenses also make the defender an attractive target to massed indirect fire.

Within NATO the "typical" mechanized infantry battalion represents a compromise between depth and density. At the initiation of battle a platoon of lightly armored vehicles, firing long range ATGM begin picking off the lead attacking vehicles. As the attack closes, the platoon is joined by a cross-attached tank company which, with their high rate of fire, armor protection and mobility attempt to break the momentum of the offensive by offering an intense resistance. If the attack maintains its vive, the defending tanks withdraw to overwatch positions behind the dismounted infantry, and, joined by the cannons of the ICVs, create a barrage of fire against the exposed attacker. If the attack is decisively beaten, the defending armor will counterattack, retake the original position, and start the process over. If, during the target servicing phase, the attacker appears too strong, the defending infantry can withdraw to the next position with the armor (and hopefully a reserve) covering their retrograde.

The "active defense" thus attempts to achieve maximum density of fire with minimum loss of depth. It is designed to take advantage of substantial pre-attack terrain preparation (obstacles, minefields, infantry entrenchments, hull defilade tank firing ramps, pre-established "killing zones", etc.) without making the defense static or positional. While it seeks to maintain a disproportionate and highly favorable loss/exchange ratio, in order to rob the attacker of his quantitative superiority, organizational cohesion and initial momentum, its use of attrition does not preclude (indeed it produces the necessary conditions for) maneuver. The stress on "activeness" is recognition of the need to keep the attacker off balance, uncertain of the next impending engagement, and precautiously over-concerned with the security of his own flank.[8]

As a tactic "active defense" was predicated on unique operational realities. The dominance of broken terrain in the border areas of the FRG - many small gaps separated by closed areas (forests, small towns etc.) which open into and diverge from a series of "traffic circles"; the location of the most favorable defensive terrain close to the interbloc border; and the necessity of covering every potential approach, while responding to the attacker's selected concentrations of main effort, have dictated both the force structure and technological emphasis of NATO's armies. Operationally the "active defense" admits the necessity of decisive engagement but unlike its traditional antecedents - it attempts to accept central battle on its own terms (unlike the positional defense) without giving up or risking the irretrievable loss of the territory and people that the defense is there to protect (unlike the mobile defense). A defense which offers the best hope for early war termination or the best deterrent for delayed nuclear escalation should be disgarded with no small caution.[9]

II. MODELING OF ALTERNATIVE DEFENSE CONCEPTS

The purpose of the symposium was not to invent an alternative to NATO's strategic concept of Forward Defense but examine the contribution alternative tactics, technologies, and force structure designs might make when employed as an implementation of, or supplement to, Forward Defense. One of the most interesting and useful aspects of the symposium was the large number and wide variety of alternative concepts to current forces that were proposed. Independent of the analytical insights and modeling results, the presentation of the documentation and comparative structuring of alternative concepts juxtaposed with current tactics was a major contribution. [10] In all, twenty-three specific proposals were developed and analyzed for the purposes of the symposium. The level of analysis of the modeling ranged from theater to battalion level combat and likewise the purposes for which the simulations were conducted ranged from heuristic excursions to experimental force structure design to cost/benefit tradeoffs.

At the level of <u>battalion</u> the work of Hofmann, Huber, and Steiger, "on Reactive Defense Options" (hereafter cited as Huber, et al), utilizing one of the most realistic computer simulations (designed to portray tactics and terrain in a direct fire battle), investigated fourteen different unit structures covering a wide range of concepts. These were organized into several categories:

ACTIVE DEFENSES

    Option A   Panzer Grenadier Bn. (Current Structure, No Tanks)

Option B Reinforced Panzer Grenadier Bn. (Current, with Tank Company)
Option C Reinforced Panzer Bn. (Current, with Infantry Company)
Option D Reinforced Panzer Grenadier Bn. (1990 Infantry Structure with Tank Company)

REACTIVE DEFENSES

Static Area
Option E Technokommandos (Afheldt's concept)
Option F Swiss Territorial
Option G Area Defense (SAS infantry concept)
Option H Austrian Hedgehog

Dynamic Area
Option I Shield Force (Loser concept)
Option K Cavalry Delay (SAS mobile concept)
Option L Cellular Defense (Fureder concept)

Fire Barrier
Option M Antitank-Air Defense Belt (Gerber concept)
Option N Fire Barrier (Hannig concept)
Option P Barrier Brigade (Huber selective fire barrier concept)

Huber, et al portrayal of active defenses most closely resembles NATO's current tactical approach in that their focus is on attrition of attacking forces at a favorable loss-exchange ratio, while yielding territory as necessary to maintain defensive integrity. In addition, they rely on subsequent use of armored maneuver against the weakened attacker to destroy his forces and regain lost territory. Static Area Defenses reflect a number of approaches for the use of infantry, from Afheldt's area defense concept employing Technokommandos (Option E), to the more conventional Swiss positional and Austrian "tout azimuth" hedgehog defense concepts. One can argue that the Swiss concept is not an "area defense" tactic (certainly the Swiss do not categorize it as such) in that it concentrates a high fire density by employing the secure flanks of Alpine territory, however, all of these options do show a reliance on a high saturation of infantry antitank weapons to succeed in destroying enemy armored formations. The Dynamic Area Defense options are distinguished by their use of tactical mobility and space to maintain a favorable loss exchange ratio. In this sense, they resemble the covering forces of the "active defense". Unlike the latter, which uses the covering force to shape the attackers ingress as a means of setting up a decisive battle, the Dynamic Area Defenses seek to avoid decisive battle with continued retrograde in depth. As a result, these options tend to limit the employment of defending forces on the battlefield to delaying actions only. Fire Barrier defensive options propose a fire belt along the line of force employment (in conjunction with mines and obstacles) to slow the penetration of the attack, obstacles which are reinforced with mobile maneuver units. Thus, the attack can be slowed and disrupted initially through means of the fire barrier, and if successful, the remainder of attacking forces are then engaged by maneuver units.

While the depth of insight and range of application of the Huber, et al model has only been scratched -- given their conclusion that Reactive Defense modules could contribute as a supplement to NATO existing structure, the proof of this will necessitate a simulation with a much broader scope at the brigade/corps level.

At the <u>brigade</u> level the work of Schmitz, Reidelhuber, and Niemeyer on "Long-Term Trends in Force Structuring" (hereinafter Niemeyer, et al) also addressed a number of options, several of which overlap with those already discussed.

    Option A. Active Defense (very similar to Huber, et al Option D)

    Option B. Tank Destroyer (comparable to Huber, et al "Dynamic Area Defense", Option L)

    Option C. Dispersed Anti-Tank Infantry (comparable in density to Huber, et al "Technokommando" Static Area Defense, Option E)

    Option D. Tank Destroyer with Infantry (a variant of Huber, et al "Fire Barrier", Option N)

    Option E. Mobile ATGM (a less dense version of Huber, et al "Fire Barrier", Option M)

By taking a battalion slice of the combat assets these can be compared to those of Huber, et al in terms of direct fire weapons density and tactical depth, as is illustrated in Figure 2. The Niemeyer, et al work provides a unique approach to relate combat effectiveness into the broader structural confines of procurement and sustainability costs. While they portray a range of tactics, unfortunately the impact of terrain upon their outcomes is not addressed - leaving no evidence as to either the "optimized" applicability across the breadth of the front, nor the best composite "mix" of terrain specific formations.

At the <u>corps</u> level, the idea of mixing dismounted Static Area infantry as a series of dispersed hedgehog defenses with the employment of heavy armored counterattack reserves was discussed at length in terms of the British experiments with the "Framework Defense Concept".[11] Although under this concept the proportion of static versus maneuver battalions appears to be no higher than 1:4 (or 20%), there appears to be considerable uncertainty as to: the size of the individual dispersed infantry elements;

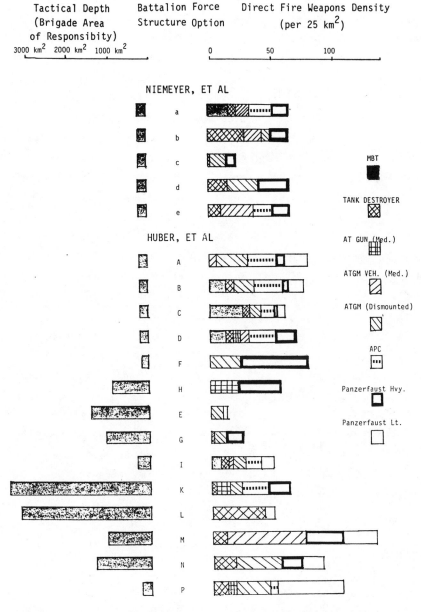

Fig. 2. Comparison of battalion options: depth vs. density

their required mobility; C³ and logistic support within the Corps structure; not to mention the combat effectiveness of the static option relative to heavy mechanized infantry. These are issues which must be addressed before the British "Framework" experience can be sufficiently evaluated.

The only theater level modeling results that were presented were those conducted by Weiner in his "Analyzing Alternative Concepts for the Defense of NATO." This work contrasted the requirements of three options: Fortified Barrier (a static but indepth version of Huber, et al Fire Barrier Options M,N,P); Forward Response (a combination of Air/Land Battle and FOFA with futuristic technology to create an extensive second echelon interdiction belt); and Distributed Area Defense (a variant of Huber, et al Static Area Defense, Opt. E). Weiner presented these concepts as pure or "ideal" types - not as a methodology to question relative effectiveness but instead, given equal performance in stopping an attack, to ask what level of resources would be required to implement these concepts. The contrasting of "ideal" types is useful, in that it clearly defines the fundamental differences of alternative concepts. But while theater level simulation is sorely needed to address the battalion/brigade level questions raised by Huber, et al and Niemeyer, et al, this presentation neither provided the detail of combat results nor the intermixing of static/barrier units with the maneuver forces to provide the necessary answers.

In summary the symposium provided a wide range of modeling approaches, with much substantive insight. However, both the comparability of results and the assessment of the attractiveness of individual options must be limited to the tactical level. Given the absence of at least a corps (and preferably a theater) level simulation little can be inferred as to: the overall attractiveness of the "defensive efficiency" hypothesis; the overall cost effectiveness of any single option; the advantages of a mix of concepts when employed synergistically; or the relative strengths and weaknesses of NATO's current force structure as a "theater" implementation of Forward Defense.

OPERATIONAL ROBUSTNESS

In providing a critique of the "new" alternative defense concepts, one is faced with several concerns. On the one hand, it is always easier to criticize than create. Many of these alternatives are still in the conceptual stage -- subject to change and considerable latitude in interpretation. Without the paternal designers present to defend or at least clarify their arguments and assumptions, we are evaluating their prodigy third hand: as translated from the conceptual level to the specifics (types and numbers of weapons, force structure design, etc.) needed for wargaming; as then applied to a Forward Defense operational mission; and finally as tactically portrayed in a combat simulation. At least some of these proponents do not even believe in Forward Defense and would be quick to denounce these bastardized offspring as illegitimate. On the other hand, with the growth of political and public interest in the issues of conventional defense, there is the danger of popular misconception -- that there is a magic tactic or technological silver bullet which would provide equal protection for a fraction of the financial sacrifice. If there is an easy formula for a secure defense, the evidence presented in this volume suggests we haven't found it. It is in that spirit that this critique is presented.

Most of the "new" defense concepts were developed from the bottom up (as they should be) from an experimental small unit tactic or innovative technological application. But what may work wonders at the squad, platoon, or company level, and be applicable to the battalion, may be disasterous when generated across the Central Front or, even worse, applied to only one individual national sector. Thus, our interest in lifting the focal plane from the tactical to the operational level -- division, corps and wider. Simultaneously, however, the issue of robustness applies to all levels of combat. This raises questions as to how dependent a particular concept is upon a potentially weak link such as: a given weapons technology that is either potentially obsolescent or so immature that the unproven performance claims of its developers must be viewed with skepticism; a force structure so preoccupied with solving one problem that it leaves itself extremely vulnerable to others; or the application of a tactic, which must be employed by draftees, but requires each to have the genius of a Clausewitz. This is not to say that NATO's concept of Forward Defense or "active defense" tactics do not suffer from problems of operational robustness, but at least it is not a lack of professional military awareness of where the weaknesses are - just a lack of political will and financial resources to solve them.

A. Command and Control on an Entropic Battlefield

The most memorable feature of tactical combat is the uncertainty, confusion, disorganization, misunderstanding, unreceived communications, lost formations, and just plain stupidity which are best described in the age old epitath of failed command - "the fog of war." There is a reason military establishments are traditionally associated with discipline, structured thought and simplicity -- in the chaotic environment of battle, military units need all the order they can muster. One of the major problems with the "new" alternative tactics, those that call for wide dispersal or retrograde over extended depth, is that they attempt to make an art form out of anarchy.

The term Technokommando is indicative of the problem. There is no doubt that a highly trained professional can: operate in small units behind the advancing enemy with little hope of return, rescue or relief; engage a column of enemy armor using a single weapon (within range of small arms grazing fire from the targets); move across an unsecured countryside in a civilian vehicle; rearm at a lager which has miraculously remained a NATO secret during peacetime; and then repeat it all again the next day. An elite commando, maybe, but an 18 year old draftee, a reservist with less than a weeks call up, a G.I. "Joe" or "Tommy" in a foreign land? This isn't a description of a conventional defense; at best, it is "high tech" sabotage.[12]

One of the major problems of the Distributed Area Defense is that its' proponents do not give the attacker the benefit of adjusting his concept of operations -- from a broad front attack with forces concentrated for a breakthrough to a rapid occupation strategy emphasizing deep, albeit narrow, penetrations to quickly seize strategic objectives with subsequent policing of bypassed areas. Based on the data presented by Huber, et al, what Soviet Western TVD commander wouldn't consider himself worthy of his Marshall's baton to march his columns from Pilsen to Munich, Meiningen to Karlsruhe, Thuringer Wald to Frankfurt, Magdeburg to the Rhine, the Elbe to the Dutch border, with an excursion to the Kiel Canal, all in seven days for the loss of 180 battalions -- less than a quarter of the active Warsaw Pact forces deployed in Central Europe (only 13.5% after reinforcement)? In Weiner's test/simulation where the attacker did not adjust his concept of operations the amount of FRG territory lost was between 40,000 and 80,000 Km^2 - which if measured as deep strategic access corridors rather than a shallow broad front acquisition would be consistent with the above claim. The nature of a campaign against an area defense thus resembles less traditional battle than a road march through a hostile environment - similar to the Soviet invasion of Afghanistan.

If the Soviets can stoically cope with six years of resistance in Afghanistan, what would be the risk in a residual policing action if the prize was West Germany? The guerilla adopts his tactics because he is weak, not because he wants to be weak. He employs the ambush to achieve local superiority rather than disperse his assets to attack outnumbered and lose. Historically, the turning point in a successfull guerilla campaign is marked by the structured transition from dispersed small unit tactics to battalion and larger size concentrations. By distributing armed combatants randomly about the country, todays Technokommando may serve as the cadre for a future resistance movement to a Soviet occupation of Western Europe -- but the dismantling of NATO's "active defense" is the surest way to make this a self-fulfilling event.

The disintegration of command and loss of unit cohesion are endemic to the dispersed area defense or deep retrograde tactics. If anything, the modeling of these "new" concepts is too generous, since modern simulation and war gaming methodologies typically do not include such intangible factors as troop morale, leadership uncertainty, and confusion induced misconceptions of the tactical situation. For example, in both the Weiner and British modeling of the Distributed Area/Framework Defense concepts three dimensional terrain boards were employed in the war gaming. While this approach can be uniquely insightful, the portrayal of an ambush when the defender is omniscient in knowing where the targeted unit is, its strength and combat formation, is certainly less than realistic.

Many of the "new" concepts do not depend solely on light, dispersed infantry, but would support them with mobile reserves and indirect fire or use their static structure as a framework around which to maneuver. However, these tactics are not self-organizing, they require extensive coordination and communication. This requires a level of command attention which is not nearly as manpower efficient as the conceptual proponents assume. While emerging technology in electronic communications has the potential to support a greater dispersal of non-hierarchically structured subunits (through the use of packet radios, burst digital transmission, and jump-modal relay subscription nets), the state-of-the art is still embryonic, and attempts to model such a system as could be available in the mid-1990s would be hypothetical at best. In many cases the infrastructure overhead and procurement costs of these advanced electronics would be no small fraction of the Technokommando armament budget.

Huber, et al are correct when they cite theoretical and experimental research in the US which showed that the "dynamic density defense" permitted an outnumbered defender to exploit tactical depth in a series of short engagements -- the trading of space for an efficient loss exchange ratio <u>vis a vis</u> the attacker. However, the same work also highlighted several key aspects of this type of defense which the proponents of deep retrograde have tended to ignore in their conceptual designs. First, the purpose of this tactic is not cost effective attrition, but rather the whittling down of the attackers quantitative superiority (through losses, disorganization and the presentation of a situation in which his massive preplanned indirect fire bombardment is less effective) in order to seek out (not avoid) decisive engagement on more favorable terms for the defender. Second, the effectiveness of the "dynamic density defense" is not spatially unlimited. There are a finite number of successive engagements a given defending unit can be exposed to after which the rebounding process itself introduces disorganization and command entropy. It works best when each successive fall back from position to position becomes shorter. Third, when conducted beyond the depth of the battalion sector, the need to stablize on prepared positions or introduce heavy armor reserves becomes a necessity. Lastly, a successful "dynamic density defense" puts a premium on direct command orchestration, careful coordination with adjacent formations and extensive reliance on communications. It is a tactic to offset some of the mass and momentum of a concentrated breakthrough on carefully selected and narrow sectors of the front. When pursued in depth, across a broad front, in the absence of prepared positions, without a strong body of main battle tanks and reserves, or if conducted with open flanks, it is the attacker, not the defender who gains the most from NATO's employment of this concept.

In summary, the new concepts can not violate the traditional requirements of troop control. Cheap solutions are either ineffective in sustained combat or expensive to command. Dispersal and deep retrograde demand more communications, not less, and the technology needed to replace upper echelon structures for an army of "Technokommandos" is still in the realm of science fiction.

B. The ATGM Fetish

The antitank guided missile plays a major role in virtually all of the "new" alternative defense concepts. Indeed, to the extent that most of them differ structurally, it is in the mix and density of the three different classes of ATGM: the specialized Tank Destroyer mounting a long range heavy (5" to 6" warhead) missile (such as the US ITV TOW and FRG HOT): the collateral ATGM mounted on infantry vehicles for secondary antiarmor protection (US IFV "Bradley" with TOW and FRG Marder with Milan); and the man-portable systems for dismounted infantry (Dragon and Milan). Given the level of ATGM saturation -- most of the alternative concepts, with the exception of the two neutral examples (Swiss and Austrian), could be characterized less as infantry formations with their traditional dismounted mobility than antitank units which are structured around infantry.

The possibility of an infantry team killing a $1,000,000 + main battle tank with a $10,000 weapon at a couple thousand meter range with the accuracy of a sharp shooter has had a narcotic effect on force structure designers. Recognizing that for alternative concepts to have credibility as options for NATO's "active defenses", they must be able to address the Warsaw Pact armor threat, would-be tactical inventors have become ATGM "junkies" -- in which a realistic appreciation of the dangers of over reliance on a single technology has been dulled by the dependence of a given structure's viability on that technology. In fact, the ATGM has long had a number of significant limitations, and current developmental trends do not bode well for a disproportionate overemphasis.

o ATGMs have a slow target servicing firing rate, determined by the need to capture and maintain effective guidance of the missile in flight and slowness of reloading the launcher. To make up for this when facing a massed high speed armored attack the defense needs a large quantity of systems deployed.

o The dismounted short range ATGMs are only marginally man-portable, requiring several infantrymen to move the launcher and just a few reloads. The more difficult the terrain, the harder to resupply the firing position. In order to engage enemy armor at night, in smoke or on a "dirty battlefield, they require a high technology sight (light intensification or thermal imaging) which adds both weight and expense.

o ATGM launchers are very vulnerable. Because the man-portable systems cannot be fired from bunkers, buildings, or with overhead protection, the crew must be exposed during the firing, flight, and reloading to both small arms and artillery fire. This is exacerbated by the obvious signature at firing and the difficulty of changing positions quickly. Light armored vehicles provide considerable protection from suppression but are themselves vulnerable to the proliferation of antitank weapons and thus are best used from ambush rather than a stand up fight. All ATGM controls are vulnerable to the introduction of low level laser counteroptics technology -- an area where the Soviets are already testing a prototype.[13]

o The introduction of Chobham and "Special" armor on fourth generation main battle tanks effectively defeats most ATGM HEAT warheads on the frontal area of the vehicle. Larger warheads (or tandum charges) require larger missiles, and will thus make the ATGM even less man-portable and launching vehicles will be able to carry even fewer missiles than the current basic load. New developments in ceramic applique, siliceous core, and explosive armor suggest that the threat of ATGMs against heavy vehicles (40 tons or more) will continue to fade substantially over the next decade. On the other hand, the inexpensive light armored vehicles of the "new" alternative concepts will be increasingly vulnerable to a growing quantity of antiarmor systems.[14]

o The much vaunted accuracy at extended range of ATGMs is significantly overrated. The long-range systems can acquire only a fraction of the targets within their maximum reach. The short-range man-portable systems, with their lack of mobility, can only cover narrow sectors.

o While broken, undulating terrain (represented by hills, forest patches, or suburbs) provide ATGM a good combination of concealment, protection, and target exposure, this only represents an average of 50% of the terrain in the Forward Defense area. In open terrain (where armor can deploy in mass and at high speed but ATGM intervisibility is reduced by even small obstructions) and closed areas (dense forests or large cities) where range is short the ATGM is of only marginal utility. And, as illustrated in Figure 3, the difference within and between corps severely limits the general applicability of ATGM tailored defenses.

o The alleged cost effectiveness of ATGM is misleading. With missile costs fifty to one hundred times more expensive than the tank round, NATO countries have greatly reduced live fire training (in some Western Armies as few as four live rounds per battalion per year) which has had the effect of dropping ATGM crew proficiency from the advertised 90% hit probability to 30%. To the extent reserves are expected to man ATGM defenses, training and the high cost of maintaining crew proficiency must be considered.

A common theme among most of the proposed concepts is their aversion to the main battle tank. In its fourth generation design, this pariah of the modern battlefield can hit, with its high velocity cannon, 93% of targets which can be attacked by the heaviest ATGM. At average engagement ranges it can service five times the targets with near equal probability of a kill. Unlike the ATGM, its gun is not limited to minimum range restriction and it fires effective infantry support ammunition - high explosive, smoke and illumination rounds. Modern tanks mount effective thermal and night vision devices, can move rapidly across country, and can deploy through the heaviest artillery bombardment. With advanced armor, it is primarily vulnerable only to another MBT, and then, when firing from hull defilade in a hasty defense, can consistently extract a favorable loss/exchange ratio against an exposed attacker. In fact, in the Huber, et al simulations, where a company of tanks was added to the infantry battalion (never exceeding 20% of the direct fire antiarmor assets) they accounted for more than half the attrition of all attacking armored vehicles and virtually 80% of the opposing MBT losses.

If the MBT is the best antitank weapon NATO possesses, why do the "new" concepts abandon it? The appeal of the ATGM is that it can provide infantry with an antiarmor capability at a fraction of the high procurement expediture of an MBT -- thus more systems can be fielded and the density of the defense effectively strengthened. However, the operational limitations of ATGMs are numerous and serious. Thus, the financial incentive to field large quantities of ATGM has the potential of fostering self-defeating force structures. Given current trends in technology, a more effective strategy than the proliferation of ATGM would be to focus on increasing quantities of tanks with high-velocity antitank guns that can penetrate modern armor. To the extent that financial constraints do not permit a meaningful increase in tank inventories, viable alternatives

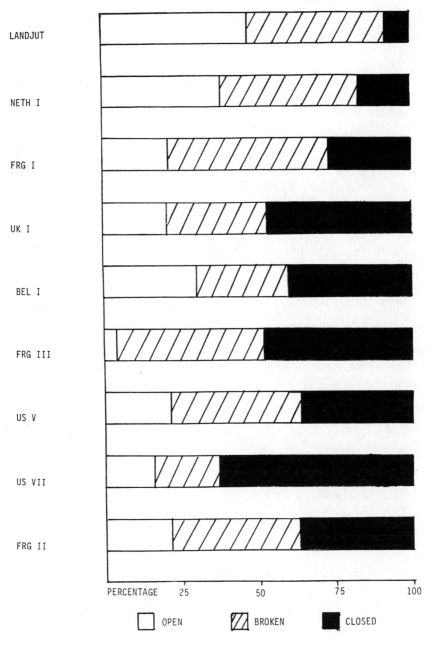

Fig. 3. Terrain distribution on central front by corps sector 15 (100 km depth from FRG Eastern border)

to ATGM in the form of both antitank guns and tank destroyers (using high velocity kinetic energy guns) may prove to be an effective compromise. Less expensive than tanks, and more effective than ATGM, these systems should be seriously considered in the context of defense options, and receive greater attention that they do currently.

C. Counterattack

Within NATO, the offensive role of maneuver forces is readily acknowledged, but generally not discussed in polite company. Strategically, the alliance has a self-prescribed defensive mission, and talk of driving East in sweeping counteroffensives (whether advocated by proponents of maneuver theology or denounced by those so preoccupied with Soviet paranoid sensitivities that they would deny the West any modern defense lest it be "provocative") is sheer rhetoric -- as inflamatory as it is ill-informed. At the operational level, however, NATO Forward Defense doctrine under Flexible Response has always recognized the political need to restore the territorial integrity of its borders and the military advantage in counter attacking the exposed flanks of a Warsaw Pact breakthrough. The problem is that under the current and growing imbalance of forces, NATO's conventional forces will be lucky to maintain a cohesive defense that is being pushed back let alone free up enough forces to decisively attack and take the initiative from the aggressor.

Tactically, the stark distinction between offense and defense breaks down under the "active" tactics NATO currently envisages. While taking advantage of favorable and prepared terrain, a high proportion of the maneuver companies/battalions are in a continual process of maneuver and used as fire "brigades" to:

- o Momentarily shore up a faltering position;
- o Replace depleted formations on line;
- o Initiate an attack to cover a retrograde;
- o Desperately run "head on" into the face of an enemy OMG to plug a gap;
- o Overrun an air assault or armored raiding detachment which has penetrated into the depth of the defense;
- o Exploit the disorganization and exposure which the offensive suffers after a unsuccessful attack;
- o Counter the establishment of a bridgehead over a major river obstacle;
- o And, last but not least lead a break out when out-flanked and in danger of being enveloped.

The dynamics of this level of combat, with its unpredictable volatility of outcome, is extremely difficult to model -- particularly when it occurs randomly across the breadth of the front. Yet it is the structural weakness, by intentional design, of the Reactive Defenses that they can not react offensively. This limitation is brilliantly illustrated in the work of Huber, et al. In the various battles they report on, every case in which the defense had the advantage of considerable terrain preparation (minefields, pre-selected firing positions, field fortifications), the results of the combat ended in one of four generic results: <u>Breakthrough</u> - the cohesion of the defense is broken, unable to stop the remaining attacking forces from deep exploitation; <u>Attack Thwarted</u> - the defense remains intact and decisively inflicts such high attrition that the attacking elements must disengage; <u>Attack Narrowly Stalled</u> - the assault grinds to a halt because of the severity of the attackers' losses but the two forces remain in contact; <u>Penetration</u> - the attack achieves a break "in to" but not "through" the defenses, both sides remain locked, the combat action falling off due to heavy losses, mutual exhaustion, and problems of ammunition resupply over a contested battlefield.

The good news of the Huber, et al study is that on the average, the defense holds twice as often as the attack achieves a breakthrough. The bad news is that in over half the cases modeled, the defense becomes weakened to the point of being interpenetrated. The lower the defensive density and/or the shorter the range of intervisibility, the more likely the threat of interpenetration. This is the classic situation in which the timely arrival of a "2nd echelon" can dramatically overrun the defenders isolated positions and reverse the disproportionate attrition expected from a successful defense. The tragedy of an interpenetrated battlefield is that in many of these cases the defenders had substantial strength left (over half were within 20% of the attackers quantity of weapons). But because of the enemy within their ranks the defense could not reestablish its cohesion even if the "2nd Echelon" was delayed by interdiction. In essence the likelihood of interpenetration is an unaudited cost inversely proportional to the "defense efficiency hypothesis.

The evidence presented on the interpenetration problem is a powerful argument against a heavy reliance on light infantry/light armored formations. The value of a "2nd echelon" to break the stalemate works both ways -- the timely arrival of a NATO reserve can sweep the defenses clear of the penetrators or, at a minimum suppress the attackers to permit an orderly withdrawal.[16] The problem with Reactive light infantry/light armored forces is that they:

o Are more likely to fall victim to interpenetration;

- o Are more vulnerable to sustaining heavy casualties in the process of withdrawal during and after the penetration (due to their lack of armor protection and mobility);

- o Cannot be used to save a penetrated "light" unit due to a "designed-in" lack of counterattack capability;

- o And, because of these weaknesses, siphon off heavy mechanized assets from where they are most needed into cross-attached "penny packets" where they take heavier losses by being forced into more exposure during rescue operations.

The lack of counterattack capability is not in and of itself sufficient to rule out a given conceptual design for a battalion or even a brigade size supplementary force, if carefully deployed on terrain which minimizes its chance of interpenetration. But, until proposed Reactive Defense concepts can be demonstrated to both withstand penetration better than "active defenses," and at least launch successful extractive counter attacks, any claims as to their relative cost efficiency or general replaceability relative to todays mechanized infantry ought to be severely muted.

D. Crisis Stability and NATO's Deterrent

NATO's operational concept of Forward Defense does not operate in isolation as the ultimate arbiter of tactical acceptability. Rather, it is a reflection of the broader strategy of Flexible Response which, as the doctrinal incarnation of NATO's political will, focuses on a much broader spectrum of deterrence which subsumes defense but also transcends it. Because NATO cannot predict in advance what contingency might trigger the outbreak of hostilities, it requires its conventional forces to cover a multitude of potential scenarios. Unfortunately, versatility for all eventualities comes at the expense of maximized effectiveness in one.

For example, if the West could know with certainty that the only threat posed to Central Europe was that of a short warning attack by in place forces, enormous efficiencies could be obtained by not needing to maintain and modernize mobilizable reserves, preposition equipment for reinforcement, or invest billions in maintaining a maritime defense of the Atlantic SLOC. This would provide more than sufficient resources to procure and maintain a fully ready and heavily mechanized maneuver force in Central Europe. At the other exteme, if an attack was presumed possible only after months of extensive Warsaw Pact mobilization and reinforcement, the Western Armies of the Central Front could reduce their active units to cadre and training strengths and, instead, reinvest those resources required for active force readiness into large scale weapons procurement, extensive ammunition stocks, and a mobilization structure for millions of reserves. In this case, NATO would be able to afford supplementary permanent field fortifications, multiple belts of Barrier Brigades backed up by dense, but Distributed Area defenses in depth. If NATO designs its force structure to be maximized for only a single scenario, it automatically increases the attractiveness of other offensive contingencies.

One of the problems of many of the "new" alternative defense concepts is that their proponents are not content to view them as tactical supplements to current mechanized forward defenses which would in fact be an added expense, and in competition with already programmed resources. Instead, they claim operational universality and, as a replacement force structure, large financial savings. One of the ways to achieve this is to employ non-active manpower drawn from the reserves upon mobilization. The problem is that given the growth in the Warsaw Pact forward offensive capabilities, NATO's existing active forces, as currently structured, would be hard pressed to conduct an effective defense with less than seventy-two hours of mobilization and deployment. These are formations with a high percentage of manning, the majority of the troops involved in day-to-day training, and with sufficient densities of heavy armor and mechanized assets to at least conduct a delaying/mobile defense to provide time for the fleshing out of the higher echelon supporting infrastructure.

Thus, NATO's peacetime requirement for a rapidly deployable defense places several severe restraints on the attractiveness of many of the alternative concepts. First, those that would gain economic efficiency by depending upon reserve manpower would automatically fail this requirement on the basis of inadequate readiness. Second, to the extent that some of these concepts demonstrate defensive viability in the simulation and war game results, they all depend more heavily than the "active defenses" for time in position prior to attack. The greater the dependence on minefields and barriers and/or the lower the level of mechanized resources available within the structure, the more a given concept is vulnerable to the exigencies of a short warning attack. Third, in an environment dominated, at least initially, by a high degree of fluidity, a concept which depends upon dismounted infantry firing ATGMs lacks the mobility to be deployed to critical sectors and, in the event of a meeting engagement, is in danger of being overrun from the march before it can deploy a sufficient density of its own antiarmor fires.

On the other hand, the structures involving a heavy concentration of tank destroyers, designed to be employed in deep retrograde tactics, may in fact serve a valuable function in screening and slowing deep penetrations of the attacker. Likewise in this environment ready but dismounted infantry formations taking up a distributed defense in the rear area, particularly on high speed axes of advance, might, by using the cover of local built-up areas, provide a containing role against raiding parties and the advance elements of an OMG, or serve as a framework around which the mechanized forces can restablize the defense. The point is that our understanding of tactical defense concepts (whether the current "active" or hypothetical Reactive) needs to be broadened beyond the relatively favorable posture of a prepared position. This is an area which, (along with the nature of fluid battle, armored maneuver, and the dynamics of meeting engagements) existing simulation methodologies have not addressed in much detail, and clearly needs further research and systematic development.

Another aspect of NATO's deterrent which conventional force design cannot ignore is the requirement that its defenses not only fight throughout the conventional phase of battle, but also participate in the transition to nuclear fire. With the large-scale introduction of nuclear artillery into the Warsaw Pact ground forces during the early 1980s, and the growing possibility that Soviet higher echelon artillery may be equipped with enhanced radiation warheads, NATO can no longer dismiss the vulnerability of its own formations. One of the greatest challenges for the defense in the nuclear transition process is redeploying its formations (originally concentrated to provide sufficient density to withstand a conventional assault), so they can be quickly dispersed laterally, and in depth, lest they be an attractive target for a nuclear strike. If we were harsh with respect to the Distributed Area and deep retrograde concepts for their command and control problems when operating widely dispersed, this same criticism is equally valid for the "active defense" under a nuclear-scared posture. In this environment, some of the static, high density concepts would automatically be ruled out due to their lack of organic mobility and thus vulnerability. On the other hand, if the Distributed Area Defense has any relevance as a tactic generally applied across the breadth of the front, its most natural habitat would be the nuclear battlefield. Despite their irrelevancy as a forward element in a conventional defense, NATO may yet need to address the requirement for "neutron" Technokommandos. Hardly what the designers had in mind, it is a direct consequence of their political efforts to weaken the modernization of NATO's mechanized Forward Defenses.

IV. FUTURE DIRECTIONS FOR COMBAT SIMULATION

In summary, what was presented at the symposium was compelling evidence that modern operations research techniques - combat modeling, simulation, and wargaming - while not providing conclusive answers or finding "new" solutions are in a very significant way asking the right questions and producing valuable insights with respect to the nature of the modern battlefield. Insights which, as a function of the rigorous and auditable methodology by which they were derived, can be subjected to empirical testing, field experimentation, and professional military commentary.

Nevertheless, if combat simulation is not to lapse into a pseudoscience - eminently rational but woefully irrelevant - the current trend away from mathematical abstractions of lethal physics to the representation of tactics, terrain, unit formation and force structure must continue. Specifically:

- o As broad as the representation of alternative tactics illustrated in the symposium was, notably absent were not only maneuver defensive concepts (mobile defense, FOFA and Air/Land Battle counter-mobility interdiction, and large unit flanking counter attacks) but also newly emerging Soviet offensive innovations: the short but intense "fire strike"; verticle envelopment and aerial descent; not to mention raiding tactics and the Operational Maneuver Group (OMG).

- o Given the importance the Soviets attach to the "encounter battle" or "meeting engagement" the absence of this combat form from such a wide sampling of modelers and methodologies suggests a serve limitation with respect to any generalization of results.

- o Much remains to be done in terms of testing proposed "new" force structures <u>vis a vis</u> both a wider sampling of terrain and in the dynamic combination of differing alternative structures in a combined operation. (For example, the British "Framework Defense" is a variant of a Distributed Area Defense at the battalion/brigade level, but from the perspective of a corps is a minority element of a much larger mechanized/maneuver concept). Similarly, many other combinations of two or more differing structures need to be investigated in terms of their complementary synergy and/or incompatibility.

- o Nor have all the technological options been adequately represented. The data represented in the modeling does not reflect the Soviet fielding of: tanks with "active armor"; their development and offensive employment of new fire support munitions (scatterable mines, ICM submunitions, "liquid fire", fuel/air explosives, and particulate smoke); or the introduction of close support aircraft such as the <u>SU-25</u> "Frogfoot" and <u>MI-28</u> "Havoc" attack helicopter. On the other hand, also ignored was Western interest in the development of a heavy mechanized infantry fighting vehicle (protected with "special armor" against ATGM HEAT warheads) or a high mobility tank destroyer mounting a rapid fire hypervelocity gun, which are as credible options as many discussed at the symposium. Combat simulation of future force structures ought to include new (or potential) technological developments of both sides.

- o One of the least understood problems of modern combat is the "transitional defense" - a conventional defense that is attacked in the process of converting from a peacetime posture to wartime deployment, a conventional defense which must transition to a nuclear battlefield. Both of these situations: represent potential defensive vulnerabilities which, to date, have been swept under the analytical rug; are relevant to the consideration of alternative NATO force postures, technology and tactics; and raise many issues which need to be addressed with the rigor and insight of simulation and modeling.

These comments should be taken not as a critique but a challenge. The development of sophisticated simulation techniques - as illustrated in the Huber, et al BASIS model and the Niemeyer, et al hierarchical war game/simulation have the capacity to address these issues both with methodological rigor and militarily relevant insight. As interest in improving NATO's conventional defense continues to increase, and the Warsaw Pact threat to Europe expands unabated there will be a pressing need for combat simulation. Combatant simulation will play an important role in Western defense decision making if the practitioners of operations research continue to develop their techniques so that they can address important issues.

REFERENCES.

1. The two best informed and innovative of the reformers being: Steven L. Canby "Territorial Defense in Central Europe" Armed Forces and Society, Fall, 1980; Steven L. Canby "Light Infantry in Perspective" Infantry July/Aug 1984; and F. Uhle-Wettler Gefectsfeld Mitteleurupa: Gefhr der Untertechnisierung von Streitkraften (Stuttgart: Bernard & Graefe Verlag 1980).

2. For two recent surveys of the historical evolution of infantry see: Paddy Griffith Forward into Battle: Fighting Tactics from Waterloo to Vietnam, (Sussex: Antony Bird Pub. 1981); and John A. English On Infantry, (N.Y.: Praeger Pub. 1984). The classic and still unrivaled work on mechanized infantry is F. M. von Senger und Etterlin Die Panzergrendaiere: Geschite und Gestalt der Mechanisierten Infantry, 1930-1960 (Munich: J. F. Lehmanns Verlag 1961); and for the best current appreciation see Richard E. Simpkin Mechanized Infantry (Oxford: Brassey's Pub. 1980).

3. Comparable data for NATO and the Warsaw Pact were derived from: David C. Isby Weapons and Tactics of the Soviet Army (London: Janes Pub. 1981); David C. Isby and Charles Kamps Jr. Armies of NATO's Central Front (London: Janes Pub. 1985).

4. For an up-to-date historical survey see: Rolf Hilmes and Gunter Lippert "Die Mechanisierung der Infantry in Ost und West" Part I and II, Soldat und Technik April/July 1984.

5. For comments on this problem see: F. M. von Senger und Etterlin "Trends in the Mechanization of Armies", Defense Yearbook 1976/77 (London: RUSI, and Brassey's Pub. 1977); G. Brugman "The German View of the Role of Infantry on the Battlefield", RUSI Journal, December 1980; F. Uhle-Wettler "Infantry Versus Tank: Common Sense and High Technology" NATO's Sixteen Nations, June-July 1984.

6. Comments by Gen. Donn A. Starry quoted in P. A. Karber "Force Restructuring and New Weapons Technologies: Relationships in NATO Armies and Operations" Paper presented at the European-American Workshop, Ebeuhausen, FRG: September 1978.

7. P. A. Karber, "The Soviet Anti-Tank Debate" Survival, No. 18, June, 1976.

8. P. A. Karber "Battlefield Leverage: Hierarchy and Transition in Central Battle" Paper presented at Division '86 conference, Ft. Monroe: February 1979.

9. P. A. Karber "Pladoyer fur die Vorneverteidigung" Pro Pace: Beitrange

10. This unique contribution can be found in the work of Karl Steiger who conducted an extensive survey of current and proposed alternative tactical concepts. Steiger takes the debate out of the realm of theory and hyperbole by placing each alternative structure in a comparable context (forced to address a specific threat on real terrain). His exhaustive review of this diverse literature and careful portrayal of tactical manuevers represents the highest realization of the potentials of military operations research. Steigers documentation, produced at Fochbereich Informotik, Hochschule der Bundeswehr Munchen, includes: "Die Konzeption der Vorneverteidigung aus einem Panzerabwehr und Luftverteidigung sraketengurtel - nach Generalmajor a.D. Dr. Johannes Gerber", (Concept M), March 1984; "Die Konzeption der Heeresstruktur 4 - Bundeswehr der Bundesrepublik Deutschland" (Concepts A,B,C), March 1984; "Die Konzeption der Vorneverteidigung mit konventionellen Feuersperren - nach Oberstleutnant a.D. Norbert Hannig" (Concept N), April 1984; "Die Konzeption der Raumverteidigung der Republik Osterreich" (Concept H), April 1983; "Die Konzeption der Landesverteidigung der Schweiz", (Concept F), June 1984; "Die Konzeption der Panzergrenadiertruppe 90" - nach Oberst i.G. Gero Koch" (Concept D), July 1984; "Die Konzeption der Raumdeckenden Verteidigung - nach Generalmajor a.D. Jochen Loser" (Concept I), July 1984; "Die Konzeption der konventionellen zellularen Vorneverteidigung - nach Oberst a.D. G. Fureder" (Concept L), July 1984; "Die Konzeption der Angreifer", September 1984; "Die Konzeption der Verteidigung im Fangnetz (SAS)" (Concepts G,K), November 1984; "Die Konzeption der Sperrbrigaden" (Concept P), November 1984; "Die Konzeption der Raumverteidigung - nach Dr. H. Afheldt und BrigGen a.D. E. Afheldt" (Concept E), November 1984; and, "Ubersicht uber die geplanten Untersuchungsfalle mit dem Gefechtssimulationssystem BASIS", November 1984.

11. For a discussion of the field tests of the "Framework Defense" see comments by NORTHAG Commander Gen. William Scotter "A Role for Non-Mechanized Infantry" RUSI Journal, December 1980. Subsequent British views: On the coordination of an infantry anvil for the mechanized counterattacking hammer, Richard Simpkin "Maneuver Theory and the Small Army" British Army Review December 1984; employment of mobilized territorial infantry in the largest BOAR post war Corps level exercise, Charles Messenger "Impressions of Lionheart" Defense, December 1984; and the use of heliborne infantry to bloc a penetration, B. W. Barry "An Airmobile Battalion: the Experiences of 1st Battalion - The Light Infantry" British Army Review, April 1985.

12. Concerns over the difficulty of using reserves and the ineffectiveness of small units as expressed by sympathetic observers of the Area

Defense concept: B. R. McCaffery "Infantry on the High-Intensity Battlefield of Central Europe" Military Review, January 1978; and James M. Garrett "Conventional Force Deterrence in the Presence of Theater Nuclear Weapons" Armed Forces and Society, Fall 1984.

13. On Soviet counter optics application of laser technology see: Caspar W. Weinberger Soviet Military Power (Washington: GPO 1982); and B. F. Schemmer "Three Threats NATO's Not Addressing" Armed Forces Journal, May 1984.

14. For Soviet views on and development of HEAT warhead defeating protective armor for main battle tanks, see: V. Slavin "Survivability of Armor" Technology in the Armed Forces (Moscow) September 1983; B. F. Schemmer "Soviets Publish Some of West's Most Secret Anti-armor Techniques" Armed Forces Journal, December 1983; the retrofitting of an extra protection T-54/T-55, "Soviet MBT's with applique armour" Janes Defense Weekly, 20 April 1985; composite steel/ceramic laminate on some models of T-64, T-72 and T-74, Steven J. Zaloga "Soviet T-72 Tank" Jane's Defense Review Vol 4, No 5, 1983; add on overlay of reactive (explosive) armor (similar to Israeli developed "Blazer" armor) for selected models of T-80 effective against HEAT warheads less than 6" in diameter, D. G. Meyer "The Great T-80 Debate: Is It or Isn't It a New Tank" Armed Forces Journal, May 1983; "The T-80 Main Battle Tank" Review of the Soviet Ground Forces, (Washington: Defense Intelligence Agency, December 1983); David C. Isby "Tracking the T-80" Soldier of Fortune, January 1984; J. R. Burniece and P. A. Hoven "T-62, T-64, T-72, T-80, T-?: Understanding Soviet MBT Development" Military Technology, May 1984; "Blazer add-on reactive armor for MBTs" Jane's Defense Weekly, 9 November 1985.

15. Statistics derived from terrain trafficability map in Karber op cite "Pladoger." These statistics are consistent with Uhle-Wettler op cite "Infantry" and G. Brugman "Setting the Scene - The European Battlefield" RUSI Journal, December 1980.

16. This defensive requirement is drawn from a series of BDM hierarchical combat simulations using the BAM model. For comments on the modeling see: James Clay Thompson and A. Grant Whitley "Evaluating NATO's Efforts to Achieve Standardization and Interoperability" in NATO in the 1980s, ed. L. P. Brady and J. P. Kaufman (N.Y.: Praeger Pub. 1985).

MEMBERS OF THE ASSESSMENT GROUP

Prof. H.W. Hofmann, HSBwM
Dr. P.A. Karber, BDM
Col. T. Stone, USAWC
Dr. W.P. Payne, TRADOC ORA

POLITICO-MILITARY ASSESSMENT

John Despres

Director
Institute for National Strategic Studies
National Defense University, Fort McNair, Washington, D.C.

New, alternative concepts of force employment and development in NATO's central region need to be assessed in a strategic framework that:

o articulates the goals of NATO's strategy, to deter aggression by the Soviet Union and its partners in the Warsaw Pact;

o recognizes both nuclear and non-nuclear forces as essential to NATO's deterrent strategy of flexible response and forward defense;

o anticipates the demographic trends, popular attitudes, political forces, and fiscal constraints that are likely to challenge NATO's defense planners and policy-makers in the 1990's;

o identifies the strategic concepts, strengths, and difficulties that will influence Soviet international behavior, especially if recent patterns of politico-military involvement in Angola, Ethiopia, Vietnam, and Afghanistan entail growing Soviet ambitions and possible future miscalculations elsewhere, including menacing campaigns of intimidation and even coercion against individual NATO countries or the Alliance as a whole;

o represents the decision-making process through which precautionary security measures and deterrent mobilizations can be undertaken by NATO;

o takes NATO's existing forces, plans, and arrangements as the starting point for constructive innovation.

Within this strategic framework, new concepts to employ permanently fortified defensive positions, distributed area defenses, anti-armor interdiction systems, and larger reserve forces are supplements or complements to the status quo rather than complete substitutes for it. They could thus incrementally strengthen NATO's security with available resources and without relying any more than necessary on the possible use of nuclear weapons to deter non-nuclear aggression.

Still, if they are viewed separately from each other and from a general plan for improving defenses in the Central Region, each of these concepts has apparent shortcomings. Proposals for defensive fortifications either along the entire border or just across important invasion routes would be expected to incur opposition from those who hope for an early de-militarization or elimination of the inter-German border. Plans for distributed area defenses and more active combat in built-up areas would raise new problems of collateral damage to civilian residents and assets. Moreover, if they were developed as complete substitutes for rather than as complements to combined-arms maneuver forces, area defense forces would not only be vulnerable to concentrated breakthrough operations, especially at night, but they would also lose the deterrent value of larger-scale and longer-range counter-attack capabilities. Concepts for interdiction operations, especially by short-range strike systems in a shallow belt along the border, would similarly be vulnerable to saturation by densely concentrated invasion forces. On the other hand, if Soviet planners could reasonably regard these systems as highly effective against Warsaw Pact forces in a strictly defensive state of alert, their large-scale introduction might create instabilities because of possible new incentives for offensive operations in the event of a deep crisis. Finally, greater use of reserve forces makes deterrence more dependent on precautious mobilization; that is, timely warning, prompt decision-making, and prudent action. These shortcomings can be largely mitigated, if not altogether avoided, by using these concepts in force mixes that are suited to the particular terrain, populations, and other conditions in specific sectors. In any case, a certain overall density and availability of ready maneuver forces and air defenses will be essential to deny the Warsaw Pact low-risk options for a sudden offensive.

To design and evaluate new force structures that employ these concepts effectively, a variety of specialized and competitive studies is needed. They should not only try to derive the best mixes of forces in particular sectors, but they should also examine alternative mixes across the entire region in a wide variety of politico-military situations, from one of protracted tension and gradual mobilization to one of sudden crisis and unreinforced attack. Additional concepts are also worth considering in these same contexts, including shifts in the international as well as inter-service divisions of labor, new ideas for the composition and organization of active forces, and specific options for attacking follow-on air as well as ground forces. Moreover, normally these studies should be jointly reviewed, if not actually conducted, on a multinational basis. Otherwise, common understandings within the Alliance on the relative merits of new ways to strengthen deterrence will be more difficult to reach.

In sum, future studies and well-prepared workshops should compare the assumptions, information, calculations, and implications of measures proposed to improve NATO's conventional defenses. Moreover, proposals should be tested and evaluated by multiple methods and models. Based on the results of such diverse analyses, the most promising measures to improve NATO's security will be easier to recognize and support. Finally, the value of measures to strengthen NATO's defenses can be communicated to policy-makers more vividly and persuasively in the future by demonstrating the results of politico-military simulations, including combat modeling, computerized games, and graphic displays. Thus, well-focused analytical research and development efforts can contribute to strengthening NATO's future security.

MEMBERS OF THE ASSESSMENT GROUP

Prof. K.C. Bowen, Royal Holloway College
Dr. D. Dare, DOAE
Dr. P. Davis, Rand
Mr. J. Despres, INSS/NDU
Mr. J. Fichtner, HSBwM
Mr. U. Nerlich, SWP
Lt. Col. C. Richter, MOD Germany
Lt. Col. I. Schoneweiss, MOD Germany
Dr. K.P. Stratmann, SWP

TECHNOLOGY IMPLICATIONS

Vincent P. Roske Jr.

Director Operations Research and Joint Analysis Directorate
Organization of the Joint Chief of Staff
Washington, D.C. 20301

1. Five concepts for the conventional defense of NATO were assessed for technology implications. These concepts were: 1) Barriers and fortified zones, 2) a Forward Response characterized by an interdiction zone on the eastern side of the FRG/GDR border, 3) a Distributed Defense characterized by in depth defense by small units distributed over a large area, 4) a Framework of small but mutually supporting defensive positions spread over a wide area, and 5) Reactive Defense concepts covering ten different employment options based on variations of traditionally armed and improved armed battalion sized units. The first three concepts were presented to the workshop by Dr. Milton Weiner. The fourth concept was presented by Dr. David Dare and the fifth concept was presented by Dr. Reiner Huber.

2. The Technology implications of each of the five defense concepts were assessed in four categories. First, the development of technology to support a concept was assessed for risks relating to scientific feasibility, cost, development schedule, and trends which may yield technologies which could subsequently dominate the subject technology. Second, the technologies were assessed for the amount of tactical flexibility provided by the configuration of the technology in each defense concept. Third, the command, control and communications implications derived from the proposed use of the technology in each defense concept was assessed. Fourth, the anticipated reliability and the burden of maintenance required by the configuration of technology in each defense concept was considered.

3. The technologies identified for each defense concept and the assessment of these technologies concluded by the assessment group are enumerated below:

a. Barriers and Fortified Zones

1. The technologies required for this defense concept include guidance, propulsion, and warhead technologies associated with advanced precision guided weapons, advanced sensors, robotics, remote control systems, advance anti-air defense systems, information processing systems for sensor corellation and weapons allocation, and the realm of electronic, optical, and infrared counter measures and counter-counter measures.

2) The application of robotics to barrier warfare was assessed to carry a high risk. Development of the other technologies were assessed to be of only moderate to low risk. Technologies associated with the use for advanced sensors were associated to be vulnerable to the dynamic trends in the counter measures and counter-counter measures technologies. The application of information processing systems was assessed to be of low technical risk, but it was noted that command and control aspects and the role of information processing systems receive an uneven and generally inadequate treatment in the description and analysis of military concepts.

3) The technologies were assessed to provide little tactical flexibility when configured for use in fixed barrier and fortified zones.

4) Recommendation: The barrier and fortified zone concept was not recommended for further study. The recommendation was based on the negative assessment of the fixed, inflexible tactical configurations, the risk to successful adaptation of robotics to use in land barrier warfare, and the vulnerabilities of the sensors and precision guided weapons to counter measures.

b. Forward Response

1) Technologies associated with the Forward Response concept were configured as advanced precision guided weapons; advance reconnaissance sensors; rapid targeting and weapons delivery; counter measures and counter-counter measures; and area munitions.

2) None of these technologies were assessed to have a high development risk. There was moderate vulnerability assessed to the dynamic trends in counter measures technology. The potential for flexible tactical applications provided by the technologies in the Forward Defense configurations were favorably assessed.

3) The Command, Control, and Communications technologies were characterized by rapid information processing techniques and a need for a centralized command and control to exploit advantages and respond to break-throughs.

4) Recommendation: The Forwarded Response concept was recommended for further study.

c. Distributed Defense

1) The technologies assessed to be required for the Distributed Defense concept were the warhead, propulsion, communications, mobility and target designation capabilities characteristic of light, highly mobile direct and indirect fire weapons. These are traditional weapons technologies. They were assessed to have low development risk and to offer considerable operational flexibility to the tactical commander.

2) Recommendation: The Distributed Defense concept was recommended for further study.

d. Framework

1) Traditional weapons and secure, covert communications characterize the technologies inherent in the Framework concept of defense. There

is little risk associated with the development of technologies for the framework concept.

2) Recommendation: The Framework concept is recommended for further study.

e. Reactive Defense

1) The Reactive Defense concept could employ advanced technology versions of mobile anti-armor and anti-helicopter weapons. The technology risk to develop these weapons is assessed to be low.

2) Recommendation: The Reactive Defense concept is recommended for further study.

4. The relative attractiveness of the defense concepts was ranked based upon the technology risks in the areas of feasibility, cost, schedule, trends, tactical flexibility command, control, and communications, and maintenance burden. From the most attractive to the least attractive the defense concepts were ranked as:

a. Forward Response

b. Distributed Defense

c. Reactive Defense

d. Framework

e. Barrier

Two comments are noteworthy concerning this ranking. First, only the barrier defense was not recommended for further study. There was little of technical significance to base a preference for one of the four remaining concepts over another. Second, the potential effectiveness of combinations of the proposed defense concepts was not prevented or considered by the working group. Such combinations may be very attractive defense concepts.

RECOMMENDATIONS

1. The parameters of information processing (such as what information is required, how it is acquired and processed, by whom it is used) are as essential to the definition and assessment of defense concepts as are the parameters of mobility, firepower, supply, logistics, etc. The analytic community should increase attention to the early definition of these C3 information processing/battle management parameters.

2. The effectiveness of combinations of the Forward Response, Distributed, Reactive, and Framework Defense concepts should be studied and assessed.

MEMBERS OF THE ASSESSMENT GROUP

Dr. Hubert Feigl, SWP
Air Vice Marshal RAF (Ret.) P. R. Mallorie
Dr. Otto Reidelhuber, IABG
Dr. Robert L. Rinne, Sandia National Laboratories
Mr. Vincent Roske JR., JAD-OJCS

ECONOMIC IMPLICATIONS, COST AND MANPOWER

Michael G. Sovereign

Naval Postgraduate School
Monterey, California 93943

Among members of the assessment group there was general agreement that the economic evaluation of conceptual alternatives in defense is a highly complex issue. Developmental alternatives have different time spans and horizons and risks. There is the difficulty, if not impossibility, of measuring all resources on a monetary scale particularly impacts on tactics and doctrine. In addition, there are a number of important resource dimensions that are difficult to quantify such as technological growth and opportunities for cooperative international ventures. Finally, structural alternatives cannot replace existing force mixes in a turn-key fashion. Rather, they tend to come about in an evolutionary manner through a gradual integration of individual new elements into current force structures which, in NATO's case, are of a multi-national nature. Thus, a comprehensive assessment needs to consider planning across many disciplines, transition of national budgets and the offsets required by the introduction of new systems. None of these issues has been addressed to any significant degree during the workshop.

Nevertheless, the group attempted a first cut of a relative assessment of the resource requirements of the presented alternatives. In doing so, the group focussed on the options evaluated by Milton Weiner of the Rand Corp. and Huber/Hofmann/Steiger of the German Armed Forces University Munich (HSBwM). To aid the assessment, the authors provided some additional resource estimates in addition to those contained in their papers. Yet, several important resource-related questions could not be answered within the time available at the workshop. These are related to the alternatives' sensitivity to warning (cost of mobility versus readiness), the overall posture compatibility (e.g., capability for air defense and contingencies), and the participation requirements (e.g., share of NATO contributions for implementation and management of uniform alternatives with regard to allied funding and hardware procurement).

Based on the information available at the workshop, the group produced a comparative assessment on seven resource dimensions:

(1) initial investment cost

(2) operating cost

(3) manpower requirements

(4) expected casualties

(5) infrastructural requirements

(6) real estate requirements

(7) operational depth required for the defense

Table 1 shows the results for six options evaluated by the HSBwM-researchers and Table 2 for the three concepts presented by Weiner.

For each resource dimension, the requirements in Table 1 are stated relative to those of option P. They imply the resources needed to absorb the successive attacks by three Soviet motor rifle regiments (BMP) as represented in the combat simulation model used in the study. The estimates account only for items included in these rather small-scale simulation experiments (i.e., battalion-level for the defense). Therefore, an assessment on a full NATO front basis might reveal significant infrastructural requirements due to re-basing, etc. On the other hand, an increased use of reservists in some of the options might reduce their operating cost requirements, which are based on a full peacetime manning. Also, the small scale of the simulation experiments does not give sufficient credit to the more traditional concepts such as C and D which have higher mobility and could be used elsewhere and for other missions.

The assessment of Weiner's alternative concepts in Table 2 could only be done in qualitative terms. The group agreed that the Barrier concept should be deleted from any further considerations due to its excessively high investment cost, on the order of one hundred billions of dollars. Except for the resource category of operational depth, the Distributed Area Defense dominates the Forward Response concept. However, strong views were expressed from the workshop floor considering the possible disabling social costs of re-basing to be expected for both concepts.

The summary conclusions of the group are compiled in Table 3. It is clear that all of the concepts must be refined before serious resource assessments can be considered. Cost of training, logistics, command and control, and the impact of other forces (such as air defense) must be estimated. However, the group could not find reasons to reject reactive defense concepts on the basis of resources required as known at this time.

There was some discussion as to whether these resources are to be considered additional or whether there can be offsets in other forces. Most of the group does not belive that the strategic situation can be safely allowed to remain as it is. Consequently, any additional capability should be exactly that. However, there are several reasons why the offsets should be identified. It was pointed out that the United States has doubled procurement and increased defense expenditures by 50% during the Reagan administration. The agreed 3% growth in NATO amounts to hundreds of millions of dollars over the (average) 10-year life of new military systems, so there should be opportunities for selection of more efficient programs.

The discussion above indicates the importance of extreme care in assessment of resource implications of the broad defense concepts. In studies of a more limited scope, resources can more easily be quantified, as shown in the other major study referred to below.

In support of concept generation and analysis it is very important to have studies which demonstrate that new weapon systems have potential cost-effective contributions so that new mixes of weapons should be considered. This was well illustrated by the study presented by Schmitz/Reidelhuber/Niemeyer of the German defense analysis establishment IABG. It showed that more efficient mixes of <u>specialized</u> combat vehicles can

Table 1: Relative Resource Requirements for Selected HSBwM-Options

Option / Origin / Res. Dimension	C Tank Btl German Army	D Arm.Inf. Btl 90 German Army	E Techno Cdo Afheldt	F Swiss Terr.Def. —	M ATM/SAM Belt Gerber	P Inf.Btl. of Barrier Brig HSBwM
Init.Inv.Cost	3	3.6	1	0.3	0.5(?)	1
Operating Cost	2	2	0.5	?	?	1
Manpower Reqm't.	8	10	20	14	10	1
Casualty Exp.	0.8	1	3.5+	4	2	1
Infrastructure	—	—	no substantial impact		—	—
Real Es.Rqm't.	none	none	small	sizeable	none	none
Ops Depth	1	1	100+	1	?	1

Table 2: Resource Requirements for Rand-Alternatives

Option / Res. Dimension	Barrier Defense	Forward Response	Distributed Area Defense
Init.Inv.Cost	> 100 bill. $	> 10 bill. $	~10 bill. $
Operating Cost	low	high	medium
Manpower Reqm't.	no change	no change	no change
Casualty Exp.	low	moderate	high
Infrastructure	very high	low	low
Real Es.Reqm't.	20 km belt	low	low
Ops Depth	none	low	high

be generated. In this analysis, the effect of different missions on the performance of the mixes was analysed. The recommended mix showed interesting variations from both current and planned forces.

MEMBERS OF THE ASSESSMENT GROUP

        Mr. J. Elliot, OSD-DCSOPS
        Dr. D. Fischer, IABG
        Lt.Col. P. Hesse, German Army Staff
        Prof. M.G. Sovereign, NPS
        Capt. K. Steiger, HSBwM

        Table 3:   Conclusions

- Differing technical assumptions make resource comparisons difficult

- Most concepts have not been refined to permit absolute resource estimates

- Life cycle cost including personnel, training, logistics and medical support must be estimated

- Peacetime manpower impact (active and reserve) is critical: Use of Reserves offers only practical prospect of more forces in combat

- Losses must be measured, but not monetarily

- Command and Control cost estimates must await refinement of concepts

- Planning for any transitions should begin early: Resources change slowly

- "Reactive Force" concepts cannot be ruled out on the basis of resource requirements

- Cost of readiness and of associated forces must be examined

FINDINGS OF THE ASSESSMENT GROUP ON MODELING AND METHODOLOGY

Robert L. Farrell

Vector Research, Incorporated

P.O. Box 1506, Ann Arbor, Michigan, 48106

This workshop has heard nine presentations. Four of these provided specific concepts or force structures and supporting analyses and five dealt with more general methodological issues. Although this report concentrates on effectiveness assessments, methodology, and models, it does so principally in the context of the specific concept and force structure proposals. Thus it is not a critique or review of the state of methodology in general, but a commentary on the modeling and methodology which we have seen demonstrated in the five concept studies discussed at this meeting.

There was a convergence of the results of several analyses of concepts which were built up around distributed area or reactive force defenses involving small units in some depth, all of which suggested a potential for significant, possibly cost-effective, military contributions, at least at a small scale. Additionally, there were results presented concerning an interdiction-belt concept variant of deeper attack concepts which showed some promise and a barrier defense concept which appeared to have less continuing interest, at least in the form presented.

Each of these concepts was supported by a quantitative analysis of the potential consequences which might result from its use. These analyses used various models and modelling techniques. All of the results showed potential positive payoffs for the concepts. As presented, each of the studies seemed to involve the use of state-of-the-art models.

The concepts and analyses presented were limited in several ways. The rappoteurs remarked particularly on:
(1) the absence of considerations of offensive elements in the analyses. (This, while a limitation of the methodology of the studies, does not correspond to any inability in existing models and current modeling techniques to deal with the offensive. Thus, no new developments in modeling are required to improve on this lack of treatment of offensive operations.)
(2) the limited scope and scale of most of the analyses in terms time and the scale of the units involved. (Again, this is a of limitation in the methodology used in the studies, not a limitation of current models or existing modeling technology. It is understandable in such preliminary analyses as most of those presented, and it is worth noting that the scale of the

more thorough study of the interdiction-belt concept -- and less interesting barrier concept -- was at a higher level than the more preliminary analyses of the reactive defense options.)

(3) the limited breadth of measures of effectiveness considered. (This generally reflected the low tactical level of the analyses, rather than a failure in models or methodologies available.)

(4) the lack of consideration of large-scale and international coordination problems. (This problem is of particular interest in a context where new defense concepts for NATO forward defense are being discussed. Presumably such concepts must be evaluated in terms not only of their tactical applicability in a small battlefield region, but in terms of their integrability into a coherent defense of at least central-region scale. The lack of study of this issue is not only a reflection of the tactical level of the analyses, but of a real limitation in most methodologies and models today. New developments may be required to address this issue properly.)

(5) the limited degreee to which joint air and ground concept designs were addressed. (This applies principally to the reactive defense concept analyses and does not apply to the interdiction-belt analyses. It is again a reflection of the tactical level of the studies which were carried out, and not a limitation of the capability of our current models. Improvement in this area requires no new model development, but some creativity on the part of proponents of the reactive defense concepts, who must design an appropriately integrated concept for air operations. This concept might involve elements taken from the interdiction-belt concepts discussed.)

(6) the absence of consideration of potential chemical or nuclear operations by either side. (This problem was addressed in the opening paper. It involves a shortfall that must be admitted to be quite frequent in analyses of NATO defense posture. While there are some models and games which allow treatment of both conventional and nuclear and chemical operations or the preparation for them, they are too little used in actual studies.)

Because of these shortcomings, the current analyses must be considered as initial, or preliminary, work only. As such, we believe that the investigators have demonstrated the capability of our community to apply existing methods and models, making modifications where necessary, to perform useful (and even exciting) work concerning possible variations in defense concepts for NATO. At the same time, it is clear that significantly more work must be done before a convincing case can be made for a change in defense concept.

Where do we go from here? The rapporteurs felt a need for continuing analyses of concepts drawing on elements of at least two of the general concept areas presented: the various versions of distributed area or reactive defenses (with which we included the framework concept) and the interdiction-belt (forward response) concept. In such additional analyses, there are certainly some methodological and model developments which would be required, but there was general agreement that the program of analysis should go forward, with methods and models modified only as necessary and feasible in the context of such analyses. This approach may be contrasted with the too-frequent recommendation that we first develop models and only after they have been developed proceed to study real problems. The continuing analyses should involve more investigators and groups studying concepts with which they are not yet associated.

This will have two major benefits:
(1) improved analysis, as new methods and viewpoints broaden the study of conceptual alternatives, and
(2) the spread of understanding of the replicable key results relating concepts and their potential contributions (or deficiencies), which is necessary to the influence of the large, consultative process which defines NATO defense policy.

With regard to the continuing analyses, we felt that the most immediate and highest priority needs included:
(1) the broadening of concept definitions to involve the entirety of the forces in the central region of NATO, or an adequate representative subset;
(2) the inclusion of military officers and organizations in the definiation and analysis of these concepts;
(3) the consideration of <u>combinations</u> of elements from both concepts in the extension of the concept definitions;
(4) the inclusion in analyses of additional concepts not proposed at this meeting, including concepts involving at least tactical level offensive actions.

There are many other areas in which we could improve our methodology in the continuing examinations of the forward defense problem. We would expect many of these to be undertaken as analysis continues. Some of the areas we remarked on are listed earlier. Others include:
(1) the use of multiple tools (and diverse kinds of tools) to study a concept,
(2) the improved use of information from military experience and history, and even from the history of military analysis (and its past errors),
(3) the involvement of exercises and trials in concept evaluation and definition.

In conjunction with the continuing analysis of these and other concepts for forward defense, we felt that continuing workshops such as this one would provide a useful framework for the international exchange of information among active investigators in this area.

MEMBERS OF THE ASSESSMENT GROUP

D. Blumenthal, Lawrence Livermore Laboratories
R.G. Coyle, STC
D.W. Daniel, RAF Strike Command
K. Niemeyer, IABG
M. Weiner, Rand Corp.

WORKSHOP PARTICIPANTS

LtCol Ulrich BARNER, Ministry of Defense FRG
Mr. Don BLUMENTHAL, Lawrence Livermore Laboratories,
    Livermore, Calif., USA
Dr. Seth BONDER, Vector Research Inc., Ann Arbor, Mich., USA
Prof. Ken C. BOWEN, Royal Holloway College, Egham Hill, UK
General (ret.) Jürgen BRANDT, Bonn, FRG
Dr. Richard G. COYLE, SHAPE Technical Centre, The Hague, NL
Mr. D. W. DANIEL, Research Office HQ RAF Strike Command,
    High Wycombe, UK
Dr. David P. DARE, Defence Operations Analysis Establishment,
    West Byfleet, UK
Dr. Paul DAVIS, RAND Corp., Santa Monica, Calif., USA
Mr. John DESPRES, National Defense University, Washington, D.C., USA
Cdr Albrecht DETTMANN, Ministry of Defense FRG
LtGen (ret.) Lothar DOMRÖSE, German Strategy Forum, Bonn, FRG
Mr. John ELLIOTT, Department of the Army, Washington, D.C., USA
Mr. Robert FARRELL, Vector Research Inc., Ann Arbor, Mich., USA
Dr. Hubert FEIGL, Foundation for Science and Politics,
    Ebenhausen, FRG
Mr. John FICHTNER, Federal Armed Forces University Munich, FRG
Dr. Dietrich FISCHER, Industrieanlagen-Betriebsgesellschaft,
    Ottobrunn, FRG
LtCol Eberhard FISCHINGER, Ministry of Defense FRG
MajGen (ret.) Alexander FREVERT-NIEDERMEIN, German Strategy Forum,
    Bonn, FRG
LtGen (ret.) Heinz von zur GATHEN, Essen-Werden, FRG
Mr. John W. GIBSON, SHAPE Technical Centre, The Hague, NL
Captain (GN) Siegfried GÜNTHER, Office for Studies and Exercises,
    Bensberg, FRG
LtCol Peter HESSE, Ministry of Defense FRG
Prof. Hans W. HOFMANN, Federal Armed Forces University Munich, FRG

Prof. Reiner K. HUBER, Federal Armed Forces University Munich, FRG
Dr. Phillip A. KARBER, BDM-Corporation, McLean, Va., USA
Colonel (ret.) Carl-Albert KEERL, German Strategy Forum, Bonn, FRG
LtCol Klaus KLEFFNER, Ministry of Defense FRG
Air Vice Marshal RAF (ret.) Paul R. MALLORIE, SHAPE Technical
   Centre, The Hague, NL
Mr. Louis MICHAEL, Department of Defense, Washington, D.C., USA
Mr. Uwe NERLICH, Foundation for Science and Politics,
   Ebenhausen, FRG
Mr. Klaus NIEMEYER, Industrieanlagen-Betriebsgesellschaft
   Ottobrunn, FRG
Cdr Bernd OLDEWURTEL, University of Kiel, FRG
Dr. Wilbur P. PAYNE, TRADOC Operations Research Activity,
   El Paso, Tex., USA
Dr. Rolf Friedemann PAULS, German Strategy Forum, Bonn, FRG
Dr. Otto REIDELHUBER, Industrieanlagen-Betriebsgesellschaft,
   Ottobrunn, FRG
LtCol Claus RICHTER, Ministry of Defense, FRG
Dr. Robert L. RINNE, Sandia National Laboratories,
   Livermore, Calif., USA
Mr. Vincent ROSKE, Department of Defense, Washington, D.C., USA
Rear Admiral Elmar SCHMÄHLING, Office for Studies and Exercises,
   Bensberg, FRG
LtCol Immo SCHÖNEWEISS, Ministry of Defense FRG
Mr. Walter SCHMITZ, Industrieanlagen-Betriebsgesellschaft,
   Ottobrunn, FRG
General (ret.) Franz-Joseph SCHULZE, German Strategy Forum, Bonn, FRG
Prof. Michael G. SOVEREIGN, Naval Postgraduate School,
   Monterey, Calif., USA
Captain Karl STEIGER, Federal Armed Forces University Munich, FRG
Colonel Tom STONE, US Army War College, Carlisle, Pa., USA
Dr. K. Peter STRATMANN, Foundation for Science and Politics,
   Ebenhausen, FRG
Dr. Thilo WEDLICH, Industrieanlagen-Betriebsgesellschaft,
   Ottobrunn, FRG
Dr. Milton WEINER, RAND Corporation, St. Monica, Calif., USA
Mr. Bernt WOBITH, Federal Armed Forces University Munich, FRG

INDEX

ACE, 19
ADATS, 110
ATGM-limitations, 181
Acceptability
  political, 7
Acceptance of models, 71
Active defense, 114, 120, 171, 172, 174
Afheldt's Area Defense, 112, 173
Aggregated attrition model, 21
Aggregation of data, 144
Airland Battle, 84
Alert system, 18
Alternative
  brigade structures, 147
  defense concepts, 83
  strategic concepts, 55
Analysis of conceptional alternatives, 206
Analytic war plans, 37 51
Analytical model, 23, 29, 86, 145
Archipelago System of Defense, 97
Area defense, 84, 97, 112, 173
Armoured Division Equivalents (ADE), 18, 30
Arms control, 84
Army Strategy Processing Model, 56
Artillery
  barrages, 128
  vulnerability, 122, 128
Assessment criteria, 15, 118, 149
Asymmetry NATO-WP, 17
Austrian area defense, 112, 173
Automated game agent, 50
Automated wargaming, 36

BASIS, 98
BDM, 113, 167
Balance
  assessment, 47, 71
  conventional force, 1, 15
  nuclear force, 8
Ballistic missiles, 12

Barrier
  brigades, 113, 173, 187
  concept, 87, 110, 176
Barriers, 84, 110, 176
Basic military missions, 52
Battalion-level model, 98
Battlefield
  extended, 10
  integrated, 10
Bean counts, 31
Border crossing operations, 10
Brigade structures, 147

CONUS, 30
Campaign model, 61
Cellular Defense Concept, 113, 173
Central
  front, 17
  region defense, 86
Checkerboard defenses, 12
Chemical
  operations, 206
  weapons, 12
Colloquium on Alternative Strategic Concepts, 55
Combat model requirements, 205
Combat simulation, 32, 91, 97, 144, 188
Combat support effectiveness, 154
Command and Control, 4, 12, 33, 69, 177, 197
Complex Strategies, 52
Complex models, 32
Conditional loss order, 106
Confidence building, 10
Conflict
  dynamics, 59
  termination, 6, 13
Contingency
  design, 16
  employment of nuclear weapons, 6
Controlled Escalation, 6

211

Conventional
  balance, 19
  defense, 2, 5, 15, 26
  deterrence, 188
  nuclear linkage, 23, 33
Cooperative ventures, 201
Corps
  structure, 174
  level model, 145
Correlation of forces, 17
Cost, 201
Cost effectiveness, 30, 136, 152, 202
Counter attacks, 13, 135, 184
Counter offensive capabilities, 14
Covering force area, 85
Credibility of models, 31
Crisis
  management, 19
  stability, 9, 98, 186
Critique of alternative concepts, 177

DOAE, 3
DYSMAP, 71
DYSMOD, 71
Data aggregation, 145
Decision rules, 38
Declaratory policy of NATO, 34
Deep battle, 10, 90
Defense
  efficiency hypothesis, 109, 136, 176
  mindedness, 89
  planning, 25
Defensive defense, 9
Defensivity, 9
Deliberate Escalation, 11, 16
Denial, 6
Department of the Army, 55
Detente, 18
Deterrence, 1, 5, 194
  criteria, 18
  intra-war, 5
Differential Equation Model, 19, 59
Direct fire engagement, 107
Dirty battlefields effects, 122, 130
Disintegration
  threat of, 8
Dispersed Anti-Tank Infantry, 83, 147, 174
Disruption of offensive concepts, 6
Distributed Area Defense Concept, 93, 178
Division of labor, 194
Doctrine
  chemical, 5
  nuclear, 5, 8
  operational, 5
  standardized, 17
  tactical, 5

Dual-capable systems, 12
Duel simulation, 146
Dynamic Area Defenses (DAD), 110, 173
Dynamic density defense, 179
Dynamic measures, 21

Economic implications, 201
Effectiveness
  assessment, 205
  measures of, 15, 19, 85, 118, 206
Efficient frontier, 137
Elevated platforms, 110
Emerging technologies, 11, 84, 98, 167
Engagement processes, 106
Entropic battlefield, 177
Escalation, 6, 8, 16, 172
  control, 33
  deliberate, 6, 8, 11
  threshold, 89
Evaluation criteria, 15, 19, 85, 118, 206
Experimental tactics, 167
Experiments
  planned simulation, 79
  random, 79
Extended Battlefield, 10

FEBA, 19
  battle, 11
Federal Armed Forces University, 97
Feedback loop, 66
Field fortifications, 128, 187
Fire Barrier Defenses, 110, 174
Flexible Response, 17, 184
Follow-on forces attack (FOFA), 90, 176, 194
Force Agent, 37
Force
  balance, 1, 19
  build-up, 19
  design, 15
  enhancement, 21
  improvements options, 22
  improvement proposals, 3
  mix, 15
  modelling hierarchy, 143
  modernization, 167
  movement, 19
  ratio, 30
  comparisons, 18
  structure, 2, 15, 83, 97, 141
    asymmetries, 17
    defensive, 12
    design, 15
    mixed, 13
    offensive, 12
    planning, 142

Fortified Barrier Concept, 87, 176
Forward defense, 23, 27, 85, 98, 141, 167
Forward Response Concept, 90, 176
Framework Defense Concept, 174

Game paradigm, 49
Game-structured analysis, 25
Gerber's ATK-SAM Belt, 113, 173
German defense objectives, 141
Global wargaming, 25
Gradual defensivity, 98

Hannig's Fire Barrier Concept, 113, 173
Hedgehog defense, 110
Hierarchic force structure, 143
Hierarchical aggregation, 145
High tech sabotage, 178

IABG, 141
In depth defense, 27
Indirect fire engagement, 107
Infantry, 167
   fighting vehicles, 170
   mechanized, 170
   mix, 170
   role of, 168
Influence diagram, 62
Infrastructural requirements, 202
Initial investment cost, 201
Innovation, 4
Institute
   for Applied Systems and Operations Research, 97
   for National Strategic Studies, 193
Integrated
   battlefield, 10
   planning, 34
Interactive models, 36
Interdiction belt, 90
Interdisciplinary dialogue, 28
Interface
   conventional-nuclear, 5
Intermediate effectiveness measures, 15
Interoperability, 11, 206
Interpenetration, 185
Inter-German border, 194
Intra-war deterrence, 6
Investment cost, 133
Iterative model application, 145

Joint Analysis Directorate (JAD), 197

Joint Strategic Planning Document (JSPD), 56

Key operational parameters, 170
Killer-victim scoreboard, 119
Kola peninsula, 66

Ladder tactics, 113
Lanchester model, 86, 97
Launch on warning, 12
Life cycle cost, 149
Line of communication (LOF) attack, 90
Löser's Area Defense, 113, 173
Long-term
   defense planning, 60
   defense program (LTDP), 84
   force trends, 141
Loss exchange ratio, 136, 171
Low density defense, 130

MASTER model, 86
MC 14/3, 84
Maintenance requirements, 197
Maldeployment, 17
Maneuver warfare, 13
Manpower requirements, 149, 201
Maximization of effectiveness, 155
Measures of effectiveness, 15, 19, 85, 118, 206
   dynamic, 19
   static, 18, 31
Methodological
   aggregation, 145
   limitations, 205
Military judgement, 167
Mine effectiveness, 154
Minefields, 109
Minimization of cost, 156
Mission area
   capabilities, 15
   priorities, 60
   requirements, 15
   mix, 15
   trade-offs, 16
Mixed force structure, 13
Mobile defense, 27
Mobility, 171
Mobilization, 19, 30, 194
Model
   acceptance, 71
   aggregated attrition, 21
   analytical, 23, 29, 86
   Btl/Rgt level, 98
   complexity, 32
   corps-level, 145
   credibility, 31

Model
  differential equation, 19
  interactive, 36
  Lanchester, 86, 97
  theater level, 19, 23, 61, 83
Modelling, 205
  problems, 32
  requirements, 35
Modernization programs, 27
Multifront crisis, 26
Multinational study review, 195
Multiscenario
  analysis, 25, 44
  balance, 47
Multitheater conflict, 33
Multi-mission platform, 170
Multi-purpose combat systems, 146, 163

National Defense University, 193
National doctrines, 35
NATO
  defense concept, 83
  defense programs, 34
  long-term defense planning (LTP), 60
  strategic doctrine, 10
Naval Postgraduate School, 201
Non-conventional threats, 4
Non-provocative defense, 6
Northern Region Model, 63
Nuclear
  battlefield, 170
  deterrence, 26
  dilemma, 8
  escalation, 6, 172
  forces, 6
  free zones, 10
  operations, 206
  posture, 5
  preemption, 12
  relationship, 5
  response, 6, 16
  threshold
Nuclear weapons, 5, 18
  employment flexibility, 8

Objective function, 15, 141
Offensive Counter Air (OCA), 11, 15
Offensive
  defense, 10
  operations, 10, 205
Operating cost, 201
Operational
  depth requirements, 132, 170, 202
  doctrine, 5
  flexibility, 24
  maneuver groups, 33, 188
  robustness, 176

Operational Concepts, 17
Optimization
  model, 3, 149
  of force structures, 149
Out-of-area activities, 16
Overseas reinforcement, 66

PGM, 93, 97
Pay-off function, 12, 15
Perceptions
  soviet, 17
Planning
  constraints, 34
  model, 149
  scenarios, 34
Political-military
  structure, 35
  wargaming, 25
  assessment, 193
  simulations, 195
Preemption, 12
Pre-attack intelligence, 91
Procurment decisions, 23
Projectability of forces, 18

Qualitative model, 69

Rand Corporation, 25, 83
Rand Strategy Assessment Center, 26, 36, 58
Random experiments, 79
Reactive defense, 97, 123, 172
Real estate requirements, 202
Relative force value ratio, 119
Reliability, 197
  of allies, 17
Reservists, 202
Resource dimensions, 201
Retaliation, 6
Risk
  of escalation, 8
  technological, 197
Role of analysis, 15, 29, 190

SAS-cavalry, 113, 173
SAS-infantry, 112, 173
Scenario, 16, 118
Scenario Agent, 38
Scripted models, 44
Sea control, 66
Search and detection, 106
Second echelon interdiction, 90
Selective
  nuclear employment options, 12
  response, 12
SHAPE Technical Center (STC), 15, 59

Short warning attack, 27, 187
Simple models, 30
Simulation, 98
Simulation
   Control, 104
   model, 32, 71, 97, 145
   political-military, 195
   stochastic, 98
Single scenario analysis, 41
Small unit defense, 94
Smart munitions, 11
Soft issues, 35
Southwest Asia, 27
Soviet
   motor rifle regiment, 115
   operational concepts, 17
   perceptions, 17
   submarine operations, 66
   tank regiment, 115
Specialized combat systems, 146, 163
Stability
   crisis, 9, 98, 186
Standard scenario, 41
Static
   Area Defenses (SAD), 110
   defenses, 12
   indicators, 16
   measures, 18, 31
STC, 15, 59
Stochastic battle simulation, 98
Strategic
   Processing Model, 57
   concepts, 6, 17, 25, 55
   doctrine, 10
   employment, 7
   flexibility, 24
   framework of assessment, 193
   nuclear capability, 16, 84
   objectives, 6
Strategy assessment, 26, 55
Swiss Territorial Defense, 112, 173
Synergism
   conventional/nuclear, 9
System Dynamics, 19, 59

Tactical
   air, 91
   flexibility, 197
   lines, 106
   Nuclear Doctrine, 5, 16
Tactics generator, 99
Tactics program, 106
Tank destroyer with infantry, 147, 174
Target
   aquisition, 11, 92
   engagement, 107
   search and detection, 106

Technokommandos, 112, 178
Technological
   growth, 201
   risk, 197
Technology implications, 197
Termination
   of conflict, 6, 13
Theater
   level model, 19, 61
   nuclear forces, 16
   nuclear war, 9
Threat perception, 16
Transitional defense, 189
Trigger events, 104

Uncertainty
   analysis, 42
   area of, 17
Unquantifiable factors, 18

Vector Research Inc., 113, 205
Visibility sensitivity, 120, 130
Vulnerability, 122, 128

War fighting capability, 18
War
   game, 19, 36, 83, 145
   termination, 13, 19, 172
   winning capability, 18
Warning, 4, 17
Warsaw Pact, 5
Weapon mix calculation, 149
Weighted Effectiveness Index (WEI), 18
Weighted Unit Value (WUV), 18